ESSENTIAL DESIGN

ESSENTIAL DESIGN

CATHERINE McDERMOTT

BLOOMSBURY

In loving memory of my mother

Acknowledgements

I would like to thank my friends and colleagues in the
Faculty of Design at Kingston University for their help
and support in writing this book.

All rights reseved, no part of this puiblication may be reproduced,
stored in a retrieval system, or transmitted by any means,
electronic, mechanical, photocopying or otherwise, without the
prior written permission of the Publisher.

Published in 1992
by Bloomsbury Publishing Limited
2 Soho Square, London W1V 5DE

The moral right of the author has been asserted.

Copyright © Catherine McDermott 1992

A copy of the CIP entry for this book
is available from the British Library.

ISBN 0 7475 0896 8

10 9 8 7 6 5 4 3 2 1

Designed by Elizabeth Pitman
Typeset by Hewer Text Composition Services, Edinburgh
Printed in England by Clays Ltd, St Ives plc

CONTENTS

Cross references

In both the essays and the reference entries, names, terms and topics are frequently marked with an arrow > to guide the reader to the appropriate entry in the reference section for a more detailed explanation.

INTRODUCTION

DESIGN AND THE INDUSTRIAL REVOLUTION

The modern industrial age in which we live and in which design has come to play such an important role is still relatively new. Two hundred years ago the Industrial Revolution laid the foundations for the new industrial age and ushered in the first of many sweeping changes. Mass production and mass consumption were made possible by the development of new technologies, the introduction of large factories and new patterns of urban living. And 200 years later the impact of those changes remains a vital area for discussion and debate.

The 18th century is a fascinating watershed. England enjoyed political stability, trade links established overseas trade, advanced banking and credit systems were created, and new ideas of retailing developed. London became a fashionable European city, attractive to foreigners because of the cultural life offered by its theatres and pleasure gardens, and the intellectual freedom offered by the city's coffee houses. London also enjoyed another important difference to other European capitals in that fashion and taste did not revolve exclusively around the Court as it did, for example, at Versailles in France. The direction of style and taste was spreading outwards as a new, affluent middle class emerged. Luxuries such as tea, tobacco, imported textiles and lace were available for the first time to large sections of the population. Indeed, a December 1791 issue of the *Observer* newspaper indicates the diversity of 18th-century consumer culture with advertisements for a patent washing machine invented by a Mr Kendall of Charing Cross, travel guides to America and the South Sea Islands, patent medicines, beauty products and a sale of imported Italian cheeses, German sausages and French mustard. For the first time, too, books, newspapers and magazines were available to large sections of the population.

Alongside this burgeoning consumer spending were developments which played a key role in the foundation of modern British design culture. Throughout the 18th century the role of the designer underwent important changes. The artisan-craftsman who produced traditional objects in ceramics, metal and glass continued to exist, but significant changes of definition were taking place. The first was the growth of printed information on design. While makers had always borrowed or copied ideas from actual objects, access to printed images from engravings and books was generally limited. Now, design publications became popular and could be bought from the flourishing book trade centred around Covent Garden. By the 1750s it was possible to make a living simply by publishing books of new designs, as demonstrated by the designer Thomas Johnson. Contemporary novels, plays and engravings began to refer to this new culture of fashion and taste in a familiar way, joking about the dangers of becoming a fashion victim or a slave to the latest taste in interior design. William Hogarth's popular moral engravings, *Marriage à la Mode*, allowed his audience the pleasure of disapproving a young couple's expensive French rococo interiors. These were markers of a new society's confidence and interest in design, highlighted by the career of Britain's legendary furniture designer Thomas Chippendale.

Chippendale was part of a large, successful and fashionable London furniture trade, but his activities and aspirations as an independent designer provide a fascinating study. The son of a Yorkshire joiner, he moved to London in the 1750s and opened a showroom in the city's then most fashionable shopping street, St Martin's Lane. The area had a distinct social and cultural character, being the heart of the artistic community, and Chippendale's workshop was directly opposite Slaughter's, the famous coffee house, which was patronized by numerous artists. The workshop was no mere outlet for quality craft skills; Chippendale offered clients a complete interior design service, importing luxury goods from abroad, providing access to avant-garde taste through his catalogues and even offering credit facilities.

In 1754 Chippendale published *The Gentleman and Cabinet Maker's Director*, which had an immediate and lasting impact. In fact, it is hard to exaggerate its importance as a design catalogue. It set new standards of production and established the designer as an important figure in fashionable London. Copies of *The Director* found their way into hundreds of country house libraries at home and abroad, including that of Catherine the Great of Russia. It was also a successful advertising strategy, generating business for Chippendale's company and making his design work popular in the widest sense. His furniture was acquired by the aristocracy but was also absorbed into the vernacular provincial tradition and was copied throughout the growing British colonies in North America and India.

This 18th-century atmosphere of expansion, intellectual experimentation and exploration opened up a period of change for designers, pioneer industrialists and inventors, including Josiah Wedgwood, Thomas Boulton, Sir Richard Arkwright and James Hargreaves. Their impact was to reshape industry and production into the new patterns of the Industrial Revolution.

Inventions affecting the textile industry provide a model for this industrial change. Spinning was the first area to be mechanized, with the invention of Arkwright's water frame, Compton's mule and Hargreaves's spinning jenny. This first wave of inventions in the 1770s shifted the production of textiles from small workshops in the home to centralized factory production. The second process to be mechanized was weaving, followed by calico printing, which was revolutionized by the invention of a roller-printing machine in 1783. The rapid expansion of textile production in the Lancashire towns of Manchester, Oldham and Rochdale was to change the industrial landscape forever.

Towards the end of the 18th century technological change was also beginning to affect other traditional industries. In 1759 Wedgwood inherited the family business in Staffordshire and set about reforming it. He introduced steam power, and during the 1760s and 1770s he set ground rules for industrial production that were copied all over the world. He was also one of the first manufacturers to introduce systematic scientific research methods in his factory. He pioneered new methods of marketing and business, being one of the first manufacturers to use newspaper advertising and to develop retail display. Even more important were the changes he introduced to the manufacturing process. Wedgwood broke down ceramic production into separate activities, thus creating the fundamental principle of the Industrial Revolution – the division of labour. It was a simple but profound change which overturned the practice of individual workers controlling the complete process of production. Now each worker specialized in one single activity, and the increased use of specialized machines led to the idea that design could be separated from manufacturing.

Wedgwood's approach reflected the wider economic theories of his age, particularly those of Adam > Smith. Smith's *Wealth of Nations* was the first analysis of the economic implications of the Industrial Revolution; he also noted the changes it would engender in labour, production and marketing. To illustrate his argument on the division of labour Smith used the now famous example of a worker manufacturing pins. If, Smith pointed out, the worker were responsible for all the manufacturing operations, his output was small, but if the worker concentrated on a single aspect of production, output increased dramatically. It was the beginning of a production process that would finally lead in the early 20th century to the car assembly lines of Henry > Ford. Smith also pointed out that increased production on its own was not enough for economic success. Marketing and, although Adam did not identify it as such, design were the factors on which the success of the new industries of the Industrial Revolution would depend. These issues were to dominate the debates on industry and design in the 19th century.

THE NINETEENTH CENTURY

Looking back at the 19th century our view reveals a period of energetic change and progress. Powerful images come to mind of new industrial centres, of Welsh mining communities, of Clydeside shipbuilding and of Lancashire cotton mills. Great deprivation contrasted with staggering affluence, and a comfortable middle-class lifestyle was supported by apparently inexhaustible numbers of cheap servants. Against this backdrop of rigid class structures was a society that promoted and encouraged research and learning. It was a period of great engineering achievements and of radical scholarship and research by such people as Isambard Kingdom Brunel, Charles Darwin and John > Ruskin. The 19th century was an extraordinary combination of repression and intellectual experimentation. There was a confidence and belief in progress, amply displayed in the vigour of Victorian civic buildings that still dominate British cities; banks, libraries and town halls display pride of progress in every brick. People from all classes could also experience that progress through the new inventions of the age – the railways, photography, the telegraph, cars, telephones, electricity and aeroplanes.

In this new consumer culture design became an important issue. The role of the designer and the social function of design were important debates taking place alongside the appearance of the first mass-produced products, department stores, advertising hoardings and mail-order catalogues. The energy and confidence with which these early industrial developments were put into force make the 19th century a fascinating area of study from our 20th-century perspective.

The Industrial Revolution, which originated in the 18th century, developed not in a planned way, but as a gradual, almost random process determined by trial and error and the simple principle of survival in the market-place. The ideas of standardization and mechanization only began to take real effect on design in the 19th century. By the 1830s social commentators and manufacturers were beginning to analyse the social and environmental effects of the Industrial Revolution, and many found those effects alarming. A romantic nostalgia for Britain's rural past began to take hold of some commentators, but those working in industry were alarmed for different reasons. They subscribed to the view that Britain, although advanced in technology, had not paid sufficient attention to design and that the growth of a mass market for consumer goods had led to a drop in aesthetic standards. So serious was the problem that Parliament, worried that standards of British design would affect trading levels, ordered the appointment in 1835 of a Select Committee on Arts and Manufactures to discuss the problems and plan the way forward. This government intervention led to a number of important innovations which were largely a response to the way in which design had developed in the rest of Europe, especially France. The Committee decided to invest in design education and trade exhibitions as the principal ways of promoting design.

Lavish, large-scale design exhibitions were a feature of the 19th century, and the published catalogues of these events provide an important chronicle of contemporary design developments. They reflect the aspirations, achievements and ambitions of the age, and even though exhibitions present a specialized view of design, they provided a forum in which to air the key arguments and debates on quality, style, taste, education, industry and commerce.

Exhibitions showing the history of design started in France, and soon spread to the rest of the Continent. The first French government trade show, called 'Exposition de l'Industrie', was organized in 1798, and there were 11 more over the next 50 years. France continued to mount exhibitions which, in design history terms, were the most important of the century. In 1889 Paris played host to the largest international exhibition mounted in the 19th century. It had the Eiffel Tower as its centrepiece and was the first to be illuminated entirely with electricity. These events encouraged trade exhibitions all over the world. The United States organized the 1876 exhibition in Philadelphia, and Italy organized the 1901 exhibition at Turin.

However, it was the early trade shows in France that prompted the British Government to organize perhaps the most famous design exhibition of the 19th century – the > Great Exhibition of 1851. Opened on 1 May in Hyde Park, it was an outstanding success, attracted millions of visitors, made a profit and the building constructed to house the exhibition became world famous. Designed by Joseph Paxton, it was built of iron and glass panels and nicknamed the Crystal Palace.

The Great Exhibition turned out to be a celebration of the new technologies and inventions of the Industrial Revolution. Manufacturers showed their most extravagant pieces and naturalism was the order of the day; popular design was confident, large-scale and ornate. These products were not greeted with much enthusiasm by contemporary critics. They argued that standards of taste were generally felt to be low and that the way to improve the situation was through education. One interesting result of the Crystal Palace exhibition was the establishment in 1852 of the Museum of Manufactures. Intended as a teaching source for designers, it later became known as the South Kensington Museum, changing its name for the last time in 1899 to the > Victoria and Albert Museum. It now holds the world's largest collection of decorative arts and design. Its first director, Henry Cole, started to collect contemporary and later historical design as a teaching collection and the idea of such a museum was imitated all over the world. In 1863 the Paris Union Centrale des Arts Décoratifs was opened, and the following year saw the foundation of the Vienna Museum of Applied Arts.

Education was seen as the most important way of improving standards of design in industry, and in the 1830s the British Government recommended the establishment of design schools to train teachers. The project expanded quickly to 80 schools in 1860, and the student body rose from 3000 to 85,000. But there were, however, different views about what and how design students should be taught.

Controversies raged about the syllabus, which reflected deep divisions concerning the role of design in society – a debate that rages to this day. One important school of thought believed that design students needed direct contact with industry, but more controversial was the style and approach designers should practise. That debate is central to understanding design in the 19th century.

The key design debate of the 19th century concerned what style of > ornament design should use. From the Industrial Revolution onwards ornament – its appropriateness, production, quantity and method of manufacture – generated endless discussion. It was central to 19th-century design, so much so that an attempt was made to raise ornament to the status of an authentic art form in its own right. Research into the common language of design gave way to research into decorative forms appropriate for the new consumer products of the Industrial Revolution. There was a huge publishing industry of design source books, ranging from the scholarly to the popular, providing information on design traditions from all over the world. The most famous of these, and endlessly reprinted since, was Owen Jones's *Grammar of Ornament*. Jones's taxonomy of ornament demonstrates the century's obsession with > historicism (borrowing from the past). Even for the most progressive designers, historicism was an integral part of the 19th-century view of design. It provided designers and manufacturers with source material on designs as diverse as Aztec, Elizabethan, Roman and Islamic. From this body of research important theories and approaches to ornament and design were developed. Designers were required to meet public demand for pattern repeats on virtually all consumer goods and the > School of Design believed that this ornament should have a geometric basis. Sources such as Islamic art were important in this context because they provided examples of abstract pattern-making which avoided the pitfalls of extreme naturalism, the trend that had attracted so much adverse criticism at the Great Exhibition.

In 1842 William Dyce, then director of the School of Design, published a teaching manual called *The Drawing Book*, which put forward the guiding principle that geometric forms provided the most appropriate style for decorative patterns. Other experiments suggested that plant structure and the science of botany provided a rational way forward for design. Visual experiments at the > Ecole des Beaux Arts in France and the School of Design in England viewed nature as a

7

laboratory which should be investigated by scientific methods, and its principles then applied to design. This approach, to create a rational set of rules for ornament and design, suggested new training methods from which the design student could usefully learn. Leading educationists believed that exercises in simple geometric design developed the hand and eye, as well as the manipulative skills needed in the modern industrial world. Such ideas became extremely fashionable. Prince Albert, for example, encouraged his children to mix mortar and lay bricks, while educationist Frederick Froebel introduced the concept of constructive play by creating building blocks for children. These ideas have retained their popularity over the years. Games like Lego work on the same principle, and even such advanced schools as the > Bauhaus in the 1920s reintroduced simple geometric exercises for the students.

The counter position to these theories saw the School of Design position as cold, rational and even barbaric. It was a view of design that ignored the powerful forces of religion, nature and, indeed, the human spirit which, it was argued, was not mechanical and could not be reduced to a set of principles. An alternative group of design reformers saw the Gothic style as the way forward, and from the early 1860s the > Gothic Revival, in several stages and forms, dominated 19th-century attitudes and taste. As early as the 1840s Gothic became part of a protest movement against the forces of industrial change and mechanization. A well-known example of this protest came from Augustus Welby Pugin. From the 1830s Pugin's writings contained a simple message – that the past, and in particular the medieval past, which he called Gothic, showed a level of achievement and simple beauty that the 19th century could not rival. For Pugin Gothic, from a visual and moral point of view, was the only style in which to work.

This simple idea underpinned the attitude of other design reformers in the 19th century, and many designers began to regard the medieval past as a way of achieving social reform through design. In this they were influenced by John > Ruskin, the most important design writer and critic of the 19th century. More than anyone else of his age, Ruskin helped to shape the taste and attitudes towards design, and his writings became sacred texts for his and subsequent generations. Ruskin despised the industrial world England had pioneered, reserving particular dislike for machine-made ornament. His most famous books, *Seven Lamps of Architecture* and *Stones of Venice*, were passionate, monumental defences of the Gothic style, and underlying his research were two important principles: the first was that ornament and design should be based on stylized natural forms, and the second was that the production of design had a strong moral dimension. Although the Gothic Revival tended not to use specific Gothic details in design, the spirit of Gothic underlay attitudes about vernacular form, truth to materials and the role of design in society. Although it is possible to criticize these ideas as naive, none the less it is through them that the influence of the Gothic Revival remained strong. Gothic as a style for progress and reform is a difficult concept for us in the 20th century, but it is true that in the hands of the Victorians it was a design language and approach to objects that could be interpreted endlessly and with great imaginative effect. The vitality of the > Arts and Crafts Movement is proof of that.

What is somewhat ironic is the fact that Britain, the first country to experience the Industrial Revolution, also developed an anti-industrialization faction that quickly found a name – the Arts and Crafts Movement. Without a doubt the most important of its designers was William > Morris, a writer, socialist and the most influential design thinker of his day. Trained as an architect, Morris used his wealthy family's connections to commission furniture designs from such friends as Dante Gabriel Rossetti. In 1861 he took the logical step of starting his own company called Morris, Marshall, Faulkner & Co. The company and its products remained at the centre of Arts and Crafts ideas. Its first principle was truth to materials. Morris and many other designers associated with the movement believed that every material has its own value, for example the natural colour of wood, or the glaze of a well-made pot. Like any other Victorian designer, Morris also spent a great deal of time researching naturalistic patterns from sources as varied as Elizabethan plasterwork and Islamic tiles. He admired traditional vernacular forms that reflected a long process of creative and practical evolution.

The final component of hardline Arts and Crafts idealism was a commitment to social reform through design. Morris viewed himself as a revolutionary, and in some respects his political ideology and his designs seem at odds. The products of 'The Company', as his firm was affectionately called, were sold and still sell (in endless reproductions) to the affluent middle classes. Morris himself acknowledged this when he commented rather bitterly that he had spent his life catering to 'the swinish luxury of the rich'. He believed that beautiful design enriched the quality of life and that the designer had a moral responsibility in his or her work towards the greater good. Unfortunately, it simply was not within his power to bring those changes about.

In recent years an interesting re-evaluation of Morris has taken place. For so long considered a hopeless dreamer and idealist in the face of industrial and capitalist realities, Morris has recently been acknowledged for the revolutionary nature of his ideas – ideas that could still have relevance for the 20th century. But if there are implicit contradictions in Morris's life and work, there is no question that after 1880 his influence on design assumed an international importance. He quite simply became the most important designer of his generation. He also sparked off something unique in British design. The Arts and Crafts Movement produced a unique flowering of talent in this country, which meant that by 1900 Britain had become the international centre for new design ideas. It was a surprising turn of events for a country whose design tradition, though a vital one, had always suffered from a touch of inferiority and isolation from mainstream Europe. Now, for the first and possibly the only time, British designers made the running on a huge international scale. A selected list of British Arts and Crafts designers makes for impressive reading: Walter Crane, Edward Godwin, Charles Voysey, Charles Rennie Mackintosh, W.A. Benson, Philip Webb, Lewis F. Day, Heywood Sumner, J.D. Sedding and Kate Greenaway. These designers, apart from organizing their own society and exhibitions, made another important contribution to the development of design – they wrote extensively about their ideas and approach. It was part of the cultural tradition of their age; the printed word was the medium of communication, and they have left a huge body of essays and books which were and remain influential both at home and abroad.

Another important influence on design that deserves a mention here was the cult of Japan. When the American naval captain Commodore Perry arrived in Japan in 1854, he ended 250 years of isolation imposed by the Tokugawa shoguns. The European obsession for Japan, which replaced the previous interest in Chinese culture, resulted in a thriving trade in imported furniture, lacquerware, prints and porcelain. Western designers began to recognize that Japanese design and culture offered a unique aesthetic, and in the same spirit also developed an interest in what were seen as other primitive cultures. Although there were very few attempts to integrate these forms into 19th-century design, there were some interesting experiments which were to become more important forces in the 20th century. Dresser, for example, copied Aztec vessels for his ceramics, and in 1886 the Colonial and Indian Exhibition in London showed elaborate African sculptures from the Gold Coast for the first time. To Western eyes these were powerful icons which provided justification for radical experiments in form and decoration.

At the end of the 19th century Arts and Crafts ideals were not the only design ideas. This period also saw the flowering of the last great decorative style called > Art Nouveau. This became internationally popular from 1895 to 1905, and was famous for its sinuous, naturalistic style using plants, insects, the female nude and evocative symbolism. It introduced sensual elements into design, and often used explicit sexual imagery. The French took the lead with the work of Emile Gallé and Louis Majorelle, the so-called School of Nancy. But Art Nouveau is now used as a general term to cover the last great 19th-century revival of the decorative arts that spread internationally from such cities as Brussels, Milan and Vienna to the USA. Popular books on the subject interpret Art Nouveau very loosely, including, for example, the work of the Scottish architect Charles Rennie Mackintosh and an important Austrian group, the > Wiener Werkstatte, particularly the work of architect Josef Hoffmann. Founded in 1903, the Werkstatte was based on the British designer C.R. Ashbee's Guild of Handicraft. There are some important differences, however. In general, the Werkstatte products, based on a distinctive aesthetic using simple geometric forms, repeated grid motifs and rectilinear forms, were more > avant-garde.

Unlike the Arts and Crafts Movement, the work of the Werkstatte was not involved in bridging the now growing gap between avant-garde design and the problems of manufacturing industry. It was more concerned with matters of style than the transformation of society through Morris's ideal of joyous labour. This distinction helps to explain why Britain, such a design force at the end of the 19th century, actively rejected the Art Nouveau movement. Its aims and ambitions had no social context, its roots were foreign and the undercurrents of sexuality made it appear excessive and extreme set alongside the honest values of Arts and Crafts principles. This British attitude is reflected in the Glasgow School's nickname – the Spook School. The major British experiment with alternative avant-garde, linked to the writings of Oscar Wilde, the illustrations of Aubrey Beardsley and the interior design work of Edward Godwin, came to an end with the Wilde trial for indecency. That single traumatic event confirmed the British public's suspicions that Art Nouveau, as a Continental exploration of new directions and ideas, was fundamentally unsound, unsavoury and un-English.

Important though these European styles were for design, the USA was tackling other problems related to manufacturing, production and marketing that were to prove of fundamental importance to design and marked a shift from the 19th century to the modern age. In this context the United States and Germany are important. The US faced very special problems, namely the sheer size of the territories opened up by mass immigration of European settlers. At first these settlers relied on themselves to produce simple products like soap, clothing and furniture. The gradual spread of industrialization placed production in the hands of large corporations, who, by the end of the century, provided Americans with standardized household goods. And to overcome the problems of distribution, chain stores, starting with Woolworth's, were promoted in the 1880s, and mail order became an effective selling technique. By 1900 Sears, Roebuck & Company was dealing with 100,000 orders per day. This American retail revolution was matched by important manufacturing changes that became known as the American system. The principle was simple: design a product using standardized parts so that it could be produced or repaired anywhere in the country. The Colt gun, icon of the American West, provides an example of the new approach. The idea of breaking down a product into simple component parts led on to important new theories of factory organization, such as Frederick Taylor's *The Principles of Scientific Management*, published in 1911. Taylor advocated breaking down the labour process into its smallest tasks, a streamlining of capitalist production from which all might benefit. His ideas, known as > Taylorism, were influential on manufacturing pioneers like Henry Ford, who developed the assembly line process for the production of cars. Fordism, as it became known, came to represent the ultimate achievement of 20th-century production and was to have an important influence on the European > Modern Movement.

With the outbreak of World War I, the design attitudes of the 19th century inevitably suffered a reversal. The war tore Europe apart, its effects were devastating and the appalling loss of a whole generation of men killed in the trenches shifted society's aspirations and perceptions. A new direction was required, and in design terms that came with the emergence of the Modern Movement. The debates that had so preoccupied the Victorians – craft versus machine production, and the purpose and function of design – remained important, but what designers now wanted was an opportunity to meet the challenges offered by the > Machine Age of the new 20th century.

THE MODERN MOVEMENT

The Modern Movement describes a group of architects and designers who set about creating a new aesthetic for the 20th century, an aesthetic which for most of its practitioners was no mere style but an article of faith. The key feature of Modernism was a spirit of rationalism and objectivity that provided a sharp cut-off point from the 19th century and its obsessions with style revivals and decoration. Modernism, unlike the Arts and Crafts Movement, believed in the city as the future for all, made possible by the new inventions and products of the Machine Age. Another key concept of Modernism was 'Form follows Function', a slogan that reflects the movement's rational, ordered, Modernist approach to design.

Modern Movement designers also explored the belief that mass production led inevitably to pure geometric form, and in doing so totally rejected decoration. The great slogans of the Modernists that 'Less is more' (Mies van der Rohe) and Le Corbusier's description of the house as 'a machine for living in' have underpinned attitudes and approaches to design throughout the 20th century. This purist approach was not, however, the whole story, and Modernism during the 1920s and 1930s was never a single homogeneous movement. That view was largely constructed in the post-war years by carefully editing out the individual, expressionist contributions to 20th-century design made during those years.

An interesting case in point is the > Bauhaus, the most famous design school of the period and a centre for new ideas and progressive design. Founded in 1919 in Weimar, Germany, the school's first director was Walter Gropius, who was responsible for moving it to Dessau in 1925. Gropius designed the school and its furnishings to

13

provide staff and students with a complete modernist lifestyle. He also succeeded in attracting some of the most important design practitioners of the Modern Movement, including Herbert Bayer, Moholy-Nagy and Johannes Itten. Post-war histories of the Bauhaus stressed a single Modern Movement approach to design, a dedication to pure geometric forms based on the circle and the square, primary colours of red, blue and yellow, modern materials and industrial production techniques. That view edited out the complex and diverse arguments that beset the school, and the hardline Modernist position was always balanced by Expressionist theories, and in the case of Itten a belief in mysticism and alternative religions. This diversity of approach can also be seen in the very different schools of Modernism that developed on a worldwide scale. The Modern Movement was also called the > International Style, a tribute to the enormous impact the new direction had.

Modernist activity centred around > De Stijl in Holland, > constructivism in Russia, Le Corbusier in France, > Futurism in Italy, the work of Alvar Aalto and Gunnar Asplund in Scandinavia, and > streamlining in the USA. While there are common links in their work, their writings and manifestos reveal a more complex picture. De Stijl, for example, was the Dutch art and design movement that promoted a rigorous aesthetic using primary colours, as well as white, grey and black, and which restricted design to flat planes and strong geometric shapes. (The best-known example is Gerrit > Rietveld's Red-blue chair of 1918.) Members of the movement were also inspired by a religious system called theosophy, whose strict, puritanical element reflected the prevailing Dutch Calvinist culture. They rejected decoration in favour of formal abstraction, and that formed a link with > Russian constructivism. The Soviets, however, had a rather different ideology in that their work, although only for a short period of time, formed part of the political movement. They concentrated on practical products for the Revolution: clothes, books, workers' cafés and housing.

In complete contrast were the experimental ideas of the Italian Futurists, who, alone among Modern Movement practitioners, allied themselves to right-wing Fascist ideology. It had started as a literary and social movement to create a new, modern country free of the past and ready to engage with the industrial culture of cars, machines and aeroplanes.

More individual was the work of Le Corbusier in France. His approach to architecture and design represents the embodiment of the purist Modernist spirit. In his famous book *Towards a New Architecture* Le Corbusier advocates a universal and timeless geometry using simplicity and pure form. In this respect his work has a direct relationship to classical antiquity, but he believed that mass-produced products could share these timeless qualities and be integrated into a new architecture appropriate for his time, which enjoyed comfort, sunshine, light, order and harmony. What this meant was new, open, internal spaces to his buildings and dramatic white concrete outlines to his most famous buildings, including the Villa Savoye.

Other countries toed a less hard line. Sweden and the US, for example, developed a more popular and accessible modern style for the general public. The Scandinavians and, indeed, the British preferred a less extreme approach. This is particularly true in their attitude to materials, in general preferring to use natural materials and less extreme geometric forms. American design also played an important role in the development of a style which was called streamlining. During the Depression years of the late 1920s, a small group of pioneer industrial designers emerged in the US, who applied the styling of the Machine Age to such products as trains, fridges, vacuum cleaners and cars. These designers included Raymond Loewy, Walter Dorwin Teague and Norman Bel Geddes, and their achievements were shown at the 1939 New York Worlds Fair which took as its theme a vision of the future. Although hardline Modernists attempt to dismiss the American contribution as mere 'styling', a more recent view is that their work creates a vital and important contribution to the 20th-century search for an appropriate design language.

During this time, too, decoration remained important. Popular design used the language of architectural geometric forms to create a highly successful style which took its name from the famous 1925 Paris exhibition, the Exposition des Arts Décoratifs – Art Deco. Some commentators felt this style merely copied the appearance of Modernism with little understanding of its principles and theories. Such criticism did not prevent the flowering of a popular decorative arts and design style in the 1930s, which proved extremely popular but which was dismissed by the Modernists who called it > Moderne.

Challenged in this way by popular taste, Modern Movement practitioners themselves were encouraged to explore and debate their ideas. And although the group never produced a single manifesto, it did come near to it via the Congrès Internationaux d'Architecture

Moderne (>CIAM), a campaigning body of architects, writers and designers who met and debated Modern Movement ideas in the 1930s. But two important Modernist design writers did emerge. The first was the writer and CIAM secretary Sigfried >Giedion. His 1948 publication *Mechanization Takes Command* is a key design history text and the first book to argue that the anonymous, technical aspects of design history are just as important as the history of creative individuals. To explain the history of conveyor-belt production techniques, Giedion selected some fascinating examples, including the Colt gun and killing methods used in Chicago slaughter-houses. His approach suggested a wider cultural context to design history, which proved extremely influential.

Rather different in approach, but equally influential, was the Modernist writer Nikolaus Pevsner. He arrived in Britain as a refugee in 1936 and published the legendary *Pioneers of Modern Design*, for nearly 60 years standard reading for every design student. This book had a single and powerful ideology: that the history of design in the 19th century prepared the ground for the inevitable forces of Modernism. Pevsner helped to create a popular perception of design as a series of male heroes, and at the same time virtually invented the history of the subject as an area worthy of serious academic study.

It was not until the post-war period that these assumptions and values were effectively challenged, first by >Pop Design in the 1960s and then by >Post-Modernism in the 1970s. Modernism was now exposed to some major critical re-evaluation, and its critics were loud and forceful. It was argued that its rules on material and form were dictatorial. Modernism was too narrow an approach to design. Its reverence of the machine played down the creative, imaginative nature of the human spirit. Equally, it ignored the complex meanings and emotional functions individuals gave to objects. The idea that a single design approach could be right and appropriate was clearly not the case.

In the post-war period Europe and the United States applied many Modernist ideas to the massive rebuilding programmes undertaken by devastated cities. Some of the results were less than inspiring and too often the dreams of gleaming cityscapes degenerated into miserable high-rise concrete developments. The legacies of these reconstruction programmes have proved so traumatic and so profound that they go a long way to explaining the revisionist views and attitudes that have found a voice in Britain in the Prince of Wales. Nonetheless, the

Modern Movement remains the 20th century's great giant of design. It is also true that the majority of the 20th century's pioneer architects, designers and theorists were, in one form or another, dedicated Modernists.

The Modern Movement also has a claim to occupy the moral high ground because of the importance it placed on the mass-produced object for all, and on the relationship between design and social function. For these reasons the Modern Movement is generally linked with left-wing values and the pre-war period. However, its great achievements were not restricted to that time. After 1950 Modernism found expression in the distinguished industrial design work of Dieter Rams, and in the ordered and rational approach of the so-called Swiss School of Typography. More recently architects such as Sir Norman Foster and Richard Rogers have reinterpreted the aspirations of the Modern Movement for the contemporary era. From the perspective of the 1990s, however, it is inevitable that the movement's history is interwoven with a legacy of hero-worship, conflicting facts and mythology that continue to fuel debate and argument.

DESIGN IN THE POST-WAR PERIOD

In 1939 the war brought to a halt the consumer culture of design and style. The energies and resources that had previously gone into the design of consumer goods were now directed towards the manufacture of armaments, gunships, transportation and other military requirements of world war. The factories which had formerly produced furniture now worked on fighter planes, the textile mills on parachute material and military uniforms. The circumstances of war therefore made the design debates of the 1930s rather insignificant. Careers, too, came to a halt. Designers, like other professionals, were called up to fight and die for their countries. Only in special circumstances were designers allowed to continue their work. These included graphic designers involved in producing propaganda material and a small group of designers entrusted with development work on military weapons and machinery. In the latter category of engineer/inventor/designer is Sir Barnes Wallis (1887–1971), chief designer at Vickers, who developed the Wellington fighter plane and the famous 'bouncing bomb' which successfully destroyed the Eder Dam in Germany. In the United States furniture designer Charles Eames was responsible for designing plywood splints, which were destined to save the lives of injured soldiers.

One unique design experiment did, however, take place in wartime Britain. In 1941 Winston Churchill ordered the introduction of a scheme called > Utility, which was to design and produce a limited range of consumer goods, including tableware, clothing, radios and furniture. Utility design meant that everyone was to be given the same choice, at the same price and under a strictly controlled scheme of ration points dependent on family circumstances rather than income. For Britain it was an extraordinary Socialist experiment that only the constraints of war could have introduced. Utility design was placed in the hands of a small group of designers who had pioneered, in a modest way, the Modern Movement in Britain. It was a fascinating design experiment, finally brought to a close in 1952, and it meant that top couturiers like Norman Hartnell designed everyday dresses for ordinary women, while Enid Marx worked on textiles and Gordon Russell produced a range of furniture.

The Utility scheme was unique to Britain and there was nothing quite like it in the rest of Europe. From 1939 to 1945 the most powerful influences on design in Europe were the buildings, insignia and products of Nazi Germany and Fascist Italy. These totalitarian states promoted types of architecture and design which favoured a return to > Classicism, figurative art and nationalist typefaces using Gothic scripts. The Nazis associated the Modern Movement with either Jewish or Communist sympathies, so it was totally unacceptable to them. The Fascist imagery of Italy, Germany and Spain will forever remain powerful, frightening and evocative, but Fascism acted as a powerful force behind manufacturing industry and design. Fascist ideology produced some key design achievements, including the Volkswagen Beetle, and it is certainly true that when, in 1945, the peoples of Germany, Italy and Japan were freed from military dictatorship, many of the developments, attitudes and enterprises the State had imposed were put to good use in post-war rebuilding programmes.

In 1945 the war had brought devastation, exhaustion and virtual economic collapse. Of those countries involved in the conflict, only North America and Australia remained virtually unscathed. To aid recovery the United States introduced the Marshall Plan, which allocated large grants of money and technical aid not only to reconstruct the countries of the Alliance, but also those like Germany

18

and Japan which had suffered defeat. A key strategy in these rebuilding plans was the role of design in helping to increase exports and boost trade and manufacturing. Britain, for example, set up the Council of Industrial Design, a government body with a remit to promote design in both the public sector and in industry. Now known as the > Design Council, this body still continues in that role. Other countries followed Britain's example: in 1950 Germany funded a design organization called Rat für Formgebung, and 1954 saw the launch of the Japanese Industrial Designers' Association (JIDA). Governments began to back design in the form of exhibitions and trade fairs at home and abroad, and famous examples include the Milan Triennales, the Festival of Britain and Helsingborg '55. Design had become an important issue. It began to attract media attention in the press and on the radio, and the international design profession, for so many years denied the opportunities for work, were anxious to play their part in the new world.

Given the legacy of war, with its shortages and rationing, it is hardly surprising that the 1950s experienced a whole new attitude to design which is often called > Contemporary. This was more than a commitment to a new design style – it was a vision of the future.

The war had left an important heritage of common purpose and cooperation to rebuild the future. In this context Contemporary was not meant as an exclusive design style, but to provide well-designed objects for everyone. In the immediate post-war years there was a great concern that modern design should be a classless style available both to the affluent and the ordinary working family. This was an important design ideology shared by designers, consumers and governments alike. The Norwegian government, for example, aimed to stimulate sales by providing furniture grants to newly married couples, while in Britain the Design Council furnished new-town show houses with Contemporary design to demonstrate its advantages and its low cost. Although this design idealism lost ground as the 1950s progressed, the design profession shared a belief that design had an important role to play in social improvement. Underlying these changes in design attitudes was the post-war economic boom of the 1950s which, although most significant for the US, also affected Europe and by the end of the decade Japan. All over the world designers were commissioned to produce objects for the post-war home, which needed to be more flexible and more compact, introducing such items as the room divider and the convertible bed-settee. At the same time there was an enormous demand for cars, motorbikes and consumer goods, including fridges, cookers, radios and televisions. The economic boom not only provided designers with work opportunities, but it also gave confidence to enlightened manufacturers that modern design products would sell.

The new styling of the 1950s was also referred to as 'organic' because of its curving, sculptural forms that took some of their inspiration from the fine art developments of such sculptors as Henry Moore, Alexander Calder and Jean Arp, and the painters Paul Klee and Jean Miró. This new attitude to form, as fluid, curvilinear and expressive, made a tremendous impact on design. It became an important liberating ingredient of Contemporary style, influencing items as diverse as sofas, ashtrays, radiograms and cocktail bars, and producing some of the most bizarre, asymmetrical shapes of the century.

Another important change to design in the 1950s was the re-emergence of bright colours and bold patterns. This was a natural reaction to the shortages, rationing and restrictions the war had imposed. Now consumer choice involved selecting colour combinations using adventurous juxtapositions of colour and pattern for tableware or for the interior. The colours of the 1950s – hot pinks, sizzling oranges, sky blues and canary yellows – found their way into post-war homes in a new range of wallpapers, textiles and carpets. Texture was another important theme. The typical 1950s home was characterized not only by vivid colours but also by various textures that might typically combine Formica and natural wood with brick and stone. This tactile theme extended to the surface treatment of household products in the 1950s which used incised, raised or impressed patterns, combining these with techniques such as frosting and acid etching. Linked to this was the growing influence on designers of Abstract Expressionist painting, which had an enormous influence on designers' attitudes to pattern.

Also important was the role of science and the post-war partnership of a new aesthetic and new technology. The 1950s was the age of atomic power and the Sputnik, and designers were deeply affected by this vision of a new future. This attitude to technology led to two developments. The first was the impact of new materials and new technological processes in transforming industrial production. Plastic technology was advanced with the discoveries in 1942 of polythene and polyester, and in 1957 of polypropylene. Plywood is an interesting example of a material that made great advances during the war. With the invention of synthetic glues and advanced kiln techniques, it became possible to bend it into dramatic sculptural shapes. Furniture was a particularly important area for new technical experimentation using materials like Perspex and Formica, and production techniques like pre-formed plywood or moulded fibre-glass. And at the same time synthetic fabrics such as Terylene and Celanese were appearing on the market.

The second influence of science on design was as inspiration and source for applied decoration. Images from the atom, chemistry, space exploration and molecular structures were quickly absorbed into the general language of 1950s' decoration, and there was widespread use of crystal patterns and molecular structures. Space exploration was another important theme. Jodrell Bank was built in 1957 and that same year the Russians launched Sputniks I and II. Rocket imagery in graphic design and textiles was widespread, and the impact of space travel, both real and imaginary, caught the popular imagination.

Another important reason why design underwent such a marked break between the pre- and post-war period was a shift in the balance of power among the important design countries. Those which had dominated the international design scene in the early 20th century, such as France and Germany, were superseded in the 1950s by Italy, the United States and Scandinavia.

Italy was a surprising country to emerge and remain as a design pioneer and innovator. In the early years of the 20th century, Italy's programme of industrialization was a slow process. The Fascist movement of the inter-war years attempted to modernize the country and to encourage industry and new industrial products such as trams, trains and cars. However, traditional craft production methods in furniture, glass and ceramics still remained the norm. After the war the country was devastated and exhausted, but a remarkable determination to rebuild the country emerged in the late 1940s, a period now called the *Riconstruzione*. The overthrow of Fascism had a liberating effect on designers, who identified design as a democratic expression of the new Italy and as an opportunity to reject the formalist style associated with the dictatorship. In less than 10 years Italy became a modern industrial state to compare with that of France or Germany, and what was even more interesting was that distinctive Italian goods and products appeared on the market almost immediately. Italian design was associated with radical modernity and Italian designers struck out in completely new directions. Typically Italian was the partnership between companies such as Cassina, Arteluce and Techno, and architects like Carlo Mollino and Gio Ponti. The showcase for the new Italian design aesthetic became the now legendary Triennales. Held in Milan every three years, they not only showed off a new Italian confidence and design lead, but also encouraged vigorous debate and discussion within the profession, which enriched the process and direction of design in Italy.

By the end of the 1950s a recognizable Italian approach to design had been achieved in fashion and cinema, and introduced to consumer design icons such as Corradino d'Ascanio's Vespa scooter for Piaggio in 1946, Gio Ponti's 1947 expresso machine for La Pavona, and Marcello Nizzoli's 1948 Lexicon 80 typewriter for Olivetti.

Scandinavia was the other powerful source of European design. While Sweden, Denmark and Finland each enjoyed its own identity, there was a deliberate attempt in the 1950s to market the idea of a single Scandinavian approach to design. So successful was this strategy that by the end of the decade Scandinavian design became the domestic style of the 1950s, characterized by simple, functional, everyday objects that everyone could afford. This achievement had its roots firmly in the pre-war period when, for example, at the 1930 Stockholm exhibition the Swedish furniture of Bruno Mathsson and Josef Franck, as well as the architecture of Gunnar Asplund, made an enormous impression on the world design community. This humanist, restrained version of Modernism now combined with the new post-war elements of expressive colour and organic forms.

During the 1950s, Scandinavian design came into its own, and the range and sheer talent displayed in glass, textiles and ceramics was extraordinary. In the area of furniture the quality and innovation of Danish design remained consistently high with the work of Finn Juhl, whose furniture explored the strength and lightness of wood as a sculptural form, and Arne Jacobsen, whose stacking Ant chair became the most successful mass-produced chair of the decade. Jacobsen's experiments combining form and new technology produced a series of design classics, including the Egg and Swan chairs, which used moulded fibre-glass and padded latex foam covered in vinyl or fabric.

Finland moved into the international spotlight rather later with a series of radical experiments in the applied arts. Typical of these is the work of glass designer Tapio Wirkkala, who explored naturalistic and abstract sources, and Kaj Franck, whose tableware looked at the industrial problems of stacking and standardization using expressive forms and bright colours. The Swedish company Gustavberg also took an international lead in the production of innovative, mass-produced ceramics, giving the consumer a wide choice of colour, pattern and form using the new aesthetic of 1950s design. The products of Scandinavian companies like this, and others, such as Marrimekko textiles, went international and shops with names like Svensk and Dansk appeared in high streets all over the world. In fact, Scandinavian designers so dominated the 1950s that no home was complete without a Danish chair or a Swedish rug.

The United States was also in the forefront of design during the 1950s. Although involved in the war, it did not suffer the same economic devastation as Europe, and during the 1950s became the world's most important economic and political power. From 1954 to 1964 the USA enjoyed a boom which enabled it to lead the world in all areas of consumer goods, industrial design and manufacture. During the 1950s it developed two important design directions. The first, in the fields of architecture and furniture, was a contemporary style comparable to that of Europe. In terms of design innovations two companies, Knoll and Herman Miller, dominated the scene. Both these companies pioneered Contemporary design as a radical rethinking of function, structure and materials. Technical innovation was the key feature of their products. Knoll Associates' most influential designers were originally Harry Bertoia, who produced the famous seat made from a grid of bent wires, and Isamu Noguchi and Eero Saarinen who designed the moulded plastic Tulip chair. During this period George Nelson was design director at Herman Miller, and his star designer was Charles Eames who put into production his experiments first with moulded plywood and then moulded plastic.

The other important American design direction arose from the country's status as the world's most advanced popular consumer culture. This was characterized by such 'inventions' as the drive-in movie, McDonalds, Disneyland, television and teenage films and music. It was consumer design at its most extravagant both in form and detail, and it was a celebration of the country's enormous spending power. The 1950s' American car remains the most enduring icon of

>Populuxe culture and its most famous designs were the work of Harley Earl for General Motors. For the Chevrolet and the Buick he used lavish chrome tail fins and details copied from rockets and jets. He introduced a whole range of colours, including the innovative two-tone paint finish.

Popular design in 1950s' USA had little in common with the design attitudes of European Contemporary. It was a celebration of design for the consumer and it remains a powerful influence on attitudes and aspirations to this day. By the end of the 1950s, however, these design directions faced a new challenge. Rather different cultural forces had started to develop. The challenge of > Pop was about to overturn the values of 1950s' design.

THE POP AESTHETIC IN THE 1960s

The culture of design underwent a fundamental change in the 1960s when > Pop Design challenged the traditions of Modernism which had dominated international design from the 1930s. The Modern Movement position was that design had to function well, use little or no decoration and be made to last. Starting in London in the 1950s, a younger generation of design theorists and practitioners were to up-end these ideals.

This alternative set of values were explored by the > Independent Group, who met informally at the Institute of Contemporary Arts (ICA) from 1952 to 1955. The group, consisting of artists, architects and writers, argued that design values need not be universal but could legitimately be ephemeral and based less on functional values than on the desires and needs of the consumer. The result of their meetings was to provide a new analysis of popular culture. They tried to break down the traditional division between high and low culture, which placed theatre, art and opera on one side of the divide, and music halls, popular entertainment and comics firmly on the other. In the 1950s crossovers between these two defined areas were virtually non-existent. What the Independent Group established was the idea that artists and designers should investigate this world of popular culture. In a series of now famous seminars they began to explore the world of science fiction, advertising, toys and comics. By the end of the 1950s the results of their explorations were a series of early Pop paintings and sculptures, some experimental architectural projects and the writings on design of Peter Reyner Banham. In 1991 a major retrospective exhibition on Pop at the Royal Academy in London reaffirmed the group as its founders. However, Pop was also to develop independently, but slightly later, in the USA and then spread outwards internationally from the art world to the world of design.

The wide acceptance of Pop was made possible by a different revolution, which also had its roots in the USA and Britain – the appearance of an independent youth culture in the 1950s. During that decade teenagers developed their own style, language and music independent of adults. Particularly interesting was that in Britain this revolution was in the hands of working-class teenagers. This group had benefited from the post-war years of expansion and for the first time had the money and confidence to create its own style. In 1959 a marketing report on working-class teenage spending patterns estimated that teenagers now controlled 10 per cent of the country's disposable income, and their taste preferences dominated the production of goods such as clothing, motorbikes and record players.

At first British teenage culture was led by things American – the music of Elvis Presley, the films of Marlon Brando, denim jeans, hamburgers and Pepsi-Cola. But by the end of the 1950s a new confidence in things European had taken hold. Colin MacInnes's cult novel of the period, *Absolute Beginners*, described the shift to expresso coffee bars, Italian shoes, tailored clothes and Vespa scooters. It was also reinforced by the appearance of a dynamic, richly talented culture in music, novels and acting. It was a revolution that infiltrated and slowly changed the establishment status quo. The best-known example of this explosion of new talent is the music of Liverpool and the Beatles. In 1956 John Lennon was a Teddy boy, wearing a leather jacket and a quiff, but in the early 1960s the Beatles were transformed into new Europeans, wearing Italian suits with tight trousers and cropped jackets, Chelsea boots and 'mop-top' hairstyles.

These changes marked the rise of London as the centre of the new Pop culture in films, photography, literature, satire, fashion and music. The 1960s were possibly the only time in the 20th century that London became the international centre for new design trends. In 1964 *Time* magazine ran an article on the city and coined the term 'Swinging London'. Alongside the article was a tourist map on which were marked not the traditional historic sights of Buckingham Palace and the

25

Tower, but the new boutiques of the Kings Road and Carnaby Street: Top Gear, Biba and Granny Takes a Trip.

During the 1960s the souvenirs and clothes on sale in Carnaby Street expressed the priorities of Pop design. It was instant and expendable, witty and ironic. Typical surface patterns from the period included flags, bull's-eyes, stripes and polka dots borrowed from Pop paintings of the period and from the popular cultures of the seaside, advertising and comic books. The visual effect of these patterns was not intended to be long-lasting, and neither was their source restricted exclusively to Pop Art. In the 1960s there was a huge rediscovery of the 19th century, particularly the more bizarre aspects of Victorian taste and imagination. Elements which found favour included the nonsense verse of Edward Lear and Lewis Carroll's *Alice in Wonderland*, with Alice drinking strange substances and talking to surreal animals. It became fashionable to appreciate artistic aspects of the 19th century; the rock group Led Zeppelin bought the Tower House designed by the Victorian architect William Burgess, and a publishing industry sprang up reviving Art Deco kitsch, Art Nouveau posters, the 'mad' paintings of Richard Dadd and books on forgotten figures, including Charles Rennie Mackintosh, of whom it is almost impossible to believe that 25 years ago he was virtually unknown outside his native Glasgow.

These revivalist elements were picked up and used in a casual, disposable way that reinforced Pop's basic premise that design was temporary. In some cases design was literally throw-away. In 1964 the British furniture designer Peter Murdoch designed furniture out of five-layer laminated paper which could be bought cheaply, replaced easily and then thrown away. The same principle applied to paper clothes, which could be worn once or twice and then simply discarded. Meanwhile, avant-garde designers in Italy devised the inflatable chair and the famous Il Sacco, called the Sag Bag in England, which used a simple fabric cover sewn in segments and filled with polystyrene pellets. Such designs could truly be described as a new aesthetic for a new age.

Another key element of 1960s' design was the fundamental belief that technology was king. The French couturier Courrèges launched his famous space age collection, featuring mini-skirts worn with short white plastic boots. Space travel was the great adventure in the 1960s, culminating in the USA's successful Moon landing in 1969, and versions of astronauts' silver suits quickly became high-fashion items.

There was a commitment to the future and to sweeping technological changes that were just around the corner. This attitude invaded the imagery of design, from computer typefaces used in popular graphics to the futuristic interiors used in James Bond films. In practical terms new materials such as PVC became available. This plasticized fabric, previously used for functional items like shower curtains, was now used for clothes when the production problems of welded seams was resolved. Plastic technology also made important advances and inspired radical experiments in Italian furniture design. However, the real impact of the promised technologies was rather slow in coming.

A notable contributor to technological advances was Japan. Although a newcomer to international design, and still heavily dependent on Western ideas, it was steadily leading the new industrial revolution – pioneering transistorization for domestic products like radios and televisions, the early use of robots in assembly-line production and computerization. However, the technological revolution suggested in the 1960s by such writers as Marshall McLuhan was not to become a reality until the 1980s with the availability of home computers, fax machines and portable telephones.

The theories behind the changes in Pop Design generated considerable writings during the 1960s, and these are also important to explore. Like designers, contemporary writers wanted to look at, and treat seriously, areas of popular culture which had previously been denigrated or ignored. Peter Rayner > Banham gave the first informed critique of Pop Design in a series of articles written between 1958 and 1965 on subjects ranging from cult films to *Thunderbirds* and folk art. Banham dismissed the idea that architectural writing provided the only forum in which to discuss such disciplines as interior design and furniture, and his insights reshaped the world of design writing. His American counterpart was the writer Tom > Wolfe, who invented the term > New Journalism to describe the style of design writing which emerged as the written equivalent of Pop Design. New Journalism used an accessible writing style that picked up on slang, colloquialisms and advertising slogans, an approach illustrated by the title of Wolfe's 1968 book, *The Electric Kool-Aid Acid Test*. Like Pop Art, New Journalism challenged the tradition of serious academic writing, which used its own language to address a small and exclusive audience. Both writers became essential reading for the Swinging Sixties and went on to influence a whole generation.

Other gurus who influenced culture and design picked up on the changes brought about by the new electronic age, and among the most important was Marshall McLuhan. In 1951 McLuhan had published *The Mechanical Bride*, which was then a unique analysis of American advertisements, and he went on to make prophetic utterances on the world as a global village. Intellectuals like McLuhan made conventional academics look hopelessly outdated and anachronistic, and their fundamental belief that technology was king was almost immediately challenged by a series of counter arguments that gained more credibility as the 1960s progressed. Design reformers like Vance Packard argued against the benefits of industrial progress, particularly the concept of > planned obsolescence, an American manufacturing strategy of the 1950s aimed at encouraging consumers to buy more goods. In his writings Packard attacked obsolescence as a social evil, and his ideas gained a great deal of sympathy among a small but growing group of designers. Buckminster Fuller's experimental design work, for example, advocated recycling techniques, imitating forms from nature and a closer relationship between design and the work of sociologists and anthropologists. In 1971 Victor > Papanek popularized these ideas in a best-selling book called *Design for the Real World*.

These alternative ideas gained ground with the > Hippy movement of the late 1960s and its rejection of consumer culture and industry. Design in the hands of the hippy idealists concentrated on do-it-yourself housing units, solar energy panels and relearning craft skills such as weaving and shoemaking. Although these alternative views reflected minority thinking, they effectively started the move towards ecology and green issues which have become so important during the last decade. The importance of hippy culture remains controversial. For some it reflected rather self-indulgent, middle-class ideas rather than a genuine movement for social change. But the hippy movement certainly introduced a rather different design approach. The mini-skirts and > Op-art patterns of earlier Pop Design shifted into a movement also described as > Psychedelia. The 1967 Beatles album *Sgt Pepper's Lonely Hearts Club Band* marked this shift. The cover, designed by Peter Blake, showed the Beatles with long hair and dayglo Victorian military uniforms, while the music and lyrics were dedicated to the culture of mind-expanding drugs like LSD.

Hippy culture sought liberation in drug use, combining this with a desire for social change. Scott McKenzie's hit single, 'If You're Going to

San Francisco', encapsulated the hippy philosophy, paying tribute to 'gentle people with flowers in their hair'. Clothes were now bought second-hand from flea markets and combined with imported ethnic clothes from India and the Far East. At the same time hallucinogenic drugs were used to explore the subconscious and release the imagination. Psychedelia used acid, fluorescent shades of green, pink and yellow to conjure up the images of a hallucinogenic 'trip', and the hallmarks of the style were improvisation, textual innovation, free-form composition and floating forms, many of which were borrowed from the intense sexual imagery of Art Nouveau.

Psychedelia had its greatest influence on graphic design. Oz magazine, launched in 1967, is an excellent example of psychedelic graphic style. It used hallucinatory decorative lettering and super-imposed images printed on pages coloured bright purple and blue. The perfect psychedelic medium, however, was the pop poster, which was cheap, mass-produced and conveyed the immediate and powerful visual impact of psychedelia. Further examples of this 2-D graphic use were the large painted murals that decorated such buildings as the Apple boutique owned by the Beatles. Psychedelia was a short-lived design style, which, in the 1970s, moved into the world of discos and pop concerts shown in the film *Saturday Night Fever*.

The international economic recession of the early 1970s, sparked off by the oil crisis of 1973, effectively brought the optimism and experi-mentation of 1960s' design to a close. The ephemeral values of Pop and its witty, experimental visual style were out of step with the new mood of conservatism. Manufacturers and consumers no longer had the confidence or money to support experimental design. This new social mood sought out the safe and the traditional, typified by such designers as Laura Ashley and her revival of country cottage products and textile prints. The era of Pop Design was over. But the issues it raised about decoration, the social context of design and the needs of the consumer were by no means dead. All these design themes were explored in the new theories and attitudes of > Post-Modernism.

DESIGN AND POST-MODERNISM

During the last few years design has become a highly conspicuous part of visual culture. It remains an important political and economic issue

29

and it enjoys a high media profile. In fact, design has become an important issue on many different agendas, and unravelling its role and direction in contemporary society has become increasingly difficult. This section aims to explain some of the important themes affecting design, starting with Post-Modernism.

Since the late 1970s the term Post-Modernism has been widely used to describe changes in design and culture in the widest sense. The term itself is a tribute to Modernism, the ideas and designers of the > Modern Movement that dominated 20th-century design from the 1920s to the 1970s. Although the word made its first appearance in the 1940s, re-emerging in the 1960s to describe the new attitudes of Pop Design, Post-Modernism only became a major force in the 1970s. Popularized by *The Language of Post-Modern Architecture*, an influential book written by the architectural historian Charles Jencks in 1977, the name applied not only to architecture, but to design and cultural change in general.

Post-Modernism initially started out as a critical opposition to Modernist principles and values. A new post-war generation felt that Modernism was too restrictive and puritanical in its approach. The Modernist ideal rejected decoration, popular taste and, as many critics felt, the idiosyncracies of human desires. Post-Modernism opened up a whole range of approaches to design, reviving ideas, materials and imagery that had been vetoed by the Modernists. One of the most important changes was a new attitude to > Historicism, a taboo area for the Modern Movement. Borrowing from the past has now become part of the pluralist approach to design in the 1990s. Another important aspect of Post-Modernism is that it became a broad cultural phenomenon, affecting much more than architecture and design. Its new approach also affected science, critical theory, philosophy and literature. In this broader perspective, Post-Modernism can be seen as an important transition in 20th-century thinking. Just as the Modern Movement can be seen as a response to the industrial > Machine Age of the early 20th century, Post-Modernism can be seen as the late 20th century's response to the age of computer technology.

As a movement of widespread intellectual change, Post-Modernism had an important impact on design. One of the most interesting developments arising from it is that many of the important ideas and theories influencing design did not come directly from the world of design. For example, new strands of thinking came from the French philosophical tradition, and a group of intellectuals whose ideas interacted with design as part of the new climate of Post-Modernism. Concepts such as > Semiotics, > Structuralism and > Deconstruction now entered the language of design debate and discussion. It was all part of a wider move to enlarge the arena of design and to shift it away from practical, problem-solving activities to the larger intellectual world of ideas. One of the cult figures associated with this move was Roland > Barthes, a French philosopher who, in 1957, published *Mythologies*, a short collection of essays on such subjects as cars, toys and advertising. The book was translated into English in 1972, but until then the work of Barthes remained obscure and largely unknown outside France.

For Barthes design was not interesting from a visual point of view; rather, it revealed the underlying framework of contemporary society. This attempt to analyse the framework governing society was called Structuralism and it attempted to provide a rational understanding of human conceptual activity. Visual culture, Structuralism suggested, could be explained by understanding the structure of the human mind. This approach was criticized because it seemed to ignore the essential, unpredictable quality of human creativity. Inevitably it led to a counter position called Destructuralism, which argued that design was an intuitive activity that could not be reduced to a set of principles. None the less, the Barthes view of design, as a series of cultural signs that could be systematically analysed, became an important part of the design debate. This approach was also part of > Semiotics, another discipline attracting widespread attention in the design world.

Semiotics is the science of signs and it provides an analytical tool with which to explore the visual world. In the 1970s and 1980s designers began to feel that semiology was a possible tool to help reveal the needs and wants of the consumer. Unfortunately, most of the writing on this subject is theoretical and, so far, designers have shown little real understanding of how to apply these theories to design. Another semiotic-derived analysis is Deconstruction, which reveals the complex layers of meaning in an image by decoding social stereotypes and clichés about sex, class and gender. It was an approach used by another important French academic, Jean > Baudrillard. He used the methodology of sociology to explore the impact of consumer culture on contemporary society, and (of particular importance to design) he also challenged the accepted idea of

31

originality. In the era of new technology, with the endless reproduction of images from television, film and advertising, Baudrillard argued that the traditional view of originality had little relevance. In this way he provided an important intellectual justification for appropriating images, and deflected attention away from the argument that design should always be original or new. Inevitably these ideas found favour with designers in the 1980s, and they borrowed images freely from any source, including art history and popular culture. The new Post-Modernist theories of Structuralism and Semiotics, developed in the disciplines of sociology and philosophy, gradually infiltrated the design debate of the 1980s. There was, however, another important new area of research, originating from the world of science, which attracted designers' interest. This was the theory of > chaos.

Developed by the scientific community at Harvard, the theory of chaos reached a wider audience with the 1980 publication of Benoit Mandelbrot's influential book, *The Practical Geometry of Nature*. The theory suggests that we have only just begun to understand the complex and apparently random chain of reactions present in nature. As a theory it presents an interesting paradigm to design, contrasting the certainties of the Modern Movement with the open-ended approach advanced by Post-Modernism. Increasingly, it has become fashionable to apply chaos theory to the world of design. Its influence on architecture can be seen in the USA with the work of Frank Gehry, in Japan with the work of Arata Isozaki and Shiro Kuramata, and in Britain with the work of Nigel Coates and Ron Arad. Creative chaos is not, however, a design movement, but part of the pluralism implied by Post-Modernism and its relationship to cultural history in general.

In the 1980s design without clearly prescribed rules explored other cultural areas which challenged the status quo. > Camp and > Kitsch, for example, represented minority areas of taste, but they now entered the design mainstream. Designers used these areas of traditional 'bad' taste in a spirit of mocking irony. Camp and Kitsch offered designers a legitimate opportunity to work in the previously forbidden territory of 'over the top'. Interior design, for example, used camp elements in a knowing, self-conscious way by using cultural references and introducing inappropriate and over-dramatic details. In this way Camp and Kitsch became amusing dismissals of certain kinds of design and sensibility, and offered the chance to exploit elements once considered beautiful but now ridiculed as sentimental or old-fashioned. Kitsch, from the German verb *verkitschen* (to make cheap), refers to objects which have no real use – ornaments, souvenirs and general knick-knacks – and opened up a new vocabulary for designers to plunder.

The 1980s enjoyed a fashion for the lurid, particularly the shock element, of removing objects from their original context and placing them in a completely different one. Thus, there was a fashion for garish religious imagery, such as the Sacred Heart and Madonna icons, of southern Europe and South America. In this context, the cheap, tacky and tasteless could be enjoyed and admired, and this exploration of the crossovers between conventional good taste and elements of Camp and Kitsch has enriched the language of contemporary design.

In the last 20 years design research and theory have also benefited from new areas of study dealing with minorities, including Black cultures, women and gays. A new and important shift of attitude has taken place. The feminist analysis of design, for example, has looked again at the contribution women have made to design, in spite of the limitations imposed on them by economics and social conventions. Feminist writings on the history of design have challenged the traditional hierarchy, which places industrial design – predominantly a male area of activity – over the achievement of women in fashion, popular culture and the decorative arts. Consider, for example, the widespread idea that the fashion designer Coco Chanel, although interesting, is essentially ephemeral and her achievements cannot seriously compare with those of her contemporary, the industrial designer Raymond Loewy. Feminism has forced design to consider the simple fact that women's experience of the design world, as practitioners and consumers, is different from that of men, but of vital importance in creating a balanced society.

The cultural background to design, described earlier, is important to explain in detail. Design is not a single-track activity with its own exclusive direction. It is part of and reflects contemporary attitudes and society. None the less, the culture of design as a specialist activity, and the nature of design as a profession and a business should also be discussed, not least because those aspects have also undergone significant change in recent years. The 1980s were quite literally the decade of design boom.

The first manifestation of that boom was the rapid expansion of design practices. The economic hothouse of the 1980s saw the establishment of a new generation of designers, which in Britain included Fitch Benoy, Michael Peters and David Davies. The emergence of the design consultancy is a relatively new 20th-century phenomenon. The idea of designers working from their own offices in the manner of other professionals, such as accountants or solicitors, started in the USA in the 1920s with such designers as Walter Dorwin Teague. But the real growth of design consultancies took off in the 1960s, and a number of practices established then, including Pentagram and Conran Design, have grown into international companies. These consultancies tried to distance themselves from the idea that design was concerned only with styling by offering clients a range of services that included graphics, product design and marketing. During the halcyon days of the 1980s many of these design practices capitalized on their new business profile by going public on the Stock Exchange, and for the first time designers such as Terence Conran and Rodney Fitch appeared on the list of Britain's wealthiest men. Although the recession of the 1990s meant that design, in common with other service industries, faced severe financial difficulties, one important principle was established: design was now seen as an important business issue, not just as a desirable extra, but firmly established on the agenda of every successful company.

In the 1990s global companies like Sony and IBM invest heavily in design, but their approach is significantly different from the design practice profile just described. For large companies, design is a team process, a mutually dependent activity. These companies have led the way in the direction of interdisciplinary design teams, who rely on inputs from different areas and disciplines. Such teams now include electrical engineers, sociologists, production managers and service personnel, as well as designers. It is an approach that reinforces the reality of modern manufacturing needs, where a product like a computer requires the services of an industrial designer on the casing, a graphic designer on the user manual, and ergonomists, engineers and programmers on the computer. Interdisciplinary teams are now expected to take responsibility for the whole project.

Ironically, alongside this development of design teams within industry was the emergence of the 1980s' lone designer superstar. In this Italy led the way with its fashion designers Giorgio Armani and Gianni Versace, who became as famous and recognizable to the public as film stars. They and other design celebrities are showered with media attention, appearing on television chat shows and featuring on the covers of popular magazines. Perhaps the best-known example of this is the prolific French designer Phillipe Starck. After a conventional career working on architectural, interior and furniture projects, Starck has become a design megastar, with one of his most popular recent designs being a named designer toothbrush. Starck epitomizes the cult status of design and designers during the 1980s.

The new status of design was fuelled by high media exposure. Books abounded on the subject; television and radio features on design, rare in the 1970s, now enjoyed frequent programming slots; newspapers, for the first time since the 1960s, gave the subject regular column inches; magazines on design proliferated, and although these often overlapped with lifestyle publications, the 1980s also saw the expansion of specialist design journals, including the American *Metropolis*, the British award-winning *Blueprint* and the weekly trade paper *Designweek*.

The 1980s was a time when design filtered into every aspect of popular awareness. Advertisements exploited the new consumer awareness, while more 'establishment' institutions like museums also took up this new public interest. Traditionally focused on design as an historical activity, museums now concentrated on exhibitions high-lighting more recent design trends. The Italian > Memphis group featured in major exhibitions all over the world, while London's > Victoria and Albert Museum gave its first one-man show to the young graphic designer Neville Brody and profiled contemporary design directions in a series of exhibitions organized by a new venture called the Boilerhouse. The Boilerhouse was the brainchild of Sir Terence Conran and only temporarily housed at the V&A. It moved in 1989 to the London Docklands in the form of the world's first purpose-built > Design Museum. In the same spirit of adventure the commercial company Vitra opened a new museum of furniture in Switzerland. The Museum of Modern Art in New York, which for over 50 years had profiled modern design in its collections, developed another interesting trend. Its shop sold design classics of the past century, and this proved to be a major retailing trend of the 1980s.

These days every > shopping mall and high street has a shop selling design objects. These 'classics' imply permanence and longevity, objects which have sidestepped the vexed issues of style and taste. Companies like Cassina enjoyed great success selling reproduction designs of Gerrit Rietveld and Charles Rennie Mackintosh. In the Post-

Modernist world of changing values such items as these had a reassuring pedigree. This 1980s' obsession with the classic was also interchangeable with the rise of the designer cult object. Here permanence was less important than the fashion and style preference of a new, upwardly mobile and affluent group of consumers who wanted to buy into the myth of designer lifestyles. Cult objects were Levi 501s, the packaging of such drinks as Perrier and Coca-Cola, and the Filofax personal organizer. Young consumers looked to design to define a stylish and distinctive identity. Fashion encouraged a reverence for the designer label; it was more important who you wore than what you wore establish your identity and status. These attitudes and values have all but vanished in the 1990s. Consumerism has been replaced by a new consciousness, often described in the press as > New Age values.

What are the new priorities and direction of design in the 1990s? Two important themes have emerged. The first is the importance of green issues. During the mid-1980s a new political movement appeared on the design agenda. Ecology issues, often referred to as 'Green', represented an important new lobby on world politics and economics. The roots of green politics go back to the 1960s, when hippy idealism and an anti-industrial stance prevailed among the young. These views, however, were regarded as the quirky ideas of a minority. The triumph of green issues in the late 1980s is that they went mainstream. All over the industrial world legislation has been introduced in an effort to curb the effects of pollution, the destruction of large areas of natural resources like the tropical rain forests, and to control the indiscriminate use of insecticides. In Britain, for example, the amount paid by industry to environmental consultants in the mid-1980s was virtually zero, but by the end of the decade the sum had risen to nearly £200 million.

The growth of social awareness inevitably affected design and the consumer. In 1989 a book called *The Green Consumer Guide* spent 44 weeks in the UK bestseller list. Designers started to question the long-term implications of their designs and the materials they used on the environment. Independent bodies such as Friends of the Earth sent out information to designers warning that the use of certain hardwoods had dire effects on precious forest resources and suggesting more ecologically sound alternatives. But while simple suggestions like these made sense, the overall picture was more complicated and the way forward for socially responsible green designers was complex in the extreme. A new wave of products and packages stamped with the words 'environmentally friendly' paid only lip service to the problem. Many of the original ideas – reusable glass bottles rather than disposable paper cartons, and an avoidance of plastic as bad for the environment – are now judged to have been over-simplistic. The current approach is called 'eco-balancing', a method of evaluating materials on the basis of energy consumption, recyclability, raw materials use, pollution and waste. The aim is to provide manufac-turers and designers with a picture of the effect materials have on the environment as a whole. For the moment, then, > green design is only scratching the surface of a large-scale, complex problem, but its underlying principles have been accepted as the basis for planning the future of design and manufacturing industry.

The second most significant trend affecting design is the develop-ment of new technologies, including computer-aided design, > robotics and > information technology. Not surprisingly, the technological changes of the last 20 years have often been described as the Second Industrial Revolution. Take a single example of the way in which such changes have affected the process of graphic design. In the Western world designers rarely use paper, drawing instruments and lettering transfers to produce finished designs. They now work on computer systems like the Apple Macintosh, thus eliminating the need for hard copy and paste-up work. Disks are now sent direct to the printer, or computer systems can 'talk' directly to each other. The traditional methods of typesetting have been overtaken by digital technology.

Another important area of advanced technology is the development of robotics. The first industrial robots appeared in the car industry in Japan in the 1960s and performed simple tasks such as spot-welding and paint-spraying. In fact, Japan still leads the world in robots, which can now perform sophisticated tasks using sensors to detect changes in temperature, pressure and texture. However, two major problems need to be overcome before robots enter the human world of the home and the workplace. The first problem is robot movement, which is currently restricted, being dependent on crawlers or wheels, and far from smooth. The second problem, still very much at the research stage, is artificial intelligence, which eventually will make robots capable of making decisions. 'Fuzzy logic', a recent term coined to describe the process where machines have begun to make decisions, allows the machine's programmer to key in a computer language that is not rigid and precise, and that deals with the variables of everyday life. Washing machines, for example, can be programmed to test how dirty clothes are and to select a suitable wash cycle.

> Virtual Reality (VR) is another important breakthrough in computer technology. VR is the name given to new developments in media technology, which promise a tactile, animated world where the viewer is an active participant rather than a passive observer. To experience this interactive computer the viewer wears a surround-vision helmet incorporating stereo sound, and gloves studded with motion sensors. So far the equipment is basic and cumbersome, and has reached the mainstream only via the leisure industry, where it is used to play computer games. The possibilities of VR, however, are endless. Designers will be able to create 3-D objects and place them in a 'virtual' world; clients will be able to see and experience completed buildings and interiors before construction begins; advertising companies will be able to produce interactive advertisements for the consumer. These kinds of advances present a revolution in the person-machine interface. The two main areas of information technology – data processing and telecommunications – are on the point of converging. The future suggests the merging of multi-media, including computers, videos and television. The first prototypes for these systems have just become available in the USA and point the way forward for revolutionary change.

Design in the 1990s does not put forward a single idea about process or aesthetics. For the moment the recession has imposed restrictions and an opportunity to rethink directions. As we approach the end of the century, design faces new challenges. The climate of Post-Modernism has helped to create a much more sophisticated consumer and opened up design to a world of diverse and rich cultural references. Designers will have to respond to that and to the fact that technology looks set to reshape all our worlds in the 21st century.

A–Z Section

A

ACID HOUSE

Acid House encouraged a revival of early 1970s' culture and a taste for
> psychedelia that remains an important design influence. It started
out in 1987 as a British youth culture movement, founded by a group
of south Londoners who spent their holidays in Ibiza and turned up for
the subsequent reunion parties at dance clubs wearing summer
clothes, no matter what the time of year. The idea caught on, and was
combined with a taste for peace and love, as espoused in > Hippy
culture. The cult clothes were T-shirts, shorts and yellow 'smiley'
badges, and a drug revival, more Ecstasy than LSD, also played its part
in the movement. However, although the drug element attracted a great
deal of media attention, Acid House first achieved notoriety from what
became known as 'warehouse parties'. These were originally held
(legally) in disused industrial buildings in London, but they eventually
spread to suburban illegal venues, including remote aeroplane hangars.
Precise details of the venue were released only a short while in
advance, and partygoers, who had often been driving around for hours,
would create traffic chaos in their haste to reach the venue before the
police did. The 'Summer of Love' in 1988 saw a police crack-down on
Acid House activities; a number of parties were raided and there were
widespread arrests. In 1989 a 24-hour party was held on Clapham
Common, but shortly after that such gatherings were declared illegal.
By this time Acid House as a new style idea was finished.

AERODYNAMICS

The study of airflow upon moving bodies. Many 20th-century designers
and scientists, including Gustav Eiffel, creator of the eponymous tower,
built wind tunnels to study the shapes which caused minimum

resistance or turbulence – factors known to impede the speed of aircraft, trains, cars and ships. In 1932 Norman Bel Geddes published *Horizons*, which contained a great deal of seductive propaganda in favour of aerodynamic-style > streamlining. He, and other American designers like Raymond Loewy, often looked to nature to support theories of aerodynamics, citing, for example, the natural forms of ice floes.

AESTHETIC MOVEMENT

Simon Jervis, an acknowledged authority on Victorian design, deliberately excluded an entry on the Aesthetic Movement in his *Dictionary of Design and Designers*, published in 1988. Quite rightly, he felt that the term was an artificial invention, encompassing as it did such elements as the taste for > Queen Anne Revivalism and for the cult of Japan. The word 'aesthetic' did come to have a special meaning for the late 19th century, however, largely through George du Maurier's cartoons, which satirized the pretensions of smart society types who took up a taste for sunflowers, peacock feathers and Kate Greenaway illustrations. These people were considered to be 19th-century fashion victims and therefore the subject of much interest and press comment. > Liberty's department store marketed a range of Aesthetic clothes for women, and these garments were worn by May Morris and other members of the > Arts and Crafts Movement. Another key figure was Oscar Wilde. He deliberately cultivated himself as the centre of Aesthetic taste – slightly exaggerated, definitely exclusive and totally dedicated to the pursuit of art and beauty. Until his trial Wilde carried the whole thing off as a wonderful performance piece, an attitude that found favour in British society, as he never appeared to take himself too seriously. Wilde the aesthete brought to London a whiff of Continental values and ultimately what was perceived to be Continental decadence. When he was sentenced to a term of imprisonment for homosexual activities it effectively closed that era of British style history.

• Elizabeth Aslin, *The Aesthetic Movement*, 1969.

ALTERNATIVE DESIGN

The 1960s was the decade of consumer growth – a time when the problems of pollution and environmental damage went largely unchecked by governments around the world. Although global waste problems were understood and recycling was a known concept, the general pattern was not to encourage Third World countries to develop their own technological needs, but to impose Western standards of progress. Many argued that this was wrong. Among them was Victor > Papanek, who developed the argument in his book *Design for the Real World* (1971). This posited the view that designers had a moral responsibility to apply their talents to solving problems in the Third World. Papanek illustrated his book with such ideas as low-tech radios, contrasting them with products found in American small ads such as parrot diapers and electrically heated Queen Anne-style footstools. In the early 1970s alternative ideas took on anti-industrialized attitudes and images of self-sufficiency. For example, the American *Whole Earth Catalog* listed suppliers of geodesic domes, solar power units and make-your-own-shoes kits. People wanted to get away from the city and live in tepee communities in isolated areas of the country. The idea of small being beautiful gained considerable ground, but only as a minority position. When the environmental group Friends of the Earth was founded in the 1970s, it was seen as part of the alternative lifestyle movement, and its campaigns to save the whale and other endangered species were considered worthy but not mainstream. That situation changed radically in the late 1980s, when > Green Design emerged as an important political force. These days not to have a green policy is widely perceived as social and moral irresponsibility.

AMERICAN DESIGN

In the 19th century the huge territories of the United States were opened up by the mass immigration of European settlers. Before industrialization, farming communities produced the goods they needed; women spun, wove and made clothes, they consumed relatively few industrial products and they made their own essentials, such as candles and soap. By the end of the century, large corporations began to dominate the production and distribution of standardized, uniform products. The Industrial Revolution removed textile manufacture from the home and brought crafts like shoemaking, formerly done by independent craftspeople, into factories. Soap, lamp oil and cast-iron stoves came from local companies. Between 1890 and

1920 mass production and mass distribution brought new products and services – gas, electricity, prepared foods, ready-made clothing and factory-made furniture – to American families.

These innovations led to several particularly American responses, one of which was the appearance of numerous books on the subject of home management. The most famous of these was *The American Woman's Home* written in 1869 by Catharine Beecher and her sister Harriet Beecher Stowe, author of *Uncle Tom's Cabin*. It was the most popular of the household instruction manuals and offered a complete guide to the management of the American home. Among the Beecher sisters' most important ideas were their detailed plans for the kitchen; they rationalized the space and designed storage areas, which are claimed to have inspired > Modern Movement ideas of the 'machine-for-living' variety. Their ideas about the status of women in the home identified the American woman, at least in European eyes, as free-thinking and independent.

The USA was also to lead the way in other areas. For example, mail order companies, such as Sears, Roebuck, were developed to deal with the problems of retailing over such a huge country. In addition, a new system of design was created, which incorporated standardized parts and methods of production, allowing products to be manufactured to a uniform standard throughout the country. This approach to design was called the 'American system', and it became part of an industrial process that ultimately led to the factory assembly lines of Henry > Ford.

The 1920s and 1930s saw an American love affair with the new > Machine Age, reflected in skyscraper architecture, the cinema, photography and industrial design. A new breed of industrial designers appeared, including Norman Bel Geddes, Raymond Loewy and Walter Dorwin Teague, and they applied their new approach of > streamlining to such diverse products as the Greyhound bus, Coca-Cola packaging and household objects.

The USA enjoyed a period of economic boom after the Depression years, and in 1939 it showed off its new prosperity at the > New York World Fair. In the post-war period design remained an important issue for companies such as Herman Miller, who employed the furniture designers Charles and Ray Eames, Eero Saarinen and Harry Bertoia. Other American furniture companies such as Knoll also maintained a high design profile, while IBM led the field in the area of industrial design. The philosophies and attitudes of these companies were influenced by the European > Modern Movement, but their outlook was international. More homegrown was the design achievement of the 1950s. Encouraged by the consumer boom and a confident approach to styling, American design was exemplified by the car-styling work of Harley Earl for General Motors – a celebration of tail fins, bright colours and chrome. Other aspects of 1950s' design included automat diners and Tupperware containers, a style sometimes called > Populuxe.

During the 1960s the emergence of > Pop Design encouraged writers such as Tom > Wolfe to explore the creative world of popular culture. Although the 1970s brought a mood of conservatism, the USA introduced new directions in design with the emergence of > Post-Modernism. Led by the example of leading Post-Modernist architects, including Robert Venturi and Michael Graves, American design enjoyed a period of revived confidence. These developments were based in and around New York, but the west coast also saw important changes. California became the centre of silicon chip technology, and the Apple Macintosh company one of the most important in the field. The Apple Mac computer has transformed the approach to and practice of modern graphics, reflected in the work of such designers as April Greiman, and Zuzana Licko, who works for the arts magazine *Emigré*. Other Californian individualists include the architect Frank Gehry and design practices such as frogdesign, Design Continuum and ID Two. The work of these designers has meant that American design in the 1990s provides a powerful inspiration for new directions.

● Hugh Aldersey Williams, *New American Design*, 1988.

ANTHROPOMETRICS

The measurement of the human body and the particular characteristics of different sexes, ages and races of human beings.

APPROPRIATE TECHNOLOGY

A term from the late 1960s used to describe the equipment supplied to developing countries. Such technology aimed to be appropriate to their needs and not to impose the structure and approach of the West. It largely involved adapting limited Third World resources to basic local needs, and appropriate technology became part of the > Alternative Design movement of the same period.

ART DECO

A design style that derives its name from the famous Paris 1925 Exposition Internationale des Arts Décoratifs et Industriels Modernes. It was a luxury style that dominated the decorative arts between the two world wars, and at the exhibition was best seen in the work of the French *ebenistes* Jacques Emile Ruhlmann (1879–1933), who combined rich materials such as ebony, shagreen, ivory and expensive veneers with refined geometric shapes, and Jean Dunand (1877–1942), who had learnt the Japanese technique of lacquerwork and specialized in elaborate lacquered panels.

Art Deco was an inevitable rejection of the twisting, naturalistic forms of > Art Nouveau. It was characterized by decorated surfaces, faceted forms and complex outlines, including a taste for wrap-around surfaces on furniture and in interiors. The sources of the Art Deco style relied on new developments in fine art: the bold colours of Fauve painting, the influential sets for the Ballets Russes, and the Cubist-inspired paintings of African sculpture. Art Deco was an amalgam of the complex visual changes affecting art and design in the inter-war years. It reflected the new vogue for Egypt, which became popular after the discovery of Tutankhamun's tomb, and, unlike other > avant-garde movements of the 1920s, it had no hardline centre. In some respects its philosophy came from the ideas of the > Bauhaus, so Art Deco also reflected the new developments of 20th-century technology. Electricity, neon lighting and the reflective surface of smooth, stainless steel became the standard components of an Art Deco style that can be seen in everything from cafés to local cinemas and smart international hotels. This popularization of Art Deco caused a number of contemporary commentators to take rather a sniffy view of the style. They felt it was a corruption of the high moral ground that Modernism had started to occupy, and the term > Moderne was used to indicate that Art Deco was a perversion of a much more serious movement.

The popularization of Art Deco was particularly important in the

United States. Everything from theatres to refrigerators got the treatment. Hollywood films turned the style into an enormous industry in the 1920s, while New York, the 20th-century city, celebrated Art Deco with some classic skyscrapers, including the Empire State Building and the Chrysler Building, and Donald Deskey's interiors for Radio City Music Hall. Art Deco style became universally popular. It was particularly influential on jewellery design, where colour and flat geometric form could be shown off to advantage in custom-made pieces or cheap costume accessories. Decorative ceramics and tableware also picked up on the style, and it crossed all class divides in the 1930s.

• Yvonne Brunhammer, Art Deco Style, 1984.

ART FURNITURE

A British term used in the 19th century to describe the furniture designed by Victorian architects. Art Furniture was essentially a design reform movement, brought to public attention by the architecture writer Charles Locke Eastlake (1836–1906) in a series of magazine articles and books. The most popular of these, Hints on Household Taste in Furniture, Upholstery and Other Details, appeared in 1868, going to a fourth edition in England and to six editions in the USA. It was a manifesto in praise of overall rectilinear forms, honest construction and geometric ornament. Basically, the book adapted the style of designer-architects such as George Street (1824–81), Richard Norman Shaw (1831–1912) and William Burges (1827–81). In 1867 the architect Edward William Godwin (1833–86) set up the Art Furniture Company and 10 years later published Art Furniture. In this context Art Furniture now came to describe the Anglo-Japanese style of the > Aesthetic Movement.

ART NOUVEAU

A sinuous, naturalistic style famous for its asymmetry and whiplash line, popular all over Europe at the turn of the 20th century. The style lasted about 10 years, from 1895 to 1905, and took its name from a gallery called L'Art Nouveau, opened in Paris by Samuel Bing in 1895. Bing was a dedicated admirer of things Japanese and started his career selling Oriental imports. His gallery attracted international admirers and patrons, and exhibited the posters of Toulouse-Lautrec, art glass by > Tiffany, jewellery by Lalique and British wallpapers and fabrics by Charles Voysey and Walter Crane. Bing's influence was widespread, and in 1890 he organized his own pavilion at the Paris Exhibition. This was the first time the style and its major exponents had been shown to a wide audience.

Art Nouveau proved influential and successful. The French took the lead first with the work of the so-called School of Nancy. Emile Gallé (1846–1904) ran a large workshop in Nancy, employing 300 craftsmen to produce furniture and glass. He was a dedicated botanist who relished literal naturalistic details and had a reverence for symbolism, which lay at the centre of his work. Louis Majorelle (1859–1926) also ran a factory in Nancy, and under Gallé's influence changed his style from > Rococo Revival to Art Nouveau. The other key French Art Nouveau exponent was Hector Guimard (1867–1942), now best remembered for his Paris Métro stations, which have come to evoke the city's *fin de siècle* taste. His style elaborated the theme of asymmetry and the flowing abstract ornament of swirls and scrolls. Guimard had developed this style under the influence of the Belgian architect Victor Horta (1861–1947). Horta, who designed the Belgian pavilion for the 1902 Turin Exhibition, had single-handedly made Brussels into the most important European city for the new style.

Art Nouveau is now used as a general term to cover the last great 19th-century revival of the decorative arts that spread internationally from Europe to the USA. It is a style famous for flowing forms which derived their inspiration from nature and more than a glance backwards to the 18th-century taste for Rococo ornament. The movement acquired several names, including > Jugendstil in Germany, and Stile Liberty in Italy in honour of the London department store. Recent books on the subject often interpret the style widely, and include the > Glasgow School and the work of Josef Hoffmann and the > Wiener Werkstatte. The German historian Nikolaus > Pevsner put forward the thesis that the style had its roots in the British > Arts and Crafts Movement, pointing to the origins of the whiplash motif in the designs of Arthur Mackmurdo (1851–1942) and Aubrey Beardsley (1872–98). The British were less keen to be associated with another key element of Art Nouveau, namely the movement's sensual and often explicitly sexual imagery. By 1905 the > avant-garde had the movement in full retreat, to be finally discredited by the > Modern Movement. It was, however, the trademark elements – natural forms such as flowers and insects, the female nude and evocative symbolism – that made Art Nouveau ripe for a 1960s' revival. Reproduction posters of the style's great practitioners sold in huge numbers and were a reminder of the evocative power of sinuous decoration. The late 1960s saw an Art Nouveau revival that was particularly important for the graphics and textiles of > Psychedelia.

● Robert Schmutzler, Art Nouveau, 1962, 1964.

ARTS AND CRAFTS MOVEMENT

A design style that grew from the disillusionment many designers felt with the changes wrought by the Industrial Revolution. Increasingly, designers saw these changes only in terms of large, ugly cities, pollution and slum housing. They felt that the traditional values of life were destroyed by industrial progress. This spirit of anti-industrialization was an instinctive reaction against the highly visible effects of industry, and the movement happened quite quickly. From the 1830s the writings of Augustus Welby Pugin (1812–52) contained a simple but influential message – that the past, particularly the medieval past, which he called Gothic, showed more understanding of beauty and design than anything the 19th century had achieved. For him, Gothic, from a moral and visual point of view, was the only style in which to work.

This simple idea underpinned the attitude of design reformers in the 19th century. Influenced by Pugin and such writers as John > Ruskin, designers thought about the medieval past as a means of achieving social reform through design, and produced objects which were useful and beautiful. Morris summed up this approach when he said that design should be 'a thing of beauty and a joy forever'. Without doubt the most important of these designers was William Morris (1834–96). Despising the values of capitalism that could destroy the quality of people's lives, he became a designer, writer and committed socialist, the most influential thinker of his generation. Indeed, the heritage of his ideas remains with us to this day. As a student at Oxford Morris was inspired by the university architecture and the powerful romanticism of the Pre-Raphaelite painters. Some members of this group – Dante Gabriel Rossetti, Sir Edward Burne Jones and William Holman Hunt –

were to become and remain his lifelong friends and collaborators. At first Morris fancied himself as a painter, but soon realized that his talents lay elsewhere. His affluent family background meant that he could afford to commission furniture and architecture for his own home, and this led, in 1861, to the logical step of starting his own company called > Morris, Marshall, Faulkner & Co. The company and its products remain at the centre of Arts and Crafts ideas.

The first principle of the movement was truth to materials. Morris, and many like-minded designers, believed that every material has its own value, for example, the natural colour of wood or the glaze of a well-made pot. Morris believed that such qualities had to be respected in every design. He also tried to revive traditional methods of production that in his lifetime had been superseded by new industrial processes. For example, Morris hated the garish synthetic dyes which had been developed by the chemical industry during the 1830s, so he set his own works at Merton Abbey in Surrey to reviving traditional vegetable dyes and printing techniques like the discharge method.

Morris was a workaholic and a man who believed in hands-on experience. He spent hours teaching himself craft techniques like weaving and book production, and researching naturalistic patterns from sources as varied as Elizabethan plasterwork and Islamic tiles at the > Victoria and Albert Museum. He admired traditional objects developed over the centuries – a slow process of creative and practical evolution that Arts and Crafts designers deeply admired.

The final component of hardline Arts and Crafts ideals was a deep concern for social issues. Morris saw himself as a socialist and revolutionary, but it is only recently that left-wing historians like Raymond Williams have re-evaluated Morris in this light. In this respect his beliefs and his designs seem at odds. His wallpapers and textiles, for example, catered to expensive middle-class taste, as they still do. Morris himself commented bitterly that he had spent his life 'ministering to the swinish luxury of the rich'. He believed that beautiful design truly enriched the quality of life and took trouble to establish decent wages and working conditions for his workforce at Merton Abbey. He also believed that the designer has a moral responsibility in his or her work towards the greater good. Whatever the contradictions implicit in Morris's ideas, there is no question that after 1880 they became internationally important.

The Arts and Crafts Movement, with Morris at its centre, was hugely influential. It spread outwards from a circle of dedicated disciples to manufacturing industries that simply copied it as one more style. The Arts and Crafts Movement also produced a renaissance in British design. By 1900 Britain had become the most important centre for new design ideas. British magazines like *The Studio* had an international readership, and design experts came to Britain to study the developments it chronicled. Architect Hermann Muthesius wrote a report for the German government. It was a new turn of events for a country whose design tradition, though vital, had always suffered a touch of inferiority and isolation from mainstream Europe. Now, for the first, possibly the only, time, British designers made the running on a huge international scale.

A complete list of Arts and Crafts Movement architects and designers makes for extensive reading. Here are the first division players: Charles Ashbee (1863–1942), W.A. Benson (1854–1924), Walter Crane (1845–1915), Lewis Foreman Day (1845–1910), Edward Godwin (1833–86), William Lethaby (1857–1931), Charles Voysey (1857–1941) and Philip Webb (1831–1915). A fuller list of designers appears in Gillian Naylor's book (see below).

In the 19th century information on the movement came from extensive magazine coverage, books by the designers themselves and a series of exhibitions mounted by the Arts and Crafts Exhibition Society. The first exhibition was held in 1888 at the New Gallery in Regent Street. William Benson, Day, George Heywood Sumner and J.D. Sedding were the main activists, and the annual exhibition proved extremely popular and influential. The group also published its ideas in a series of essays, which are still regularly reprinted.

With the outbreak of World War I the activities of the Arts and Crafts Movement came to a standstill. In the years following the war the movement rapidly declined, to be superseded by the > Modern Movement, and with it disappeared the dominance of British design. The ideas of the Arts and Crafts Movement, however, have remained a significant influence on the 20th century. The debate that so preoccupied these Victorians – craft versus machine production, and the purpose and function of design – remains controversial. The movement effectively split design and craft activity, and in the 20th century the two have come to mean very different things: design is associated with manufacturing industry, and craft with individually made objects.

In every part of the developed world creative people still choose to opt out of the system, seeking a rural idyll and dedicating themselves to craft work. The impact of Arts and Crafts taste has also been diverted into mainstream design. The same people who buy home computers and video machines also want country-look pine kitchens and floral curtains, tastes catered to by British retailers such as Sir Terence Conran and Laura Ashley. With the increased pressures of life in the industrial world people are looking again at the ideas of William Morris, for so long considered a hopeless idealist and dreamer. His ideas are once again seen as relevant to the way we live and the way we plan the future.

- Gillian Naylor, *The Arts and Crafts Movement*, 1971.

LAURA ASHLEY

Ashley (1925–85) was one of the most important designer-retailers of the last 20 years, and the 500 shops she established with her husband Bernard continue to be an international success story.

She began her business marketing Victorian-inspired clothes for middle-class hippies, and the sprigged fabrics in which they were made became her hallmark. Hers was a nostalgic, fantasy vision of urban life that suited the revivalism of the 1970s with its obsession for stripped-pine Welsh dressers, country cottages and health food. Very quickly Laura Ashley started to market a whole lifestyle based on this look, including curtains, wallpaper, furniture, lamps and other household items.

Balanced against a taste for reworking traditional designs, the Ashley company introduced the latest high technology into their garment factories and employed advanced marketing techniques, including high-quality catalogues, user-friendly shop layouts and sophisticated advertising. Laura Ashley's work has been accused of being 'twee', and because of this her contribution to design is often under-rated, indeed, often disparaged by contemporary designers and design writers. However, to consumers at home and abroad Laura Ashley remains immensely popular. Indeed, it would be hard to identify another British designer who has made such a mainstream contribution to popular design in the 20th century.

- Laura Ashley, *The Laura Ashley Home*, 1989.

ASSEMBLAGE

A fine art technique, not a style, which combines two-dimensional materials and images and three-dimensional forms and objects. It became popular at the end of the 1950s in Europe and the USA. Assemblage attempts to erase the distinction between high and low art, imagery and materials. It was used to present the fragmented, diverse and rapidly expendable signs of the new consumer culture. The materials for assemblage could be natural or manufactured. The French Nouveau-Réaliste artist Jean Dubuffet first used the term in 1953 for his assemblages of papier-mâché, scraps of wood and other debris. Other work from the Nouveau-Réaliste group included César's compressed cars, and Jean Tinqueley's mechanical assemblage, photo-montage, advertising and > found objects. Assemblage was particularly important in the work of American artists Robert Rauschenberg, Joseph Cornell and Louise Nevelson. This was part of the Dada revival of the late 1950s, and was used both as a tribute and critique of the new consumer-led society, a position that Pop Art was later to exploit. Assemblage as a serious art movement was given official recognition in 1961 with the 'Art of Assemblage' show at the Museum of Modern Art in New York.

The process of working with diverse objects and materials has remained a central one for artists during the 1970s and 1980s, and remains a potent means of expression for the ecologically aware 1990s. The techniques and attitudes of assemblage art works have certainly influenced design. Most design students experiment with assemblage as a way of freeing the imagination, and several notable individualists in the areas of furniture and interior design employ the technique in their finished commercial work. The British architect Nigel Coates, for example, uses salvaged fragments, including aeroplanes, and recycled objects with specific references to mainstream culture in his interiors.

AUSTRALIAN DESIGN

The history of Australian consumer design is the history of white colonization, first by the British and then by other Europeans. A recent exhibition in Melbourne showed some early settler furniture, and there were touching examples of domesticity, such as old chair-backs used to make a crib. When the country's prosperity and city culture became established, Australia relied on imported European design ideas. It took some time for the emergence of a distinctly Australian style. The post-war period has seen a growing confidence in things Australian, and a mainstream Australian culture has emerged in the last 20 years. New films, literature, architecture and design have attracted international focus. In 1988, for example, the > Victoria and Albert Museum in London mounted a major exhibition on Australian fashion. Other design areas of interest include new Australian furniture from Marc Newson, Kevin Perkin and Toby Stewart. These designers are especially interesting because they have attempted to create furniture which explores an Australian heritage and uses native woods such as eucalyptus and myrtle. After years of importing design and style, Australian designers look set to introduce a distinctly antipodean flavour to international design trends.

● Tony Fry, *Design History – Australia*, 1989.

AUSTRIAN DESIGN

In the 19th century Vienna was at the centre of the Austrian Empire, and was famous for its flourishing cultural and intellectual life. It was also to make an important contribution to design, particularly on the difficult question of developing a style appropriate to the new 20th century. In 1873 Vienna had staged a conventional international exhibition showing off the prevailing Austrian taste for florid > historicism. Some 10 years earlier the city had also established a museum of applied arts and a design school following the example of the > Victoria and Albert Museum. It was not until the 1890s, however, that Viennese designers began to make a truly original contribution to design, when, in 1897, a breakaway group led by the painter Gustav Klimt (1862–1918) established itself as an independent artists' association. In 1898 Joseph Olbrich designed the famous Secession building, which became a visual symbol for progressive Austrian designers and architects. The group's magazine, *Ver Sacrum*, was also the name of a room designed by Josef Hoffmann in the 1898 Secession exhibition. Two years later the group's exhibition also included work by British designers Charles Rennie Mackintosh and Charles Ashbee. Mackintosh was to provide a particularly strong direction for progressive Austrian design and for Hoffmann in particular. It was, however, Ashbee and the Guild of Handicraft, which he co-founded in 1888, who inspired the establishment of a similar group of craftsmen and women called the > Wiener Werkstatte. Hoffmann and Moser had visited the Guild in Chipping Camden and were so impressed that they persuaded a rich banker to back an Austrian equivalent. The Werkstatte design work developed a rigorous geometric aesthetic, which none the less kept a place for decoration. In this respect Austrian design, until 1915, provided a significant bridge between 19th-century tradition and the Modern Movement to come. In the 1990s Austria is now a small, wealthy country, but it no longer provides any innovative lead for design.

● *Vienne*: 1880–1938, exhibition catalogue, Centre Georges Pompidou, 1986.

AUTOMATION

The replacement of human control by mechanical devices. Simple forms of mechanization include the use of computer terminals in offices, while more advanced forms allow entire production processes to be entirely controlled by machines. Processed food production, an industry which is now almost fully automated, used the closed-loop technique, which means that raw materials are fed into one end of a machine and a finished product is delivered from the other end without any human intervention.

There are many social responses to automation. Some argue that because automation reduces the number of employees needed in the workplace it contributes to unemployment. Others maintain that automation de-skills a high proportion of the workforce and creates an élite who are trained to do the highly skilled design and maintenance of automated processes. *See also* Braverman, Henry; Robotics.

● C. Gill, *Work, Unemployment and the New Technology*, 1985.

AVANT-GARDE

A French term to describe innovators and pioneers in art and design.

B

PETER REYNER BANHAM

Britain's most important post-war design writer (1922–88). A founder member of the > Independent Group, he was closely involved in the 1950s with the new Pop aesthetic. In some respects Banham was a conventional academic; his PhD thesis on the Modern Movement, which he wrote under Nikolaus > Pevsner was later published as *Theory and Design in the First Machine Age*. From 1958 to 1965, however, he wrote a regular column in the *New Statesman* dealing with design, technology, the mass media and popular culture. Those articles, on a diversity of subjects – customized Minis, household gadgets, the cult film *Barbarella*, the children's puppet programme *Thunderbirds*, sunglasses and folk art – made a major contribution to > Pop Design theory. Banham developed a theoretical basis for Pop in terms of its cultural relevance to the 1960s, and gave the era its first informed critique of Pop design. His writing was witty and accessible and challenged the traditional hierarchy of high versus low culture. Banham dismissed the idea that architectural theory and writing provided the only basis from which to discuss such disciplines as interior design and furniture. His insights on contemporary culture reshaped the world of design writing. However, from the 1970s he virtually stopped writing on design. Banham lost his constituency in the 1980s. He became curiously isolated and during this period he went to work in the USA and devoted his attention to architecture and the city. His most notable book was *America Deserta* (1982).

- Penny Sparke (ed.), *Design by Choice*, 1981.

ROLAND BARTHES

French literary scholar and critic (1915–80) whose writings have had an enormous influence on designers. His book *Mythologies*, originally published in 1957, enjoys a near legendary status. It contains a number of essays on popular subjects such as toys and advertising, and a particularly famous piece on the Citroën DS car. Barthes found popular culture interesting not from a visual design point of view, but because it reveals the underlying framework of contemporary society. From the world of design he attempted to extract the meaning, or in his words the mythologies, of imagery and form. He sought to understand the framework that governs society, and in this sense he represents a structuralist viewpoint. His concept of design as a series of cultural signs that could be formally analysed was part of the new discipline of > semiotics.

Mythologies was not translated into English until 1972, so until that time Barthes' work remained largely unknown outside France and the enclosed world of French philosophy. The subsequent influence and popularity of his work also constitute a little bit of cultural history. *Mythologies* is now required reading for any aspiring design student, and his work as a whole is part of a wider move to enlarge the arena of debate and to shift design away from merely practical, problem-solving activities to embrace a larger world of intellectual ideas.

JEAN BAUDRILLARD

Born in 1929, Baudrillard is professor of sociology at the University of Paris. He is part of a group of French intellectuals, which included Roland > Barthes, whose ideas interacted with design as part of the new climate of > Post-Modernism. Using the methodology of sociology, Baudrillard explored the impact of advertising and consumer culture on contemporary society, and particularly challenged the idea of originality. He suggested the notion of authenticity as essentially meaningless in an era where new technology facilitates the endless reproduction of information and images via television and faxes. These ideas found particular favour with designers in the 1980s, who appropriated images freely from almost any source. Appropriation is the practice of creating a new work by taking a pre-existing image from another context. Such borrowings are the graphic equivalent of the > found object. Baudrillard called this process simulation. Something of a cult figure among a younger generation of designers, Baudrillard provided an important intellectual justification for borrowing used images and deflecting attention away from the idea that design should always be original or new.

● Jean Baudrillard, *The Mirror of Production*, 1975.

BAUHAUS

A design school founded in Weimar, Germany, by Walter Gropius in 1919. It was to become the most famous design school of the 20th century. Gropius changed the school from a local art academy to the Staatliches Bauhaus and it became a centre for new 20th-century ideas in art and design. In 1925 the Bauhaus moved to Dessau, where it opened for business on 4 December 1926. The new buildings, confident and articulate, were designed by Walter Gropius and were his most important contribution to the new Modernism. Dessau provided a complete Modernist lifestyle for staff and students. The furnishings, including the studios and canteen, were tubular steel designs created under the direction of Marcel Breuer, head of the joinery workshop. The lamp fittings, designed by Marianne Brandt, came from the school's metal workshops. Gropius attracted some of the most important art and design practitioners of the > Modern Movement, including Wassily Kandinsky, Johannes Itten, Paul Klee and Herbert Bayer. Histories of the Bauhaus have tended to stress its single Modernist approach to design, dedicated to pure geometric forms, primary colours, modern materials and new industrial production techniques. That view has edited out the complex and diverse positions developed at the Bauhaus. Gropius himself was deeply influenced by British > Arts and Crafts thinking, and the school's commitment to Modernism was always balanced by Expressionist art and theory. The curriculum consisted of a broadly based foundation year, followed by craft specializations. That educational principle is now the basis for design education all over the world.

The Bauhaus remained a small, exclusive training school until 1932, when the last director, Mies van der Rohe, took the remains of the school to Berlin and the Dessau complex became a training school for the Nazis. During its 14-year life the Bauhaus had only trained 1250 students, many of them foreigners whose fees helped to support the school. Owing to the rise of Nazism many Bauhaus staff left to begin a new life in the USA. Gropius, for example, built some of his most important buildings in North America, and as professor of architecture at Harvard University, his philosophy influenced an entire generation of students. Mies van der Rohe settled in Chicago and Laszlo Moholy-Nagy taught at the Illinois Institute of Technology. After the war Dessau became part of East Germany, and thus came under communist rule. Some of the Bauhaus buildings were left derelict, but one wing became a trade school. In 1976 the buildings were partially restored to become a hostel for visiting tourists. Then, in the autumn of 1989, the political tide turned. East and West Germany were unified, and the resulting liberalization resulted in the Bauhaus re-opening as a design institution. Some 56 years after its forced closure, the new director, Professor Rolf Kuhn, announced plans to restore buildings, organize exhibitions and seminars, and to open an experimental design workshop. Once again the Bauhaus has a future.

• Frank Whitford, *The Bauhaus*, 1984.

BELGIAN DESIGN

Belgium's major claim to design fame is its role in the development of > Art Nouveau. Its capital, Brussels, was also the home of the leading Surrealist painter René Magritte until his death in 1967. Magritte reflected the solid bourgeois values of the city, so it was something of a surprise in the 1980s when Belgium, for so long sneered at as boring, produced a whole crop of talented, new-wave fashion designers. Called the Antwerp Six, they included Dirk Bikkemburgs and Dries van Noten, and they created a sensation with their elaborate imagery and innovative approach to clothes styling.

BIEDERMEIR

A German style of the early 19th century, now greatly admired for its quality, confidence and rational form. It was inspired in part by French

Empire taste, by 18th-century English furniture tradition and not least by German middle-class, Protestant values. In fact, the name Biedermeir was meant as a put-down of middle-class values: *bieder* is the German word for 'unpretentious' and M*eier* is a German surname as common as the English Smith or Brown. The term Biedermeier was first used in the 1890s to mock the style of the 1820s, but after 1920 more and more Modernist designers drew inspiration from this period. Biedermeir furniture, which came from provincial craftsmen rather than smart city workshops, was made for the middle classes, using refined, simple neo-Classical shapes. The term Biedermeir is now applied to German-speaking countries of the early 19th century, and the description evokes pride and admiration.

BOUTIQUES

Boutiques were small, independent fashion shops that helped to revolutionize fashion retailing in the 1950s and 1960s. They introduced important new design trends in clothes, graphics and interior design to a wider public. In 1964 the American magazine *Time* coined the name 'Swinging London' and published a tourist map which highlighted the city's new boutiques and nightclubs rather than the traditional tourist attractions. These new shops centred around three now legendary London streets – the King's Road, Carnaby Street and Kensington High Street – and they enjoyed wacky names like Granny Takes a Trip, I Was Lord Kitchener's Valet, Hung on You and Gear. The boutique has now come to represent the 1960s with its explosion of youthful creativity and entrepreneurial spirit, but the retail revolution it represented had its roots in the 1940s. The name derives from the small shops of the Parisian Left Bank, which sold clothes of their own design. In 1950s' Britain clothes were sold either by department or chain stores. Fashion was the preserve of adults, and adolescent boys and girls were expected to dress like their parents. The emergence of teenage culture changed all that.

In 1955 Mary Quant opened Bazaar, a shop selling her own clothes, on the King's Road. It was an immediate success and others quickly followed. In the 1950s Bill Green had opened another pioneer shop called Vince in Foubert Place off Regent Street. It sold imported Continental casual clothes, and one of Green's assistants, John

Stephens, went on to open a series of boutiques in Carnaby Street. These were the beginnings of a huge explosion of 1960s' boutiques centred in London, but quickly spreading throughout Britain. By 1970 there were estimated to be 15,000 boutiques throughout the country. Only a few have survived, one being Boodle-am in Leeds.

As well as marketing the new clothes of the 1960s, boutiques also contributed to important changes in interior design. Like stage sets, they were designed as > installations, reflecting the new > Pop Design. They played pop music, employed young staff and aimed for a rapid turnover of stock. Barbra Hulanicki's Biba, with its dark, moody > Art Deco interior was particularly important because it marketed a complete design image. In 1968 John McConnell designed the famous black and gold Biba logo, inspired by Celtic imagery, with a mail order catalogue in the same style. In 1969 Tommy Roberts asked designer Jon Wealleans to create a Pop Art interior, using inflatable false teeth and Disney characters, for his boutique Mr Freedom. These changes affected the way the more powerful department stores sold clothes. In 1967 Harrods opened its own boutique called Way-In with a keyhole logo designed by the international consultancy Minale Tattersfield.

The word 'boutique' has now disappeared, but its heritage remains. The spirit of independence lived on in the anarchic > Punk shops Boy and Seditionaries in the late 1970s. These days, however, retailers such as Joseph still create their shops as unique selling environments, but they no longer sell cheap, accessible clothes. Instead, fashion has moved towards an obsession with expensive designer labels. *See also* Retailing.

HENRY BRAVERMAN

Braverman was an American economist whose writings have been influential on industry. Since the Industrial Revolution discussion has focused on the role of the worker. The economist Adam > Smith described the process called division of labour, and this process went one step further with the left-wing concept described by Braverman in 1974. He argued that capitalist production aims to deprive workers of control in the labour process and to give it to the managers. The work is sub-divided into small tasks, so workers, even white-collar staff, are progressively de-skilled. The workers' struggle in the workplace is not so much a concern with wages, as with attempts to retain their skill and control over production. Braverman's thesis does not stand up very easily to empirical analysis, despite the fact it has been extremely fashionable and influential. While capitalism tends to de-skill, a counter-tendency evolves when industries require new skills. Braverman's real error is to imagine that the technical labour process is capitalism's real concern; in fact, profitability is the main criterion. Capitalism is quite prepared to allow higher levels of skill in the workforce if it leads to a higher profit. Profit, rather than control, is the motive behind de-skilling the workforce. In many ways Braverman was unrealistic.

● Henry Braverman, *Labour and Monopoly Capital: The Degradation of Work in the Twentieth Century*, 1974.

BRICOLAGE

This is a design technique where fragments of already existing signs, objects and materials are combined in a single work. The *bricoleur* (artist/designer) draws from existing stocks not so much to make meaning of them as to show their unfixed or 'decentred' state in the post-modern era. The anthropologist Claude Lévi-Strauss used the term decentred in his 1962 book *The Savage Mind* as a metaphor for mythical thought, but since the late 1970s it has come to mean the appropriation and quotation of images and fragments in all forms of the arts. In the original French it has the derogatory connotation of fiddling or tampering with.

BRITISH EXHIBITIONS

In the early 19th century Britain had no tradition of design exhibitions to compare with that of the Continent, particularly the successful Paris Exhibitions of the 1840s. In 1845, however, Prince Albert set up a committee to explore the possibilities. At first small events were organized, but in 1849 the Prince decided on a larger scheme, which eventually resulted in the Great Exhibition of 1851. Eleven years later London staged another international event, designed by Captain Fowke and decorated by J.G. Crace. This 1862 exhibition included a section on

Japan and saw the emergence of a new, professional group of British designers, which included R.N. Shaw, Philip Webb and William Burges. In retrospect the exhibition of 1862 rather than 1851 marked the pinnacle of high Victorian design. It was followed by exhibitions of lesser importance in the early 1870s, and then the era of international exhibitions was over. Avant-garde designers turned to the Arts and Crafts Exhibition Society as an outlet to show their work.

In the 20th century British exhibitions enjoyed a revival. The most important official event was the 1924 British Empire Exhibition held at Wembley in west London. Only the stadium now survives. Sir Laurence Weaver organized the displays and one of the most popular exhibits was a life-size model of the Prince of Wales carved in New Zealand butter. Inevitably comparisons were made with the Paris 1925 Exhibition, and it was felt that Britain's design lead, so all-powerful in 1890, had slipped away. In 1933 *Country Life* magazine sponsored the first exhibition of British Modernism with a minimal flat by Wells Coates and furniture by R.D. Russell. The > Design and Industries Association also organized numerous design exhibitions, but the largest event of the 1930s was the 1938 Empire Exhibition held in Glasgow, which included over 100 pavilions and palaces. The timing of this exhibition was hardly fortuitous, but the onset of World War II did not end Britain's plans for future design exhibitions. In 1944 the government set up the Council of Industrial Design to promote better standards of British products. In 1946, the year after war ended, the > Victoria and Albert Museum reopened its doors with an exhibition called 'Britain Can Make it' (BCMI). It introduced the British public to the post-war belief that design was a key tool in the struggle to rebuild Britain. It also promoted the novel idea that designers should step out of their, till then, anonymous role and explain themselves and their activities to the public.

If BCMI was organized on a shoestring budget, just the opposite was the case with the exhibition to celebrate the centenary of the Great Exhibition of 1851. Called the 'Festival of Britain', it was built under the auspices of the Labour government on London's South Bank, with Gerald Barry as festival director and Sir Hugh Casson in charge of design. It introduced the public to the idea of > Contemporary Style and proved to be a great popular success, but when the Conservatives came to power in 1952 they decided to pull it down. Since then no large exhibitions have been staged by the government, but the establishment of the Design Centre in London's Haymarket has provided a permanent venue for trade and design exhibitions. There are, however, plans in hand for a major British exhibition in 2001 to celebrate the new millenium.

● Paul Greenhalgh, *Ephemeral Vistas: Expositions Universelles, Great Exhibitions and World's Fairs*, 1988.

BROWN GOODS

This term is used to describe a range of consumer products for the home, including hi-fi systems, televisions and radios. It dates from the 1930s, brown referring to the bakelite radio cases and wooden television cabinets that were then the norm. 'Brown goods' is now an inaccurate description of electrical products, as most of them are finished in > matt black. *See also* White goods.

BRUTALISM

An architectural term to describe the concrete Modernist buildings of the late 1950s. In 1966 Peter Reyner > Banham published an account of the movement, called *The New Brutalism, Ethic or Aesthetic?* which illustrated the work of some of the best-known British architects working in the style; these included Alison and Peter Smithson who had been part of the > Independent Group, and James Stirling, whose Roehampton housing estate was inspired by Le Corbusier's Unité building in Marseilles. In 1960 the World Fair in Tokyo showed off Japanese architectural experiments in the Brutalist style. In general these giant-scale buildings in rough concrete textures have not won much public affection. Sir Denys Lasdun's National Theatre, built in 1976 on the South Bank, is loved and hated in equal measure.

C

CAMP

A design style that uses obvious bad taste in a spirit of mocking irony. It is also used to describe the excessive behaviour associated with certain kinds of effeminate homosexuality. Male drag artists, for example, exploit the meaning of camp in their performances. On the other hand, the sumptuous > Art Deco set designs of Erté reflect authentic theatrical camp, as do Salvador Dali's set designs for *Salome*. Indeed, camp design often involves an element of exaggerated theatricality. Fashionable interior decorators often work in a camp idiom in that they make entirely inappropriate and over-dramatic references in their designs. Camp design can also exploit the idea of using elements once considered beautiful or valid but now thought ridiculously sentimental or old-fashioned. In this respect it overlaps with > kitsch. The use of camp references often involves a knowing self-consciousness, as noted by cult film director John Waters: 'In order to acquire bad taste one must first have very, very good taste.' Camp can often be an amusing dismissal of certain kinds of design and sensibility, so as a description it should be used with care because of the imprecision of its definition. In its purist form, however, camp offers the territory of 'over-the-top', of design without rules, which challenges the status quo and as such has been explored by Post-Modernist designers.

CCI

Centre de Création Industrielle, otherwise known as the Pompidou Centre, is the design showplace of Paris. Designed by Richard Rogers and Renzo Piano in 1977 and named after the then French president, its purpose is to educate the public and schoolchildren about the designed environment. The CCI director is the writer François Burckhart, former head of IDZ-Berlin, Germany's government-sponsored showcase for modern design. In recent years the Pompidou Centre has mounted an important series of exhibitions exploring both design history and contemporary issues. Particularly notable among these exhibitions has been a series highlighting the cultural achievements of individual cities, including Vienna and Berlin.

CHAIN STORES *See* Retailing.

CHAOS

A theory deriving from the scientific world, but which has recently been explored as an attitude to design. In lay terms the scientific theory of chaos suggests that we have only just begun to understand the complex chain reactions of events and natural phenomena present in nature. For example, it has been suggested that a butterfly flapping its wings in one continent can affect climate changes in another. Such ideas are the paradigm of, for example, the rational world of Newtonian physics. The theories and ideas of chaos were developed in the scientific communities of Harvard from the 1960s. One of the best-known publications on the subject is *The Practical Geometry of Nature* (1980) by Harvard scientist Benoit B. Mandelbrot.

Literary concepts of chaos go back even further than the 1960s. In the 19th century the French poet Charles Baudelaire refers to 'moving chaos' in one of his poems. In the 1920s *Ulysses*, by the Irish novelist James Joyce, was accused of being chaotic, while Dadaists talked about returning to 'some kind of chaos'. This tradition was kept alive by the Situationists in the 1960s, and > Punk inherited something of that way of thinking in the Sex Pistols' slogan 'Cash from Chaos'.

Increasingly, it has become fashionable to apply a touch of chaos to the world of design. The term 'creative chaos' began to be applied to design in the 1980s as a position against a single and ordered view of design. One of the most accessible accounts of creative chaos is an essay written by the British architect Nigel Coates. In it he cites some important theorists, notably the 1960s' activist Marshall Berman and his 1983 book *All That Is Solid Melts into Air*. Berman mixed literary, sociological and architectural studies in his reappraisal of the city. His pluralist approach suggested to many designers that one should go with and exploit the cultural flow of chaos – indeed, that chaos could be a much richer source of ideas than any attempt to impose order and structure. The resonance of creative chaos can be seen on an international level. For example, it shows in the work of Japanese architects/designers such as Arata Isozaki and Shiro Kuramata, as well as the American Frank Gehry's bar, Rebecca's, in Venice, California. In Europe creative chaos as a theme can be identified in the work of the British-based architect Zaha Hadid and the Italian design groups Alchmymia and Memphis.

Creative chaos is not a design movement. It is one aspect of the pluralism implied by Post-Modernism and its relationship to cultural history in general. *See also* Camp; Crafts Revival; Creative Salvage; Green Design; Junk Aesthetic; Kitsch.

● Greil Marcus, *Lipstick Traces: A Secret History of the Twentieth Century*, 1989.

CHICAGO SCHOOL

A group of architects who built the first skyscrapers in Chicago between 1880 and 1900. The term also refers to the buildings and influence of Frank Lloyd Wright, although he concentrated on private commissions for houses rather than high-rise buildings. After the great fire of 1871 in Chicago attention was paid to making architecture safe and suitable for the city's fast-growing reputation as a commercial centre. William Lebaron Jenney and Louis Sullivan developed a version of high-rise functional classicism that was ultimately replaced by a taste for the Beaux Arts style and > Art Deco.

CIAM

Congrès Internationaux d'Architecture Moderne was an international congress of architects which was active from 1928 to 1953. Its members included the architects, apostles and teachers of the

> Modern Movement, who debated and established the movement's ideas. In all, 10 conferences were held, including Frankfurt (1929), Brussels (1930), Athens (1933) and Paris (1937). The subjects under discussion were always rigorously modern, such as mass housing schemes, the planning of cities and the standardization of furniture. The Swiss architect Karl Moser (1860–1936) was the first CIAM president, with Le Corbusier, Mart Stam, Gerrit Rietveld and El Lissitsky among the first members.

CLASSIC DESIGN

A modern label which seeks to identify the enduring objects of 20th-century design – those which have stood the test of time and critical approval. These objects reflect a set of approved models and suggest values outside the vagaries of fashion, but 'classic' can also have other, very different meanings. In the 19th century, when scientific materialism was having a profound intellectual impact, Darwin's theory about survival of the fittest was applied to design, with the idea that certain objects deserved to survive on merit alone. Although the word 'classic' was not used by the Victorians, its sense was implied, and this viewpoint underlay Nikolaus > Pevsner's book *Pioneers of Modern Design*. The > Modern Movement also subscribed to this view in that leading architects and designers selected objects they felt embodied the values of excellence. Le Corbusier, for example, revered Thonet's mass-produced bentwood chair, and from the 1930s onward this attitude was also reflected in the collecting policy of the Museum of Modern Art in New York.

The concept of classic was also used to commercial ends by manufacturers who saw a reproduction market for the work of 20th-century designers such as Charles Rennie Mackintosh and Marcel Breuer. In fact, the furniture company Cassina has produced a series of reproductions, which include Gerrit Rietveld's Red-blue chair and some of Mackintosh's furniture. This category of classic, however, is still reliant on contemporary taste rather than on some absolute standard. None the less, classic implies that the object has stepped out of the issues of style and taste and that its integrity survives within the wider context of the century. These qualities are strong marketing tools, and in the 1990s there is a proliferation of designer shops selling 'classic' products. The Museum of Modern Art shop in New York is an interesting example; objects ranging from pens to tableware are automatically granted classic status simply by appearing in the shop. Classic design is sometimes interchangable with > Cult Objects.

● *Classics of Modern Design*, exhibition catalogue, Camden Arts Centre, 1977.

CLASSICISM

A reverence for the architecture and art of Greece and Rome has always been a key element in Western design. During the 18th century archaeological discoveries such as Pompeii helped to spark off a new interpretation of the style often referred to as Neo-Classicism, a style seen in the designs of Robert Adam, Thomas Chippendale and Thomas Hope. Although Classicism was not popular after the mid-19th century, it none the less remained a constant source of inspiration and ideas for designers. In the early 20th century Classicism was a theme in the work of Modernist designers such as Le Corbusier and Walter Gropius, and was an important element in the work of Mies van der Rohe. More recently Classicism has emerged as an important source for Post-Modernist designers.

COMMERCIAL ART

An outdated term for what is now described as poster, packaging, display and advertising design. The term itself was an uneasy Victorian invention, the word 'commercial' being intended to relegate these areas of graphic design to a lowly status. Its use, however, survived well into this century. The magazine *Commercial Art*, founded in 1922, survived into the 1930s.

CONCRETE

A building material which has been used since Roman times. Made from a mixture of mortar and small stones which sets rock hard, it was technically improved in the late 19th century with the introduction of

69

iron. Reinforced concrete, or ferro-concrete as it was called, became one of the 20th century's most popular construction materials.

● Peter Collins, *Concrete, the Vision of a New Architecture*, 1959.

CONSERVATION

The protection and preservation of our architectural heritage. In recent years conservation has become a powerful political issue. These concerns go back to the 19th century, which saw the growth of numerous societies and organizations dedicated to the conservation of old buildings and landscape. The Society for the Conservation of Ancient Buildings was founded in 1877 following a letter to *The Times* from William Morris. Currently, the most important British conservation body is the National Trust, now the largest landowner in Britain, with 540,000 acres and 292 properties open to the public, 87 of them large houses. The Trust was formally registered in 1895 and acquired its first property four years later. Other conservation bodies followed in its wake: the Ancient Monuments Society (1921), the Council for the Protection of Rural England (1926) and the Georgian Group (1937). In the post-war period the conservation brief on buildings was widened to include Victorian architecture, and the Victorian Society, founded in 1957, was particularly important in this work. Some 20 years later, in 1979, the Thirties Society was established, and more recently campaigns have been launched to save important examples of 1950s' and 1960s' architecture.

Although the preservation of important buildings is a worthy activity, many people consider that it has gone too far. The argument often appears to be that any building more than 50 years old is better than a modern construction. It is a fierce debate that found a focus in Peter Palumbo's attempt to redevelop a site in the City of London. The unremarkable Victorian architecture he proposed to replace with a Modernist office block was passionately defended by all and sundry, and resulted in his planning applications being blocked. Some now feel that conservation may have impeded the development of contemporary architecture.

CONSTRUCTIVISM *See* Russian Constructivism.

CONSUMER DESIGN

This term refers to commodities or objects bought for use in the home. Consumer goods, sometimes called consumer durables, include such things as televisions, videos, cameras and kitchen equipment. The term also refers to products bought and used by the customer for final consumption, such as food, beer and newspapers. The term consumer design is sometimes used instead of industrial design, but the latter includes products designed for use outside the home, such as industrial or military hardware.

• Adrian Forty, *Objects of Desire: Design and Society 1750–1980*, 1986.

CONTEMPORARY STYLE *See* Fifties Contemporary Style.

CONURBATION

A group of towns which have merged into a continuous built-up area, engulfing all villages and communities in between. The word was first used by Sir Patrick Geddes, the greatest British town-planner of his day, in 1910.

CORPORATE CULTURE

Not strictly a design term, but a company ethos that permeates many large manufacturing companies. It originally took off in the USA, with office size and furniture being determined by an employee's position on the company ladder. Other perks, such as company cars and keys to the executive washroom, were allocated on the same basis. Corporate culture is satirized in the classic 1960s' comedy film *The Apartment* starring Jack Lemmon, and it is linked to the American national need for conformity during the 1950s and 1960s. Executive man got a bad press in the 1960s and 1970s, as did the Japanese equivalent, forever associated with company songs and slogans, dedicated worker loyalty and a twelve-hour day. More recently the idea of Corporate Culture has been treated more favourably. It is now seen less in the context of staff perks and rituals than as a recognizable business approach to increased profitability. More and more companies are encouraging the idea of business identity as a marketing strategy to win customers and increase their customer profile. The strength of Corporate Culture applied to design can be seen in the architecture, packaging and graphics of the McDonalds hamburger chain.

CORPORATE IDENTITY

The name given to a company's graphic image. The tradition of designed company names, or logos, goes back to the 19th century. They were used to reinforce a strong brand identity, usually for food and drink products. In the 20th century the idea of a more powerful corporate image took hold, and the role of corporate identity became much more powerful. Coca-Cola is an example of a 19th-century pre-corporate logo that has survived.

The father of corporate identity is usually held to be the German designer Peter Behrens, who, in the inter-war years, worked for the electrical company AEG. It was in the post-war USA that the design of corporate identities became a profession in itself. Indeed, the identity designed for IBM in the 1950s by Eliot Noyes and Paul Rand is regarded as a model of its kind. Noyes went on to apply corporate identity schemes to blue chip American companies such as Westinghouse, Mobil Oil and Pan American World Airways. By the 1960s a whole series of design consultancies specializing in corporate identity had been established in the USA, including Lippincott & Margulies, and Anspach Grossman Portugal, as well as independents such as Saul Bass. European countries followed suit. A notable British consultancy is the Wolff Olins partnership.

Recently there has been a trend in corporate identity schemes to replace names with strong graphic symbols which the customer can instantly identify. The large M for McDonalds, or the track sign for British Rail are two examples of this trend.

• Wally Olins, *Corporate Identity*, 1989.

COUNTER CULTURE

A 1960s' term used to define unconventional theories about such traditional institutions as marriage and family life. Counter culture stressed the need for people to express their individual creativity, to experiment with drugs and, in the 1960s' vernacular, to 'drop out and do your own thing'.

CRAFTS REVIVAL

Part of the > Arts and Crafts Movement, which espoused a self-conscious rejection of industrial production. In the 20th century the potter Bernard Leach provided a role model for the craftsperson, working in dedicated, rural isolation and struggling to achieve a complete understanding of the craft. The lure of the simple life was irresistible to a generation of young craftspeople in the early 1970s. In fact, there was a feeling that good work could only be produced from the setting of a derelict Victorian church or a renovated 17th-century barn.

In Britain the Crafts Council (established in 1971 as the Crafts Advisory Committee) supported the role of the artist-craftsperson, but gradually came under increasing pressure to broaden its terms of reference. While the traditional role for the crafts remains strong, a rather different profile emerged in the 1980s. The USA led the way with new aesthetic ideas applied to glass, wood and iron. In Britain young makers began to challenge the whole basis of the craft aesthetic, encouraged by the culture of > Punk and its belief in the power of do-it-yourself. A change of direction can be traced through two important exhibitions organized by the Crafts Council. The first, in 1982, was 'The Maker's Eye', which helped to broaden the concept of what a craft object might be by including such things as letter-boxes and motorcycles. Then, in 1987, the 'New Spirit in Craft and Design' looked at the influence of youth culture on London's new makers, including Judy Blame (b. 1960), Tom Dixon (b. 1958), André Dubreuil (b. 1951), and Fric and Frack (Fritz Soloman and Alan MacDonald, est. 1985). These young furniture makers, jewellers and metalsmiths recycled scavenged materials and obsolete artefacts. Their work came from the streets of Dalston, Clerkenwell, Hackney and Portobello, and they challenged the conventional boundaries of craft production. These

73

designer-makers took up an extreme position, but they forced the crafts to re-examine their role and future. More recently, traditional craft values, which never went away, have reappeared as a new force. Crafts, for too long considered peripheral and marginal activities, have taken up a leading role in directing ideas in the 1990s.

CRANBROOK ACADEMY

Established in the 1920s, the Cranbrook Academy was an American design community with distinctly utopian ideals. Its founder, George C. Booth, was a Detroit publisher who felt that the commercial aspirations of American design could be enriched by wider cultural references. In 1923 he met Eliel Saarinen (1873–1950), the leading Finnish architect of his generation, who was then teaching at the University of Michigan. Booth commissioned Saarinen to design the buildings of a new design school called Kingswood, and the Finnish architect also taught there with his son Eero Saarinen (1910–61). During the 1930s the school attracted many important teachers and students, and its reputation and influence invited comparisons with the > Bauhaus design school in Germany. Cranbrook was described as a working place for creative art and its inspirations were Scandinavian. Among its distinguished students was Florence Shust, who later married Hans Knoll. Knoll Associates became one of the most influential American furniture companies, providing an important link with European Modernist designers and the American market. Charles Eames was another graduate, and from 1937 he worked with Eero Saarinen on a range of plywood furniture that won two first prizes in a competition organized by the Museum of Modern Art. With the death of Cranbrook's founder in 1949, and Eliel Saarinen the following year, the school temporarily lost its direction. In recent years, however, the Cranbrook Academy has once more become an important centre for design education.

● *Design in America: The Cranbrook Vision, 1925–50*, exhibition catalogue, Detroit Institute of Art, 1984.

CREATIVE CHAOS *See* Chaos Theory.

CREATIVE SALVAGE

A 1980s design style based on making things from Britain's industrial leftovers. It was a kind of recycled skip culture and inspired a wave of metal furniture and objects from such designers as Ron Arad, Tom Dixon and Jon Mills. In their hands creative salvage was an urban-inspired rejection of Japanese, > matt black stereo systems and Milanese designer chic. For example, Ron Arad's One-Off gallery in Covent Garden had distressed walls, a concrete staircase and chairs made from old Rover car seats; Tom Dixon opened a studio in Notting Hill Gate, where he welded bizarre metal furniture; and Danny Lane started making chairs from pieces of broken glass. In 1985 a group called Mutoid Waste started to put on performance pieces based on the new aesthetic, and Crucial, a well-known gallery in Notting Hill, started exhibiting and selling Creative Salvage objects.

CUBISM

In the inter-war period Cubism was simultaneously a style, a movement and a set of aesthetic principles. Although painting was its primary focus of activity, it also affected design and architecture. Cubism was pioneered by a small group of artists working in Paris around 1905–8. These artists formed two separate groups, working more or less independently of each other, but sometimes overlapping. The first group, which included Picasso (1881–1973), Braque (1882–1963), Gris (1887–1927) and Léger (1881–1955), was centred on Kahnweiler's Gallery and Picasso's studio in Montmartre. The second group, which included Robert and Sonia Delaunay, met in the cafés of Montparnasse and at the house of Marcel Duchamp (1887–1968) in suburban Puteaux. It was the second group that gained initial notoriety as the Cubist Movement, launching their work at the 1911 Paris Salon des Indépendants, where it was greeted with derision. None the less, their notoriety spread to New York and other European cities. In the meantime, the art dealer Kahnweiler had secured the painters he represented a faithful clientèle and a reputation as the true pioneers of Cubism.

By 1914, if not before, the ascendancy of Picasso and Braque over the movement as a whole was established. The paintings from this period had formal characteristics in common, which distinguished Cubism as a style. The first was the use of 'multiple perspective' – the subject viewed from different angles at the same time. The second was an overall pictorial composition in which the subject was broken up and which diminished the illusion of space and solid. The third was a restricted palette of colours to avoid the sharp tonal contrasts that would interrupt the overall composition of the painting.

This set of aesthetic principles also had a wider application to the new ideas emerging under the wider terms of reference of Modernism. First there was a growing concern on the part of technically radical artists in the pre-1914 decade to acknowledge the specificity of the visual medium and art practice in question. For the Cubists this ranged from Picasso's celebration of the artifice of art to Léger's attempt to find pictorial equivalents for modern, urban visual experience. Artists wanted to engage with the experience of modernity in both its positive and negative aspects. For the Cubists this was summarized in the concept of simultaneity, which referred to the collective experience of city life, the multiplicity of visual perception or the simultaneous contrast of colours. Accompanying their interest in modernity, however, was a commitment to artistic tradition and the need for the new to build on the old. For the Cubists this ranged from a concern to update > Classicism to a sympathetic adaptation of popular and vernacular images and practices. In this way Cubist theory has a direct link to the parallel experiments in architecture and design. The search for the new linked painting, buildings, furniture and products, and the heritage of Cubism continues to influence design.

● John Golding, *Cubism*, 1988.

CULT OBJECTS

This term covers a wide range of designed artefacts which reflect the style preferences of individual groups. One of the best known is the Filofax personal organizer, which came to represent the > Yuppie culture of the 1980s. It was the accessory of the successful graphic designer or journalist, challenged only by the Psion computer version. In the world of clothes the Burberry mackintosh, the Barbour waxed cotton jacket, the original Levi 501s and the Gucci loafer shoe enjoy similar status. A list of cult cars would include the Citroën 2CV, the Mini, and the Volkswagen Beetle. Drink packaging is another cult marker. Both Coca-Cola and Perrier make the grade, with a changing array of designer beer bottles and cans. If, in theory at least, > Classic Design is about permanence and longevity, cult objects are about fashion and change. These days every mall and smart shopping street has a specialist shop selling cult objects, Oggetti in London's Jermyn Street being an example. Such shops cater to the tastes of the affluent, design-conscious consumer.

- Dejan Sudjic, *Cult Objects*, 1985.

CUSTOMIZING

A popular extension of custom-making, whereby an expensive product is made to order following customer specifications. Typical examples of this are Rolls-Royce cars or pleasure yachts fitted out with luxury extras. Standard, mass-produced items can also be given this personal touch. For example, Levi jeans may be embroidered and leather jackets may be decorated with studs. Customizing in this sense has turned into a kind of folk art. Such treatment of standardized objects is not exclusive to Western culture. In the Philippines the basic American jeep is turned into a highly decorated vehicle called a Jeepney. Customizing has thus emerged as a contemporary creative art form inspiring numerous exhibitions and books on individual examples of the activity.

CYBERNETICS

The study of communication mechanisms, especially electronic ones designed to replace activities (such as adding up) previously performed by the human brain.

D

DECODING

A word appropriated from military intelligence which means translating coded messages. In design terms it is used to describe the ideas of > Deconstruction, attempting to reveal the complex layers of meaning hidden in any image. In 1978 Judith Williamson published her book *Decoding Advertisements: Ideology and Meaning in Advertising*, which applied the methods of > semiotics and post-Freudian analysis to graphic design.

DECONSTRUCTION

A > semiotics-derived analysis. It deconstructs social stereotypes and clichés about gender and the status quo which are communicated by the mass media. Deconstruction reveals the complex layers of meaning of an image. It implies that we can analyse an image and reveal its visual, cultural and linguistic meanings by applying the scientific principles derived from semiotics. The term > decoding is also used to express this process. Young designers in the late 1980s became very interested in the idea of layers of meanings, but did not examine deconstruction in its purist form. Design as an intuitive activity cannot be reduced to a set of scientific principles.

DEPARTMENT STORES *See* Retailing.

DESIGN AND INDUSTRIES ASSOCIATION (DIA)

The English equivalent of the > Deutsche Werkbund, a group that linked design with industry. In the years before World War I a number of British designers were becoming increasingly aware that European design developments were taking the lead. In particular, the activities of the Deutsche Werkbund indicated that the > Arts and Crafts Movement was lagging behind the times. In 1915 a small group of British designers including Harold Stabler, Harry Peach of the Leicestershire Dryad Works and Ambrose Heal, founder of the well-known furniture store, launched the Design and Industries Association, which operated from the Art Workers' Guild premises in Queen Square, London. Another guiding figure behind the DIA was W.R. Lethaby, then professor of design at the > Royal College of Art. Although the expressed aim of the group was to create a closer link between design and industry, the profile of the DIA was closely allied with the Arts and Crafts establishment, and in the early 1920s there is little to suggest the group responded to the European > Modern Movement. The group's conservative approach is reflected in the DIA yearbooks published between 1922 and 1930. These volumes are full of photographs of Dryad cane furniture, Brown Betty teapots and Jaeger sports clothes. None the less, there were subtle signs of change, most notably a series of transcribed radio talks on Modernism for the BBC in 1932, and a short-lived magazine, *Design in Industry*, edited by Maxwell Fry. Its successor, *Design for Today* (1933–35), illustrated the work of leading British Modernists, including Raymond McGrath and Wells Coates. The year 1933 saw an important exhibition of British industrial design held at Dorland Hall, and the new confidence this encouraged led to a rise in the DIA's membership. In 1944 the establishment of the government-supported Council of Industrial Design effectively took over the work of the DIA. In the post-war period the DIA encouraged exhibitions, lectures and publications, and continues to organize activities in these areas.

DESIGN CONSULTANCIES

The emergence of the design practice or consultancy is a 20th-century phenomenon. The role of the independent designer has a longer history. It is known for example that Josiah Wedgwood paid for freelance ceramic designs. By the 19th century the concept of a staff designer was becoming more familiar. The emergence of designers working from their own offices, in the manner of other professionals like accountants or solicitors, to provide design consultancy services, started in the USA during the 1920s. Before that designers had worked together, for example the > Wiener Werkstatte and the British > Guilds of Design.

The United States provided a different model with the pioneering work of Raymond Loewy, Norman Bel Geddes, Walter Dorwin Teague and Henry Dreyfuss. These American industrial designers were direct products of the changes in American economy of the 1920s, and in particular the effects of the Depression. To stimulate economic growth manufacturers wanted new products and looked to the emerging design profession to supply them. Teague is usually considered the first full-time professional designer. He set up his office in 1926 at 210 Madison Avenue, and his first commission was a camera for Eastman-Kodak. Norman Bel Geddes worked for the Toledo Scale Company, and the surviving correspondence between designer and client reveals a great deal about early working methods. In particular, Bel Geddes was keen to promote the use of his own name as a marketing device for the product. This showed the new status and power accorded to designers, and to reinforce this, American designers produced serious books on design. Self-promotion was the forte of Raymond Loewy, famous for designing the Gestetner duplicating machine, the Lucky Strike cigarette packet and the Greyhound bus. Glamorous and charismatic, Loewy's lifestyle resembled that of a movie star. The designers of this era, sometimes called the > Machine Age, produced a style called > Streamlining and established the models for European design consultancies. In Britain the Design Research Unit was founded in the 1930s by Milner Gray and Misha Black. By the late 1940s they had been joined by several more. Crawfords, for example, best known as an advertising agency, now developed a design office, but the real expansion of design consultancies took place in the post-war period. In the 1960s several British consultancies were formed that went on to build international reputations, including Conran Design, Pentagram, Wolff Olins, Minale Tattersfield and Kenneth Grange. They did, however, try to distance themselves from the idea that design was associated with styling. The new consultancies prided themselves on a complete service for the prospective client, and a new generation of consultancies emerged with the retail boom of the late 1970s. These included Stewart McColl, David Davies, Michael Peters, Fitch Benoy and Din Associates. For design practices these were halcyon days. Several went public on the Stock Exchange and overnight their founding partners became millionaires. For the first time designers like Terence Conran and Rodney Fitch featured in the country's list of richest men. This period in the history of design consultancies officially came to an end with the recession of the 1990s, and design consultancies now face a period of retrenchment.

• Penny Sparke, *Consultant Design: The History and Practice of the Designer in Industry*, 1983.

DESIGN COUNCIL

A body founded to encourage manufacturers to use designers, to raise the profile of design in British industry and to improve levels of public taste. It began life on 19 December 1944 as the Council of Industrial Design (COID), its arrival announced by Hugh Dalton, president of the Board of Trade. Although the name was changed in 1960 to the Design Council, its brief remained the same. The COID's first job was to organize an exhibition called 'Britain Can Make It', held at the Victoria and Albert Museum in 1946. The event was extremely successful, attracting nearly 1.5 million visitors, and marked the beginning of an exhibition programme on design which continues, at the Design Centre in London, to this day. Gordon Russell, whose furniture company of the same name promoted a safe and very British version of Modernism, became the council's director from 1947 to 1960, its most influential period. In the post-war years the idea that design should be democratic and could play an important role in reconstructing British life was widely held. The Design Council promoted the view that modern design, called > Contemporary Design in the 1950s, could play a key social role, even going so far as to suggest that it could undermine class differences. The council pursued a vigorous publicity strategy, which included the launch in 1949 of an in-house magazine, *Design*, as well as books and educational material on the subject. It also effectively targeted the media. The BBC selected Council-approved furniture for its television programmes, while popular magazines such as *Woman* regularly ran features in collaboration with the council. This popularity came to an end in the 1960s with the challenge of > Pop design, and the Design Council gradually became less of a central force. The 1970s and 1980s saw three new directors: Lord Reilly, Keith Grant and Ivor Owen. In recent years the Design Council has been under severe financial threat and its future, particularly its location in central London, looks uncertain.

DESIGN EDUCATION

See Bauhaus; Cranbrook Academy; Ecole des Beaux Arts; Royal College of Art; Ulm.

DESIGNER-MAKERS

A term which appeared in the late 1970s as a way of describing the new role craftspeople demanded for themselves. The old idea of craft as a sort of guild activity, handing down skills in making traditional, vernacular items such as ladderback chairs or woven baskets, no longer held true. Jewellery was a particularly important area in this respect. In the early 1980s jewellery-makers looked to new materials, forms and techniques to make decorative pieces that broke with the conventions of traditional jewellery. They wanted the making aspect of their activity to be recognized alongside their role as designers. *See also* Crafts Revival.

DESIGN HISTORY

When the Design History Society was set up in Britain in 1977, it marked a small but significant change in the study of design. Before this date the history of consumer products was called the history of decorative arts or the applied arts. Study in this area was the territory of the museum or the antique collector. It was not possible to 'read' design in the conventional British university sense, and design history as a subject did not exist, except as a small part of the history of art and architecture. The emergence of design history as a separate area of study was a direct response to changes in British art and design education in the 1960s. An overhaul was long overdue and the Coldstream Report recommended that the old diploma qualification for a designer should be upgraded to a degree in line with university education. Rightly or wrongly, part of this upgrading was a compulsory element of contextual studies, which traditionally occupies 15 per cent of the student's time and accounts for 20 per cent of the final marks allocated to this area.

When these changes were implemented, art history departments in British art schools and polytechnics underwent an expansion, and design students in the areas of graphics, industrial design and fashion started to demand classes in their own subject history. Academic staff had to develop new courses with little in the way of resources to help them. In the 1970s books on 19th-century design were thin on the ground. Students learned directly from hands-on experience of the objects and from such series as the post-war Faber guides, which were aimed at the antique collectors' market. There were pioneers, however. Gillian Naylor's book, *The Arts and Crafts Movement*, appeared in 1971, and Tim Benton developed the now defunct Open University course A305. In fact, Benton did a great deal to bring together young art school lecturers and encourage them to build up the new subject area of design history. He was not, however, among the founder members of the Design History Society. Those included Penny Sparke, now at the > Royal College of Art and author of several important books on design, Stephen Bayley, first director of the > Design Museum, Dorothy Bosomworth, Alan Crawford, Jonathan Woodham and Catherine McDermott, who acted as the society's chairperson in the early 1980s. The society organized a newsletter, lectures and conferences, and built up a network of members interested in design history. Gradually the new subject gained ground. Several polytechnics, including those in Brighton, Staffordshire and Newcastle, offered degrees in design history and publishers started to commission books on it. There were, however, critics of these developments.

Many distinguished museum curators felt that they were the guardians of the subject. Simon Jervis, for many years a curator at the V&A, described its growth in the polytechnics as unfortunate, and its stress on design after the Industrial Revolution as blinkered. Unfortunately, the development of design history in Britain coincided with a period of massive financial cutbacks. The possibilities for sabbaticals and research grants in design history were virtually non-existent. By and large polytechnic lecturers did not have the resources or the time to forge a strong intellectual base to the subject. That lead was taken by university academics in other fields.

In the search for a new methodology to apply to design the writings of the French philosopher Roland > Barthes suggested a new framework. Barthes provided an intellectual input and gravitas to design history that many felt it lacked. In Britain a series of books exploring issues of style and design were written by graduates and teachers at Birmingham University's famous Centre for Contemporary Studies, and a pioneer of the genre was Dick Hebdige's *Subculture: The Meaning of Style* (1979). In addition, the writings of university academics in economics and the history of technology have enriched the understanding of design. In this context American academics have made a significant contribution to design history, but their research tends to fall within the areas of contemporary studies or women's studies. From that perspective have come definitive accounts of the home, shopping, housework and the fashion industries. In the 1990s design history now draws on these sources and has become an accepted subject area and an established part of the educational agenda.

● Hazel Conway, (ed.), *Design History: a Student's Handbook*, 1987.

DESIGN MAGAZINES

The development of a specialist design press really took off after World War II. The British *Design* magazine, launched in 1949 as the house publication of the Design Council, is a good example of this. During the 18th and 19th centuries the power of the design press to publicize rising stars and help shape public opinion and taste remained the preserve of books. However, that situation saw some significant changes at the end of the Victorian era. The 19th century had developed a whole range of home improvement periodicals, but it is hard to pinpoint a journal dedicated to profiling innovative design until the appearance of *The Studio Magazine* in 1893. Financed by a Yorkshire businessman, Charles Holmes (1848–1922), *The Studio's* editorial policy was to focus on progressive artists and designers. Its first issue featured Aubrey Beardsley, and another first came with a lengthy profile on Charles Rennie Mackintosh in 1897. The magazine is also important because of the international nature of its readership. It numbered many European designers and architects among its subscribers, and constituted essential reading, much as *Domus* later did in the post-war years. An American edition of *The Studio Magazine* was launched in 1897. Its sister publications, the *Studio Yearbooks*, were published from 1907, and there was a series of special issues, including one in 1906 called *The Art Revival in Austria*, which introduced the work of the > Wiener Werkstatte.

Although individual groups of designers published their own magazines, as did design organizations such as the > Deutsche Werkbund and the > Design and Industries Association, the concept of a distinctive, specialized design press did not really take off until the 1960s. For the first time design journalism made an appearance – in the USA with the writings of Tom > Wolfe, and in Britain with those of Peter Reyner > Banham. Newspapers began to use regular design correspondents, such as Fiona McCarthy, who worked for the *Guardian* newspaper. Curiously, all of this came to an end in the recession of the 1970s, only to reappear with a vengeance in the designer decade of the 1980s. In Britain alone the 1980s saw the launch of *Creative Review*, *Designers Journal*, *Interior Design*, *Designer*, *Eye*, *Design Week* and perhaps the best known of all, *Blueprint* magazine. Launched in 1984, *Blueprint* is edited by Deyan Sudjic. Using an A3 format with distinctive layout and photography, it has charted the major international trends of the 1980s. Nowadays, it has again become established practice for the major international daily papers to devote column inches to the subject of design.

DESIGN MANAGEMENT

A theory devised to impose rational organization on factories and offices. Theorizing about design management started in the early 20th century with Frederick Taylor, whose pioneering attempts became known as > Taylorism. Design management is now firmly on the agenda of every successful company. In the post-war period it grew with the rise of middle managers, outlined by Alfred Chandler in *Visible Hands: The Management Hand in American Business*, a book which won the prestigious Pulitzer Prize in 1977 and rooted management technology firmly in the sphere of business history. More recent work on design management theory has been less thorough, generating a debased 'airport paperback' genre based on anecdotal evidence, all of which makes the task of defining design management extremely difficult.

Although the theory can often result in generalization and a blinkered view of design, it is none the less rising up the management agenda. Even though the efforts of management theorists to incorporate design in their theories has so far been decidedly weak, it is an area to watch.

DESIGN MUSEUM

Officially opened in 1989 by the then prime minister, Mrs Margaret Thatcher, the museum was the brainchild of Sir Terence Conran, founder of the > Habitat retail group. In 1981 he established the Conran Foundation as a charitable institution to fund and run the new museum, the first of its kind. Conran had been thinking about a project to promote design in this way for several years, and in 1979 he met Stephen Bayley, then a young university lecturer, whom he appointed to oversee his plans. At first the project was given space in the old boiler rooms of the > Victoria and Albert Museum, which Conran converted into a gleaming white exhibition space in return for a five-year lease. From 1982 to 1987, The Boilerhouse, as it was called, put on a series of exciting design exhibitions on such subjects as Sony, Philippe Garner, Memphis, National Characteristics of Design and Youth Culture. Bayley was nothing if not adept at generating controversy and admiration in equal measure. It was a surprise, therefore, that shortly after the new museum opened in Butler Wharf Bayley resigned to start his own consultancy called Eye-Q. The directorship was taken over by Helen Rees, Bayley's colleague of several years, who developed a lively pro-gramme of exhibitions, educational projects and lectures. Rees resigned in 1992. Although only two years old, the museum is now established on the design map and attracts visitors from all over the world.

DESIGN THEORY

Traditionally design theory has been subsumed by the parent disciplines of art and architecture. There is, however, a body of writing on the subject of design, which has a long tradition. Typical of these writings was *The Analysis of Beauty* (1756), a defence of the Rococo style by the painter William Hogarth. In the 18th century design publications took the form of pattern books or treatises, which included theories of the sublime and the picturesque. The first modern books on design theory, however, started to appear in the 19th century, and generally fell into two groups. The first group was a body of writing linked to the new theories of > Design Education and centred around the > School of Design. These writings include the work of Owen Jones (1809–74) and Christopher Dresser (1834–1904), who advocated a > geometric approach to ornament based on nature and the study of the past, including Islamic and Classical forms. The second group of writings were a response to the effects of the Industrial Revolution, and among them the writings of the architect Augustus Pugin (1812–52) are particularly important. Like Pugin, John > Ruskin and Gottfried Semper also linked design to architecture in the 19th century, but by far the largest body of design theory came from the British > Arts and Crafts Movement led by William Morris. Morris was the most important design writer of the century, and he, together with many of his followers, published his ideas that design should be related to social theory. The designers of the Arts and Crafts Movement continued to publish their ideas in books and essays right into the 1920s, and these views were widely read and imitated.

In the early 20th century manifestos from practitioners of the > Modern Movement focused on art and architecture, but design as a key part of the new > Machine Age was also included. Le Corbusier's writings praised the values of mass production and standardized objects like the Thonet bentwood chair, which he called *objets-types*. The most far-reaching ideas on design theory came from Walter Gropius, director of the > Bauhaus. He had read the works of Morris and followed Herman Muthesius's campaign at the > Deutsche Werkbund for standardization. The tradition of designers writing about design was taken up in the USA by the newly emerging industrial design profession of the 1920s and 1930s. It was then that Norman Bel Geddes published his book *Horizons* in praise of the machine.

After World War II design theory allied itself to the new theories of business management and scientific methodology. > Ergonomics, developed during the war as a scientific attempt to design machinery with human comfort and efficiency taken into full account, became fashionable. In the 1960s the British writer Bruce Archer introduced a systems method to design. This was an attempt to break down the stages of design in order to make the process accessible and easy to understand. The so-called > New Journalism also appeared in the

1960s as a direct response to the new aesthetic of > Pop Design. Writers, including Tom > Wolfe and Peter Reyner > Banham, wrote about design and the interest in popular culture using accessible language and imagery. They were not interested in the process of design but in the social meaning of style and the appearance of an object. Design theory had become eclectic. Its sources borrowed from the tradition of French philosophy in the works of Roland > Barthes, and from disciplines including sociology, anthropology and art history. Design research and theory have also benefited in the last 20 years from the emergence of new areas of study, particularly those dealing with minorities, including women, blacks and gays. Academic studies in the area of women's studies, for example, have revealed important information about kitchen planning and management. Design theory in the 1990s, like design itself, does not put forward a single idea about process or aesthetics. The approach is pluralist and the only shared aim is to place design in its widest social context.

DE-SKILLING *See* Braverman, Henry.

DE STIJL (THE STYLE)

A Dutch art and design movement and one of the most influential Modernist groups of the 20th century. The De Stijl group was committed to the efficiency and precision of machine-made form as a celebration of modernity. It took its name from a magazine founded in 1917 by the architect and painter Theo van Doesburg (1883–1931). The magazine was a vehicle to publicize the group's design work, but it also published serious theoretical writings which stressed an intense mysticism. De Stijl was particularly interested in theosophy, a religious system that believed in a direct communication between God and the soul, which was also to appear as an influence at the > Bauhaus.

Founder members of De Stijl included the painter Piet Mondrian (1872–1944) and the architect J.J.P. Oud (1890–1963), and soon expanded to include a wider group, the best known of which was the designer Gerrit Rietveld (1888–1964). De Stijl promoted a rigorous modern aesthetic which used primary colours of red, blue and yellow, as well as black, grey and white, restricted to flat planes and strong geometric shapes. In design terms the purest example of De Stijl was

Rietveld's famous Red-blue chair of 1917, manufactured in 1918 by van de Groneken. The chair, built on a series of horizontal and vertical planes, has become a design classic of the > Modern Movement. This chair and Rietveld's 1924 Schroder House at Utrecht are clear and eloquent expressions of the group's original ideals. The members of De Stijl rejected any form of naturalism in favour of a formal abstraction that allied the movement with > Russian Constructivism. Links with Moscow during this early period were strong. El Lissitzky, the Russian Constructivist, featured in *De Stijl Magazine* in 1926, and he returned the favour with a Russian article on Rietveld. The magazine was important because it provided a sense of community for such international and diverse groups as Dada, the > Bauhaus and the Constructivists. By the end of the 1920s the De Stijl movement had effectively broken up, but its influence remained strong. In the Netherlands, the design tradition it left is revered, and on an international level the visual style of the movement has influenced everything from graphic design to interiors.

- Paul Overy, *De Stijl*, 1969, 1991.

DEUTSCHE WERKBUND

A German organization founded in 1906 to promote design and industry. It was loosely modelled on the British design guilds, but with an important distinction. The Werkbund was not a social experiment or an exclusive designer club. It was established to promote the interests of manufacturers, industrialists, artists and designers. Very quickly it became a much more important organization in Germany than its British equivalent, the > Design and Industries Association, did in Britain. Founder members of the Werkbund included Peter Behrens (1896–1940), the Austrians Josef Hoffmann (1870–1956) and Joseph Maria Olbrich (1867–1908), Bruno Paul (1874–1968) and Richard Riemerschmid (1868–1957). Significantly, important manufacturers were also involved in founding the group.

In 1907 Hermann Muthesius (1861–1927), author of the influential *Das englische Haus* (1904–5) and superintendent of the Prussian Board of Trade for Schools of Arts and Crafts, made a speech at the newly founded Commercial College in Berlin in which he set out the problems facing German industry. He stressed that if Germany wished to achieve industrial supremacy, it was essential for her to produce soundly designed and well-manufactured goods. He warned of an economic recession if designs were to be copied from the 'form-treasury' of the past century. While Muthesius's views attracted some opposition, particularly from the German arts and crafts establishment, he was supported by a number of influential figures, including Peter Bruckmann, a prominent manufacturer of silverware.

The declared aim of the Deutsche Werkbund was: 'The improvement of industrial products through the combined efforts of artists, industrialists and craftsmen.' But the Werkbund was concerned not only with craft objects, but also with mass-produced objects and the latest forms of transportation. The Werkbund yearbooks illustrate examples of locomotives, aircraft, motor cars, ocean liners and urban transport systems, all of which are considered from the practical as well as the aesthetic standpoint.

Peter Behrens is the best known of the designers associated with the Werkbund. In 1906 he was invited to design publicity material for the electrical company AEG by its far-sighted managing director, Walter Rathenau. In 1907 Behrens was appointed coordinating architect to AEG. In this capacity he designed not only buildings, including a famous turbine factory (1908–9), but also electric lighting systems, fans, kettles, ovens, clocks, typefaces and shop-fronts. He continued to design for AEG until the outbreak of war in 1914.

The best example of the Werkbund's self-confidence was the large-scale exhibition it mounted at Cologne in 1914. It included buildings by Behrens, Gropius, Muthesius, Josef Hoffmann, Bruno Paul, Bruno Taut and Henri van de Velde. Gropius's model factory and Taut's glass pavilion have entered the folklore of the > Modern Movement. The buoyant confidence in industry displayed at Cologne may be contrasted with the 'backward-looking' approach of the British > Arts and Crafts exhibition, which was opened in Paris at exactly the same time.

After the 1914–18 war the Werkbund became less concerned with the problem of industrial design. In 1927, under the direction of Mies van der Rohe, it organized an exhibition devoted to housing in Stuttgart; the Weissenhof Seidlung, an ideal suburb, was the outcome. In 1934, following Nazi disapproval, the Werkbund was disbanded. It was revived after World War II and is still in existence.

● J. Campbell, *The German Werkbund*, 1978.

DUTCH DESIGN

The Netherlands have enjoyed a rich design tradition since the 16th century when the country was an important trading power. The craft tradition extended well into the 19th century with, for example, the ceramics of the Koninklikje Nederlandsche Fabriek (the Royal Dutch Factory). The introduction of industrial techniques, however, sparked off a debate about the direction of design, influenced by the British > Arts and Crafts Movement. This led to the founding of the Vereeniging ter Veredeling van het Ambacht (Society for the Enoblement of the Crafts), otherwise known as VANK, an influential body which championed the work of designer craftspeople. However, VANK was not in step with the new moves to come to terms with industry and the modern world pioneered by organizations such as the > Deutsche Werkbund in Germany. Against this background the emergence of the > De Stijl movement, the Netherlands' most important contribution to 20th-century design, is rather surprising. This small group of individuals was to make a significant contribution to the > Modern Movement, the best-known work coming from the purist geometrical paintings of Piet Mondrian and the minimalist structure of Gerrit Rietveld's Red-blue chair of 1918. De Stijl encouraged a vital Dutch Modernist Movement that affected many areas of design and architecture in the 1930s. On an international scale the Netherlands' best-known company is Philips, established in 1891, and with its own design studio from the late 1920s. Philips produces consumer products for industry and the home, although their reputation is for a safe, middle-of-the-road approach. More recently Dutch design has been best known for its contribution to graphics. Two of the best known practices are Total Design, set up in the 1960s by Wim Crouwel and continuing the tradition of clean-cut Modernist graphics, most notably for the Dutch Post Office (PTT), and Studio Dumbar, founded by Gert Dumbar, whose approach is rather different in that he encourages non-functional, witty or ironic elements in his design.

● *Dutch Design, 1945–1987*, exhibition catalogue, Stedelijk Museum, 1987.

E

ECCLESIASTIC DESIGN

This term refers to the taste for religious icons and > Kitsch that appeared as a fashion element in the early 1980s. Pop singer Boy George started it off by wearing nuns' habits, Jewish orthodox hats, crucifixes and Quaker-style shoes. Catholic images of the Sacred Heart began to appear as decorative features in fashionable interiors, and on record sleeves designed by Vaughan Oliver for the independent record label 4AD. Fashion designer John Richmond decorated a series of suits with simple crosses in the late 1980s, but the fashion for religious iconography as style has not survived into the 1990s.

ECLECTICISM

A combination of the views and styles of different sources and periods. Applied to design, eclecticism is often used in a disparaging sense, but it was originally used to describe the practice of selecting the most desirable elements from visual culture. During the 19th century, when the West was confronted not only with the panorama of its own art and design history but with the magnificence of the East, eclecticism became an important issue. Owen Jones, architect, designer and Orientalist, called for an intelligent and imaginative eclecticism as a response to the vast array of sources from which the contemporary designer could draw inspiration. He, along with Christopher Dresser, E.W. Godwin, Bruce Talbert and Lewis F. Day, were eclectic in their approaches, borrowing from Islamic, Indian, Chinese and Japanese sources. Although frowned on by the hardliners of the > Modern Movement, eclecticism remained a 20th-century theme. Eclectic design affords a freedom of selection and imagery which has proved very attractive to many contemporary designers. Current taste in interior design, for example, often combines antique furniture with aggressive, Modernist, high-tech materials. Eclecticism is very close to > Historicism, but the key difference is that the former combines diverse styles in a single product or interior.

ECOLE DES BEAUX ARTS

The 19th-century French architectural school famous for developing a method of teaching architecture which is still in use today. In the 19th century the school stood for a rational > Historicism which could still incorporate a formal, highly monumental approach to planning. The best-known building by a Beaux Arts graduate is the Paris Opera House of 1868 designed by Charles Garnier. Another famous building by a Beaux Art student was the great iron and glass Hall of Machines at the Paris Exhibition of 1899, designed by Charles Dutert. Although this building regularly featured in modernist anthologies, it epitomizes Beaux Arts principles in that formal and innovative approaches are explored and exploited.

The school itself was primarily a validating authority. Students were actually taught in *ateliers*, private architectural schools operated by former students of the institution. The Beaux Arts charged no fees and foreigners were eligible to become students if they could speak adequate French and draw copies of the plaster casts in the Hall of Antique Studies. The most famous foreign student was the American architect Louis Sullivan. In the 1920s, with the rise of the > Modern Movement, Beaux Arts ideals were largely discredited until finally, after the 1968 Paris student uprising, it was recognized as an anachronism and closed down. Its enduring influence, however, can still be seen in the current trend of architecture and design towards > Classicism.

ENGLISH STYLE

Admiring a particular kind of English taste is nothing new. At the end of the 18th century the French recognized an English gift for casual elegance in clothes and manners, which was linked to sporting interests, horses and that peculiarly English invention, the country house. By the end of the 19th century this English style could be recognized in men's tailored clothing of the Savile Row variety, and specialist sports clothes. Riding apparel, Burberry raincoats, leather brogues and Norfolk tweed jackets are some of the classic designs that remain popular in the 20th century. Combined with these things were elements of the British Empire, such as rattan furniture, gin and tonic, and the safari suit. English style was endlessly reinterpreted in the 20th century, exploiting traditions such as afternoon tea, decorated china cups, chintz curtains, comfortable sofas and patterned wallpapers. The products of English Style are a huge export business selling to Japan and the USA.

ERGONOMICS

The study of maximum functional efficiency by observing men and women in their working environments. The science of ergonomics was particularly developed during World War II in order to improve the performance of bomber pilots. Ergonomists studied the most comfortable and efficient methods of operating controls and dials, and tried to apply scientific research to the analysis of human eye range or the power of the hand grip. After the war their findings were also applied to the design of machinery ranging from cookers to cars. However, the chair, more than any other piece of design, has probably received the most study from ergonomists. These days every car seat or office chair is marketed as a breakthrough in ergonomic comfort. Ergonomics have undoubtedly improved practical considerations of comfort and use, and have been especially important in the development of specialist products for the old, the sick and the handicapped. Ergonomics, however, is not an exact science, and the balance of use and comfort still requires the intervention of the designer.

EXECUTIVE STYLE

A catch-all term for the lifestyle and trappings of prosperous business people. The rise of the executive reflected a whole new way of thinking about business, a revolution that took place from the late 1950s to the 1970s. The roots of executive style come from New York and the rise of multi-national companies. These companies, proud of their size and modernity, encouraged their managers to execute policy decisions, and invented the word 'executive' to describe them. The status of executives was reinforced by such trappings as executive briefcases, executive clothes in grey, lightweight fabrics, and executive Club Class travel. Everything was cool, shiny and new. Executive style always included the latest technologies – paging machines, computers and car telephones – and it was always male. When the style became too bland and too popular, it simply faded away to be replaced in the 1980s by > Yuppie style: unstructured Calvin Klein suits and Paul Smith accessories. In the 1990s the New Man has rediscovered the family, green issues and the well-worn, worsted jacket. Executive style has become a design history footnote.

EXPRESSIONISM

A dominant movement in art, graphics, architecture and design since the late 19th century. It is characterized by an exaggeration of the materials, colours, outlines or textures of objects in order to heighten the emotional impact. Although historically linked with northern Europe, especially Germany and Austria from the 1890s to the 1920s, the themes of Expressionism have been revived in paintings of the 1980s, with the use of large-scale, heroic themes and tactile, painterly surfaces. A well-known exponent of this technique is the American artist Julian Schnabel. Although still evident in the 1990s, Expressionism has been ousted by a cooler use of materials and a more subtle sense of irony. The major Expressionist groups of this century have been Die Brucke (1905–13), and Der Blaue Reiter (1911–14), and German architecture, theatre and film of the 1920s was profoundly influenced by the movement. The Expressionist influence on graphic design has been particularly important.

• R. Furness, *Expressionism*, 1973.

F

FANZINES

Small circulation fan magazines sent out on subscription or with membership of a traditional pop fan club. In the late 1970s fanzines became a small footnote in graphic design history with the rise of > Punk. Taking the message of do-it-yourself to heart, Punk fanzines created the new, alternative graphic design. The best known fanzine was *Sniffin' Glue*, first issued in 1977, which was put together in editor Mark Perry's flat using photocopiers, felt-tipped pen headlines, badly typed copy and a staple gun. Fanzines challenged the idea that graphic design was the exclusive preserve of trained designers, and thumbed their noses at the formal layouts of mass-circulation magazines. Terry Jones, former art editor for *Vogue*, took the fanzine mainstream with *i-D* magazine in 1980. It started life as a chronicle of London street style, but by the mid-80s Jones and his team of young photographers, stylists and designers had created a new direction for graphic design.

FASCIST DESIGN

This was the result of right-wing political movements in Europe during the 1920s and 1930s. Fascism is an Italian term, first associated with Benito Mussolini, and later with the German Nazi Party and the Spanish Falange. The fascist principles imposed on designers included a reverence for nationalism, a distrust of democracy and a belief in the single state party. Totalitarian movements promoted particular types of design and architecture. In Germany this was exemplified in the work of architect Albert Speer and in the revival of Gothic type for newspapers and propaganda materials. *See also* Italian design.

● Robert Soucy, *Fascist Intellectual*, 1979.

FEMINISM

A movement advocating equal social and political rights for women. In a design context it prompted art historians to question not only why there had been so few women artists and designers, but how these very words were part of a patriarchal culture. This questioning has more recently been applied to the younger discipline of design history, and a feminist analysis considers the efforts women have to make in order to design, overcoming the limitations imposed by economics or social conventions. As in art history, this has resulted in a re-examination of the way design history seeks only to emphasize innovation and an aesthetic avant-garde. Instead, it now encourages inquiry into an alternative tradition, particularly in such areas as fashion, popular culture and ephemera.

While recognizing the importance of documenting women's work, a feminist approach seeks to uncover the historical and cultural conditions in which the work was produced and received in order to challenge the accepted hierarchical and often patriarchal account of history. This is particularly evident in the status accorded to industrial design and the 'machine aesthetic' over the decorative arts, fashion and popular design.

In the 1980s and early 1990s the feminist emphasis has been that there is no one feminist or 'essentialist' approach, just as there is no fixed feminine or masculine experience. Both are determined by society, culture, race and class. Similarly, design historians have begun to consider that women's experience of the designed world, their role as consumers and the way in which their identities are constructed through such things as advertising are not only different from those of men, but are of vital importance to the creation of a balanced society.

● I. Anscombe, A *Woman's Touch: Women in Design from 1860 to the Present Day,* 1984; J. Atfield & P. Kirkham, A *View from the Interior,* 1989; T. Gronberg & J. Atfield (eds), A *Resource Book on Women Working in Design,* 1986.

FESTIVAL OF BRITAIN 1951

In a now famous essay the British writer Michael Frayn described the 1951 Festival of Britain as 'the Britain of the radical middle classes – the do-gooders. In short, the herbivores, or gentle ruminants, who look out from the lush pastures which are their natural station in life with eyes full of sorrow for less fortunate creatures.' In 1948 the Labour government wanted a festival which would suggest a new and optimistic future, and would also provide an international forum to promote British manufacturing skills. Its guiding spirit, Sir Gerald Barry, had been a radical journalist and former editor of the *News Chronicle*, and he wanted the festival to symbolize a turning away from the years of austerity. The event was given 27 acres of bomb-damaged rubble on London's South Bank and a budget of £7 million. The finished site included the Dome of Discovery, the world's largest domed structure, and the Skylon, the world's tallest structure, designed by architects Philip Powell and John Moya. The whole area was furnished and decorated in a style known as > Contemporary. Famous designs included Ernest Race's spindly metal Antelope chairs, Lucienne Day's Calyx fabric, her husband Robin Day's seating for the Festival Hall, and the festival logo by Abraham Games. The event gave designers, many of whom had gone straight from college into national service, their first opportunity of work.

The festival opened on 3 May and ended in September, having been visited by six million people. Dylan Thomas remembered the influence of 'strong pink . . . rose, strawberry, peach, flesh, blush, lobster, salmon . . .', and the *New Statesman* described it as 'a tonic'. A month after the festival closed the Labour government was voted out of office and the Conservatives ordered the demolition of everything on the South Bank except the Festival Hall. In 1979 the critic Christopher Brooker, in a television programme called *City of Towers*, suggested that the festival had a lasting influence in showcasing the new town-planning that was introduced into so many British cities in the 1950s and 1960s. With the benefit of hindsight the festival has been criticized as marking the point when Britain stopped trying to lead the world and began to revel in nostalgia. However, it remains Britain's most important post-war design festival.

● Mary Banham & Bevis Hillier (eds), A *Tonic to the Nation: The Festival of Britain 1951*, 1976.

FIFTIES CONTEMPORARY STYLE

For the 1950s Contemporary was more than a new design style; it was also a vision of the future. In fact, it went on to become an international movement. It was a natural reaction away from the oppression of war, with its drabness, regimentation and shortages. Contemporary was symbolic of a new tomorrow. Its priorities were colour, lightness, organic shapes and, with the help of technology, it aimed to be democratically accessible. During the war years chemical dyes were virtually unobtainable, so it is not hard to see why the 1950s loved colour combinations which included hot pinks, sizzling orange, bright blues and canary yellows. These new colours found their way into cheerful, abstract patterns which appeared on the wallpapers, textiles and carpets of post-war homes, cafés and hotels. The new interest in design can be clearly seen in the 1950s' magazines about the home and in the period boom for do-it-yourself.

Contemporary design also introduced new shapes, with objects from chairs to electric fires taking on a lighter, curving quality. This organic quality was inspired by fine art developments such as the mobiles of Alexander Calder and the sculptures of Henry Moore, but it was made possible by technological advances developed during the war. Plywood, for example, had become much more versatile with the invention of synthetic glues and new kiln techniques. Originally used in the manufacture of bomber planes, plywood was now capable of being bent into dramatic sculptural shapes. The American designer Charles Eames had started working with the material for splints for wounded servicemen, but went on to design a series of classic plywood chairs.

In England Contemporary design was first shown at the 1951 > Festival of Britain. For the event Ernest Race designed the Antelope chair, using spindly metal legs with bobble feet and a brightly coloured, machine-formed plywood seat. Designers were commissioned to produce new objects for the post-war homes, which were now smaller and more compact. Furniture needed to be flexible and to respond to social change, hence the introduction of the tele-chair, the convertible bed-settee and the room divider. There was also an important ideology underlying Contemporary design. The war had left a feeling of common purpose and of working together for a better future. In this context Contemporary was not meant as an exclusive, upmarket design style, but as a democratic development that would provide well-designed objects for everyone. In Norway the government provided grants for young married couples to buy modern furniture, and > Scandinavian Design developed and marketed an inspired version of the new style.

In Britain the > Design Council furnished show houses in new towns and ran features in popular magazines outlining the advantages and cost of Contemporary design. There was a great deal of talk about it being classless, and in the early 1950s there was an attempt to bring it into mass production. Whether people wanted it or not is another matter, but it was certainly available at moderate prices. Contemporary style coincided with the economic boom of the 1950s, experienced first in the USA and then in Europe. Jobs were relatively easy to get, and the possibilities of consumer spending, which had disappeared in Europe from 1939 to 1952, gradually returned. Contemporary design was a celebration of that spending power. By the end of the decade, however, Contemporary had lost its monopoly on progressive thinking. It had become just another style whose clichés were swept away by the powerful forces of > Pop Design in the 1960s.

- Lesley Jackson, *The New Look: Design in the Fifties*, 1991.

FOLK ART

Part of a vernacular tradition of design, which has long been admired. It includes religious figures, decorated barges, woven baskets, ceramic ornaments and cottage furniture. Folk art has slowly evolved through generations of anonymous artisans. That tradition makes it hard for the historian to document, so folk art as an important area of design creativity has been shamefully neglected. None the less, devotees and pioneers of the subject exist. The study of folk art is particularly strong in the USA, where it was 'discovered' in the 1920s and promoted by Gertrude Vanderbilt Whitney, founder of the now famous Whitney Museum. Important collections included decorated household objects, tinware, weather-vanes, toys, tavern signs, painted furniture and quilts. In the 1940s the designers Enid Marx and Margaret Lambert published an important study of British folk art, in which they argued that its role as an inspiration for modern design should not be ignored. Nowadays many designers acknowledge this inspiration.

- M. Lambert & Enid Marx, *English Popular Art*, 1951.

HENRY FORD

Ford (1863–1947) was founder of the Ford Motor Company and creator of the moving assembly line, which revolutionized the structure of the work process and the way 20th-century goods were to be made and designed. Of Irish Protestant descent, Ford was born in a rural Michigan community and was to become one of the great industrial giants of the 20th century, his company being the first to mass produce a cheap, standardized car. He started his career working for the Edison Lighting Company, becoming its chief engineer in 1893. Ten years later he established the Ford Motor Company and it became a phenomenal success, producing some 16 million Model T cars between 1908 and 1927.

Ford's moving assembly line technique, introduced in 1913, became known as > Fordism and came to represent the ultimate achievement of 20th-century industrial production. It was also to have an influence on European Modernist architects such as Walter Gropius, who wanted to apply similar methods to Modernist architecture. In fact, Ford did not actually invent the moving assembly line. It was part of a whole series of experiments being conducted at that time in the USA, including a famous example cited by the Modernist writer > Sigfried Giedion of conveyor belt techniques used in Chicago slaughter-houses at the turn of the century. Equally, the theories of Frederick Taylor, who proposed new ideas concerning the organization of factories, were to be influential. None the less, Ford has passed into history as the man who turned these experiments and theories into industrial reality. His two famous quotes, 'History is bunk', made in the witness box in 1919 when he sued the *Chicago Tribune*, and 'You can have any colour so long as it's black', about the Model T, support the myth of Ford as the tough 20th-century industrialist reshaping the modern world. His achievement in creating the popular car was imitated in the USA, with the establishment of General Motors, and throughout Europe.

● Henry Ford, *My Life and Work*, 1923.

MICHEL FOUCAULT

Foucault (1926–84) was part of the group of French intellectuals, including > Barthes and > Baudrillard, whose writings have been explored by a new wave of designers and design writers. Foucault has provided a major critique of conventional approaches to sociology and history. His research has included influential studies of asylums and prisons. The study of Foucault is part of a wider Post-Modernist attempt to involve design in a broader cultural debate. Although his writings are not concerned with objects, his theories, many contemporary teachers and students argue, should be part of the contextual study of design and its role in society. For example, a designer commissioned to produce children's toys could learn a great deal from Foucault's theories of the family structure.

• Michel Foucault, *The Archaeology of Knowledge*, 1969.

FOUND OBJECT

A found object or *objet trouvé*, is a natural or synthetic object transferred to an art or design context. Unlike the ready-made, it is chosen for its aesthetic or visual appeal and often carries connotations of chance discovery, re-seeing the ordinary and re-evaluating the meanings usually ascribed to objects. Although Kurt Switters first introduced the found object (in the form of tram tickets, toy parts and other urban debris) in his Mertz > assemblages of the late 1910s, it became a central form within > Surrealism when mixed with other media. The Surrealist found object, celebrated at the 1936 International Surrealist Exhibition in London, included driftwood, pebbles and gnarled branches, with the emphasis on discovery of the 'marvellous' in the ordinary world. Since the late 1950s, with assemblage, > Pop and environmental works, the found object has become much used because of its potential in rethinking the function and meaning of objects in our society, and in being a readily accessible source of materials and images. More recently the found object has become the basis of the > Bricolage approach, with the artist as a commentator on the fragmented world.

FRENCH DESIGN

French design has always been synonymous with style, and its products over the centuries, from Sèvres porcelain to Gobelins tapestries and couture fashion, have attracted international admiration. In the early 19th century, France pioneered the trade exhibition, opening the first government Exposition de l'Industrie as early as 1798. Napoleon encouraged this trend in 1801, 1802 and 1806, and after that time no fewer than 11 design exhibitions were held in Paris up to 1849. They were enormously successful, attracting up to 4000 manufacturers, and were imitated all over Europe. It was, in fact, the Paris 1849 exhibition which prompted Prince Albert and Sir Henry Cole to mount the > Great Exhibition of 1851 in London. France was subsequently to mount a series of international exhibitions which, in design history terms, were the most important of the 19th century. Significant highlights include the 1867 exhibition, notable for showing Japanese design from the Shogun period and reinforcing the 19th-century obsession with the cult of Japan. However, the largest international exhibition mounted was in 1889, with the Eiffel Tower as its centrepiece, a brilliant iron translation of a medieval spire. The 1889 exhibition was the first to be illuminated entirely with electricity, while other technological firsts included a demonstration of Alexander Bell's phonograph which made it possible to hear the Paris Opera with the aid of a stereophonic telephone device. Another section was devoted to primitive villages, including a Javanese kampong, and it was here that Debussy first heard Javanese music.

The Paris 1900 Exhibition saw the climax of > Art Nouveau design, showing the work of Emile Gallé, Louis Majorelle, Alphonse Mucha and Samuel Bing. After World War I the 1925 Exposition des Arts Décoratifs et Industriels marked the height of the > Art Deco style, which took its name from the exhibition. Again, French designers such as Jacques Ruhlmann, Jean Dunand and René Lalique took the lead in developing a modern geometric style using highly skilled craft techniques and rich, exotic materials. In addition, the 1925 exhibition provided an international forum for the new > Modern Movement. Particularly important was Le Corbusier's Pavilion de l'Esprit Nouveau and the Russian Pavilion, which was the only Constructivist building erected outside the Soviet Union. Le Corbusier also built a pavilion for the 1937 Paris exhibition, but different political priorities now influenced design. This was indicated by the German pavilion, dominated by the eagle and swastika. The 1937 exhibition was the last great event of its kind in Paris.

After the war an organization of architects, decorators and designers calling themselves the Union des Artistes Modernes, showed their work in a series of exhibitions called 'Formes Utiles', and in 1955 the French Ministry of Commerce initiated a design awards scheme similar to the Italian Compasso d'Oro. The > CCI (Centre de Création Industrielle) was launched in 1970, and later moved to the custom-built Pompidou Centre. French design received another boost in the early 1980s with the arrival of Jack Lang as the minister of culture and the establishment of VIA, an organization set up to promote it. New French design was epitomized by the Grapus, a graphic design practice, furniture designers, Andrée Putnam, Roland Cecil Sportes and Jean-Michel Wilmotte. The best-known French designer remains Phillipe Starck, whose prolific work in industrial design, lighting, furniture and architecture has established him as a design superstar.

● *Design Français* 1960–90, exhibition catalogue, Centre Georges Pompidou, 1988.

FUNCTIONALISM

The theory of functional design. It refers to objects designed solely for practical use without any ornamentation or decoration. The word itself appears frequently in Modernism and one of its basic tenets is the theory that 'form follows function'. Functionalism is therefore part of the rational, ordered Modernist approach to design. Its aims and objectives were clearly expressed by the > Ulm school of design and the work of its best-known student, Dieter Rams, for the German company Braun. In the 1960s Functionalism was challenged by the new priorities of > Pop, and later by the diverse approaches of > Post-Modernism. These movements argued that Functionalism was too narrow an approach to design; it ignored the social meanings individuals give to objects and it played down the creative individualist nature of the designer. In opposition to this, Functionalism is regarded as not merely a style but a deeply felt commitment to order and progress.

FUTURISM

Futurism was the creation of Filippo Tomasso Marinetti (1876–1944), an Italian poet based in Milan, who published 'The Foundation and

Manifesto of Futurism' on the front page of the Paris newspaper *Le Figaro* on 20 February 1909. Its militant and strident tone announced a new literary and social movement which was to free Italy from its 'countless cemeteries' and glorify a 'new form of beauty, the beauty of speed'. The manifesto stressed the youth of its creators ('the oldest among us is thirty'), the rejection of all past values and institutes, and the need for 'courage, audacity and revolt' to embrace the new industrial world of machines, noise, speed, danger and continuous change. Italy at this time was undergoing rapid but late industrialization. Northern Italy, united in 1860, was the centre of this rapid expansion, with such industrial cities as Milan and Turin, the home of Fiat motors. Indeed, the automobile, with its conquest of speed and its shiny, noisy forms, became one of the chief symbols of Futurism.

After publishing his manifesto, Marinetti gathered around him a group of young artists, poets, musicians and architects committed to his stirring ideas. They included Umberto Boccioni (1882–1916), painter and sculptor, Carlo Carra (1881–1966), musician and painter, Giaccomo Balla (1871–1958), artist and later an interior designer, Gino Severini (1883–1966), a painter based in Paris, Luigi Russolo (1885–1947), musician and creator/performer of 'noise machines', and Antonio Sant'Elia (1888–1916), architect and designer.

Although best known for such paintings as Boccioni's *The Street Enters the House* (1911), or Balla's *Dynamism of a Automobile* (1912), the movement was tremendously important and influential for its embracing of urban industrial culture in visual and written forms. Marinetti, a mast of propaganda, made manifestos almost a requisite for any group wishing to reach a large reading public. He developed Futurist evenings and tours to attract a broader audience to experience the multi-media performances of poetry, music, art and design in Italy and Europe. Unlike many of the modern movements, Futurism was fiercely nationalistic and Marinetti saw it as a resurrection of Italy, as well as a chance to colonize other world centres. Interestingly, Futurism was to have its greatest impact in England and Russia, both of which Marinetti visited, and which, for different reasons, had entrenched art traditions. Strongly influenced by the writings of Nietzsche on the new man (*Thus Spake Zarathustra*), and Henri Bergson's philosophy of matter, time and space ((*Matter and Memory*, 1896), the Futurists developed a new language of dynamic lines – lines of force and inter-penetrating planes evident in their paintings, graphics, sculpture and proposed architecture. Although influenced by the > Cubists' work, seen in Paris in late 1911, their various manifestos on painting, politics, music and sculpture stressed their concern with upheaval of all accepted values, whether in terms of using new, often impermanent materials like industrial glass, hair and plastics, or the glorification of war and social change (except for women). It was these manifestos, where the ideas far outstrip those contained in their work, that were to have the greatest impact.

During World War I a Futurist battalion was formed, but following the death of the most innovative members, Sant'Elia and Boccioni, the movement's impetus faded. Marinetti attempted to revive Futurism in 1916 with Balla as the main figure, but as Marinetti became a more vocal adherent of Mussolini's Fascism, the major figures dispersed.

● C. Tisdall, *Futurism*, 1977.

G

GEOMETRIC DESIGN

Geometric design has a rational mathematical or geometric origin. Simple geometric patterns can be found in nearly all prehistoric and primitive societies, but it was the Romans who invented complex geometric patterns used in mosaic floors. These Roman forms inspired later Islamic designs, which in turn influenced medieval churches and monasteries in Europe. By the Renaissance geometric patterns were part of a common language of design, but their importance gained a sharper focus in the 19th century with research into decorative forms appropriate for the new consumer culture of the Industrial Revolution. The publication from 1834 to 1845 of Owen Jones's and Jules Goury's *Plans, Elevations, Sections and Details of the Alhambra* helped to revive a Victorian interest in geometric design. At the same time a number of books were published which tried to explain the phenomenon of pattern repeats, probably as a response to the increasing demands of industrialization. Jules Bourgoin (1838–1907), former professor of ornament at the Paris Ecole des Beaux Arts, and the British industrial designer Christopher Dresser (1834–1904) explored plant structure as a way of understanding the geometry of the natural world. Another example of this approach can be seen in J. Glaisher's well-illustrated article on snow crystals as sources for designers, which appeared in the *Art Journal* in 1857. These researches influenced the education of young children and student designers at the government's > Schools of Design. Around this time the educationalist Friedrich Froebel (1782–1852), who believed in the concept of constructive play for children, developed a set of building bricks for this purpose, and it is certainly true that Prince Albert had the royal children learning how to mix mortar and lay bricks. It is believed that Frank Lloyd Wright played with

Froebel bricks in his nursery. George Ricks, a London school inspector, applied some of Froebel's ideas on a larger scale in the city's board schools. Typical of his methods was an 1889 educational textbook called *Simple Drawing Exercises on Squared Paper*. Ricks believed that exercises in simple geometric design developed hand and eye coordination, even if they did not encourage the imagination. After World War I art and design education moved towards a more craft-based approach, but geometric exercises reappeared again at the > Bauhaus in the late 1920s. Early abstract artists, such as Mondrian, also experimented with geometric form, but here the relationship is less clear. More recently, however, fine artists, such as Kenneth Martin, have taken up mathematical approaches to painting, and recent experiments with Japanese computer art suggest that geometric design will continue to exercise a fascination for the creative imagination.

SIGFRIED GIEDION

Giedion (1888–1964) and Nikolaus > Pevsner are the two most influential design historians of the mid-20th century. In 1948 Giedion's book *Mechanization Takes Command* argued that the modern world and its artefacts were continuously affected by scientific and industrial progress. His book was the first to argue that the anonymous technical aspects of history are just as important as the history of creative individuals which had dominated, and still dominates, the history of design. His view, which suggested a wider cultural approach to design, was deeply influential. *Mechanization Takes Command* looked at developments in Chicago slaughter-houses, and suggested that their use of conveyor belts could be applied to modern industry. His case studies also explored the Yale lock and the Colt gun. Giedion had trained as an art historian under Heinrich Wolfflin. He became a defender of > Modern Movement principles and devoted much of his professional life to promoting modern architecture. In 1928 he became the secretary of > CIAM. In the 1940s his Harvard lectures on the theme of Modernism were published as *Space, Time and Architecture*.

GLAM ROCK

A pop music phenomenon of the 1970s, which gave rise to gaudy satin clothing embellished with sequins and rhinestones, platform soles and exaggerated make-up. The androgynous style appealed equally to men and women. The elements of Glam Rock were to be revised in the 1980s as part of the Post-Modernist appropriation of > Camp and > Kitsch.

GLASGOW FOUR

The Glasgow Four consisted of Charles Rennie Mackintosh, Herbert MacNair and Margaret and Frances MacDonald. This group launched one of the most influential styles of the late 19th century, but its most famous member was the architect Charles Rennie Mackintosh, whose work was rediscovered in the 1960s and who has since emerged as one of the world's most famous designers, canonized by an international following, with particularly fanatical support in Japan. He and Herbert MacNair both studied at the Glasgow School of Art and fell under the influence of its remarkable head Francis H. Newbery. It was Newbery who introduced the pair to the two MacDonald sisters in 1893, and they eventually married, MacNair to Frances in 1899 and Mackintosh to Margaret in 1900. Although Mackintosh is by far the most famous of the Four, they were all gifted and versatile designers and doubtless future research will re-evaluate their individual contributions to the creation of a unique style. What we do know is that by 1892, before the Four met, Mackintosh had already developed his distinctive > Art Nouveau decorative style. But working as a group, the Four exhibited together at the 1896 Arts and Crafts Exhibition and attracted considerable criticism from their more sober English colleagues.

In 1897 Mackintosh won the competition to design a new building for the Glasgow School of Art, and the same year started to work on Miss Cranston's series of tea rooms. The Four's commissions were to be thin on the ground, so they looked to the Continent for a more sympathetic treatment of their work. Their success was secured by a triumph at the Vienna Secession Exhibition of 1900, and the following year the Secessionist magazine *Ver Sacrum* was devoted entirely to the Glasgow School. This recognition did not attract long-term projects for the group. They relied on commissions from personal friends and a small group of admirers.

By 1914 Mackintosh was embittered and frustrated; he left Glasgow first for Chelsea and finally for France in 1925. By all accounts he was a difficult, creative personality not given to making many client concessions. He and his colleagues stepped outside the received > Arts and Crafts wisdom of truth to materials and honest construction. Much of the furniture they designed is uncomfortable, poorly constructed, painted or stained – all heinous crimes to advocates of the Ernest Gimson school of furniture design. Their best works were formal stage sets. These were beautiful and poetic, with an almost mystic undercurrent seen in the recurring motif of a stylized rose.

There is something tragic about the demise of the Four. Frances died in 1924, Mackintosh in 1928, spending the last years of his life painting and virtually unknown. MacNair stopped designing in 1924, although he lived until 1953. In the post-war period their achievements were known only to the informed few. When Glasgow Council made plans to knock down several key buildings, few people protested as there was little pride in this remarkable group. However, the 1960s' revival of things Victorian changed all that. Cecil Beaton reworked Mackintosh's style for the sets of *My Fair Lady*, and slowly the work of the Glasgow Four developed into a small industry. The Italian company Cassina made reproduction Mackintosh furniture and the group's graphic style became central to the Art Nouveau revival. Their contribution to the visual language of 20th-century design is enormous.

• Roger Billcliffe, *Charles Rennie Mackintosh*, 1983.

GLOBALIZATION

A spread by Western companies to new markets, particularly those in developing countries. The trend for globalization was sparked off by the recession of 1979. Unlike old-style multi-nationals such as Hoover, now global companies such as McDonalds and Coca-Cola do not extract or process raw materials locally, but simply exploit local markets. The top 10 globals with high-profile brand names are (in descending order): Coca-Cola, McDonalds, Pepsi-Cola, Nestlé, Mercedes, Disney, Sony, IBM, Toyota and Kodak. Globalization has led to a great deal of angst about national identity and a fear that the culture of individual nation states will be swamped by an all-powerful but bland product conformity. The expansion of global industries presents complex political and economic questions.

• Michael Porter, *Competition in Global Industries*, 1986.

GOTHIC REVIVAL

In several stages and forms, the Gothic Revival dominated 19th-century attitudes to and taste in design. In the early years of the century it was part and parcel of the Romantic movement, which included such novels as *Ivanhoe* by Sir Walter Scott. In the 1840s Gothic Revival became part of a protest movement, a reaction against the all-too-visible effects of the Industrial Revolution. A well-known example of this protest came from the architect Augustus Pugin (1812–52). In 1846 he published a book called *Contrasts*, which contained a very simple message; Pugin believed that the medieval past, which he called Gothic, showed more understanding of beauty and design than contemporary architecture. *Contrasts* used simple examples to illustrate his point of view. The caring treatment of the sick in a 15th-century monastery, for example, is contrasted with the notorious Victorian work-houses so vividly described in the novels of Charles Dickens. Pugin considered Gothic, from both a moral and visual point of view, as the only style in which to work. The best place to see the results of his theories is the Houses of Parliament in London, which were rebuilt in the 1830s. Pugin was given the job of designing all the decoration, furniture, tiles, wallpaper and textiles in the Gothic style. Nearly all of this work survives today. The Houses of Parliament suggested the possibilities of using the Gothic style for business and commerce, and by the 1860s and 1870s a movement called High Victorian Gothic had appeared. Its practitioners were the architects George Street, John Seddon, William Burges and William Butterfield, and among the key buildings they designed were the Law Courts on The Strand and St Pancras Hotel.

Gothic style was a vigorous and picturesque approach, but ultimately it did not prove popular. As a source of inspiration, however, it remained constant. For many influential critics, John > Ruskin for example, Gothic became a vehicle for reform and a driving force behind

111

the ideas of William Morris and the > Arts and Crafts Movement. Although this movement tended not to use specific Gothic details in design, the spirit of Gothic underlay its attitudes about vernacular form, truth to materials and the role of design in society. These ideas may have been naive, but none the less the influence of the Gothic Revival remained powerful throughout the 19th century.

• Kenneth Clark, *The Gothic Revival,* 1962.

GRAFFITI

Words and symbols used to deface public spaces and transport. Deriving from the Italian verb to scratch, graffiti dates back to ancient Egypt, but has become an interesting subject for artists and designers only since World War II, particularly in the 1970s. With the invention of aerosol paint cans, streetwise teenagers from the Bronx, using such names as Fab Five Freddie and Futura 2000, put their marks on the walls and carriages of New York's subways. They signed their work with an individual 'tag', which used a jagged, inflated typography and vivid colours that were to influence mainstream graphic design.

Opinions as to the significance of 1970s' graffiti differ. Some claimed graffiti was a legitimate kind of urban folk art, while others said it was simply vandalism. The New York art establishment took up the movement, and Keith Haring is the best-known example of a commercially trained artist who exploited the style. Haring's imagery was widely used in graphic design and incorporated into fashion by designers such as Vivienne Westwood.

GREAT EXHIBITION OF 1851

Proposed by Prince Albert in 1849 and brought to fruition by the artist/designer Sir Henry Cole, the Great Exhibition opened in Hyde Park on 1 May 1851. It was a tremendous success, attracted millions of visitors, made a profit and the building that was constructed for the exhibition became world famous. The architect, Joseph Paxton, built it of glass and iron panels in order to demonstrate the latest industrial techniques and materials. It was immediately nicknamed the Crystal Palace. The exhibition itself was a celebration of the new technology and inventions of the Industrial Revolution, and it is possible to study the exhibits in the *Art Journal Illustrated Catalogue*. The exhibition proved extremely influential. It attracted intense newspaper coverage and critics studied the proceedings in some detail. Even allowing for the fact the manufacturers showed their most elaborate pieces, extravagant naturalism was the order of the day. Popular design was confident, large scale and ornate.

Overall the exhibition was not felt to be Britain's finest design hour, but its importance to design should not be underestimated. Even the project's harshest critics were impressed with Pugin's Medieval Court, which housed Gothic furniture and metalwork of his own design. The Great Exhibition allowed people a chance to look at the products of other nations, and the Indian section in particular was a revelation. It also confirmed another important development: that Britain had become the world's most important political and economic power. It marked the beginning of Britain's short-lived but all-powerful Empire. *See also* British Exhibitions; Victoria and Albert Museum.

GREEN DESIGN

Green design springs from a movement aimed at conserving the world's natural resources and preventing the effects of industry and pollution destroying the delicate balance of the world's ecology. Green design is still in its embryonic stage, but it is an extremely important new direction. Its roots go back to the 1960s anti-consumer movement, which started in the USA with Vance > Packard's attacks on the automobile industry and its development of built-in > obsolescence. Similar protests also found expression in the growing movement for > Alternative Design in the 1970s. These views, however, were felt to be those of an eccentric and slightly quirky minority. They were dismissed as idealistic, hippy ideas that had little relevance to the modern world.

The great triumph of Green Design is that its ideals, if not its practice, have gone mainstream. One of its most famous advocates, the Prince of Wales, has banned aerosol sprays in his household and introduced organic farming methods on his land. More importantly, however, green issues have moved on to a legislative level. The European Community, for example, has proposed an environmental policy, which would hold the polluter personally responsible for pollution damage. The EC also intends to introduce an eco-labelling system to help the consumer identify which products are ecologically sound. In fact, governments all over the world have introduced new laws to curb the adverse effects of industry. Three years ago US legislators made it compulsory for companies to have waste emissions independently measured, and they are now exploring the possibility of banning certain printing inks used for magazines and packaging. Green design has become an industry itself.

In 1985 the amount paid by industry to environmental consultants was virtually zero. It has now risen to nearly £200 million in the UK alone. Two British consultants in this field, John Elkington and Julia Hailes, published the *Green Consumer Guide* in 1989 which spent 44 weeks in the UK bestseller list. Nowadays, independent bodies like Friends of the Earth send out information to designers and architects warning against the use of certain hardwoods because of the effect on precious forest resources. At first environmentalists regarded designers with suspicion, believing them to be the people who encouraged consumerism. That view has now shifted and designers are encouraged to get involved with projects at an early stage to help solve the key resources issue. Among the vanguard are the 02 design group, based in Copenhagen, and Anita Roddick, owner of the Body Shop, who has pioneered recycling, and introduced new inks and printing techniques for her products.

Designers are being asked to consider the long-term implications of their designs and materials specifications, perhaps by avoiding non-biodegradable plastic or by using recycled products. However, some green ideas are now seen to have been over-simplistic. For example, some processes for de-inking paper produce up to twice as many damaging emissions as the process used to make virgin paper. The same confusion has affected the fashion industry's search for green fabric. Overall the situation needs much more independent information. The current buzzword is 'eco-balancing', a method of evaluating materials on the basis of energy consumption, recyclability, raw materials use, pollution and waste. The method is intended to give an accurate picture on the effect materials have on the environment as a whole. Green design is still only scratching the surface of this large and complex problem, but there are some interesting new directions. IBM, for example, has introduced a pioneering scheme to recycle old computers, while the German company AEG has withdrawn its electric carving knife on the grounds that it was unnecessary. Developments like these mark a wider change of attitude which looks promising for the future.

● Dorothy McKenzie, *Green Design: Design for the Environment*, 1991.

GUILDS OF DESIGN

The word 'guild' means an association of craftsmen. Guilds developed in the Middle Ages for the purpose of training and protecting their members. It was this idea of collaboration and mutual support that attracted many 19th-century designers. > Ruskin, for example, founded the Guild of St George in 1878, a doomed attempt to revive the spirit of medieval life. The Art Workers' Guild was founded in 1883 by pupils of the architect Norman Shaw to discuss art and architecture and quickly expanded to include established designers Lewis Day, Walter Crane and William Morris. By the 1890s the guild acted as an important discussion forum for craftsmen and designers. In 1915 its premises were taken over by the newly formed > Design and Industries Association.

The first commercial design enterprise to choose the name 'guild' was the Century Guild, founded in 1882 by Arthur Mackmurdo with Herbert Horne. The purpose of the guild was to 'render all branches of art the sphere no longer of the tradesman but the artist'. It was dissolved in 1888, but the work of its members is remembered as an early development of the > Art Nouveau whiplash line developed in graphic design and chair-backs. The most famous guild, however, founded by Charles Ashbee in 1888, was called the Guild of Handicraft. Ashbee, who was inspired by Morris, opened premises in London's Mile End to train Cockney workers in simple craft techniques. In 1901 he moved 150 workers to Chipping Camden in the Cotswolds to start a social experiment in communal living and design. The Cotswolds had become something of a cult for the > Arts and Crafts Movement, as a region rich in honey-coloured, vernacular 17th-century architecture and a rural life virtually untouched since the 18th century. Ashbee was part of an advance guard of artists and designers who moved to the region at the turn of the century. His guild advocated self-help, education for all, garden allotments and pageants. It attracted a steady stream of publicity and visitors, and produced simple silverware and jewellery that was to inspire more commercial enterprises such as Liberty's department store. In 1907 the guild, never a financial success, finally failed. Many of the Cockney families stayed on and integrated into Cotswolds life. Ashbee himself moved to Jerusalem. The idea of communities of craftsmen and women continued to find favour in the 20th century.

H

HABITAT

A British retail group of design stores established in 1964 by Sir Terence Conran (born 1931). Habitat is much more than a shop; for a whole generation of young, middle-class shoppers it represented a new lifestyle.

The first Habitat store, opened in the Fulham Road, London, sold Indian rugs, Polish enamelled mugs, and all manner of lighting and tableware stacked floor to ceiling in warehouse style. For the British shopper Habitat was a retail revolution. The shops introduced contemporary design at accessible prices, the interiors laid out with bold colours and in-house graphics. The year 1966 saw another innovation – the launch of the Habitat catalogue. Now acknowledged as a design classic, the catalogue is lavishly laid out with arty photographs and a simple but striking graphic style. Three years after its inception the catalogue offered Habitat's growing numbers of customers a mail order service. By 1980 the Habitat group included 47 stores in Britain, Europe and the USA.

Conran trained at the Central School of Art as a textile designer. After graduation he went on to design furniture, opened a famous restaurant called the Soup Kitchen and launched his design consultancy, now called Conran Associates. Sir Terence is now Britain's best-known designer, and in the early 1980s he became a driving force behind the retail revolution. In 1981 Habitat merged with Mothercare, a well-known chain of mother and baby stores, and in 1983 the company bought Heal's, the famous department store specializing in furniture. The Heal's building, something of a London institution, became the centre of the Conran empire.

Conran's expanding business interests also included property development, and he bought an area of London's docklands called

Butlers Wharf, which was to play a key role in another of his innovations – the world's first > design museum. The idea for this had first developed in the late 1970s, and in 1981 the Conran Foundation was set up to finance it. In 1989 Prime Minister Margaret Thatcher opened the museum, and it has since attracted a great deal of public and media interest.

Recently Sir Terence has moved back to retailing. He has resigned the chairmanship of his company and now devotes himself to running his upmarket store The Conran Shop. Sited in the famous > Art Nouveau Michelin building, The Conran Shop enjoys a reputation as London's leading design store, highly praised for the quality of its window displays, the directional choice of merchandise and its sophisticated approach to the international shopper. For the moment it would seem that Conran has come full circle.

- Barty Phillips, *Conran and the Habitat Story*, 1984.

HERITAGE INDUSTRY

An obsession in contemporary Britain with the past. It is also the title of a book by critic Robert Hewison, which explores the way Britain markets the past. Hewison's thesis is that Britain has an obsession with the past which has undermined the country's ability to cope with the present and the future. While the country faces a massive recession, he argues, a new force is taking over – the heritage industry – a movement dedicated to turning Britain into one vast, open-air museum. Hewison is not alone in voicing this disquiet. Tom > Wolfe has described Britain as a huge theme park filled with Elizabethan Beefeaters, Dickensian eccentrics, country cottages and shabby tea-rooms. Endemic in British culture seems to be a belief that the past is best. The commercial possibilities of the heritage industry have been exploited by popular film and television programmes, such as *Jewel in the Crown*, a dramatization of colonial life in India. This genre provides romanticized images of a safe past. Many commentators, however, worry that this obsession with the past is holding back a commitment to deal with the problems of the present and the future.

- Robert Hewison, *The Heritage Industry*, 1987.

HIGH TECH

This is not a design movement, but an approach to industrial materials used in new and different contexts. It is sometimes called the Industrial Aesthetic and as such its origins can be traced back to Paxton's prefabricated designs for the Crystal Palace and Eiffel's tower in Paris. It was the > Modern Movement, however, which developed High Tech in a big way. In 1928 Pierre Chareau designed the Maison de Verre using industrial glass bricks, shop steel ladders and factory shelving. In 1936 the Museum of Modern Art in New York mounted an exhibition that extolled the virtues of, among other items, laboratory glass for the home. Such industrial products appealed to all designers. In 1949 Charles and Ray Eames used a mail-order catalogue to buy off-the-peg factory construction components to build their Santa Monica home. This idea of putting industrial products to other uses continued throughout the 1960s and 1970s and can be seen at the > CCI (Pompidou Centre) in Paris. This controversial building, designed by Richard Rogers and Renzo Piano, made a feature of exposed heating ducts and conduits for such utilities as plumbing and electricity. It was compared to an oil refinery, but a refinery dedicated to culture, painted in primary colours and full of wit and humour. Rogers also designed the Lloyds building in the City of London, arguably Britain's last great building of the late 20th century.

In the 1970s High Tech became fashionable as a style for the home. People began to buy restaurant cutlery and warehouse storage systems. The cult was documented in Joan Kron's and Suzanne Slesin's book, *High Tech*. The cover photograph showed off the aesthetic with fruit in a concrete bird-bath placed on a table-top made from deck plate (a material used for the floors of battleship boiler-rooms). Shops selling high-tech style sprang up all over the world. One of the best known in London was Practical Styling, owned and run by Tommy Roberts.

High Tech also influenced art, the description being applied to contemporary art made with sophisticated technology such as computers, lasers, holograms, photocopiers, fax machines and even satellite transmissions.

● Joan Kron & Suzanne Slesin, *High Tech: The Industrial Style and Source Book for the Home*, 1978.

HIPPY CULTURE

A movement that stressed anti-materialism, peace and love, and encouraged individual lifestyles. After the movement's heyday in the late 1960s and early 1970s, 'hippy' became a term of abuse, and hippy ideas were dismissed as the self-indulgent posturings of middle-class students who subsequently sold out to the Establishment values they had once rejected. Undoubtedly, the movement's earnest introspection set it up for ridicule on a massive scale. In the New Age 1990s, however, hippy culture is up for a more sympathetic evaluation.

Of major importance here is the hippy attitude to technology. Young people in the late 1960s began to oppose economic concepts such as planned obsolescence and the exploitation of natural resources. Hippy culture also upturned the design status quo. Design choices now became arbitrary and often bizarre. The emphasis was placed on individual lifestyles. Clothes were bought second-hand or from ethnic shops selling Afghan coats and embroidered Indian shirts. For women the tailored clothes and obvious make-up of the early 1960s were discarded in favour of a more natural look and long hair. Furniture and interior design picked up on recycling Victorian items, and propagated DIY ideas of building storage units from planks, bricks, beer crates and other discarded industrial materials. The norms of Western culture were regarded with deep suspicion, and alternative lifestyles and religions from the East, in theory at least, provided more attractive examples of how to live out the new social revolution. Although serious principles underlay the hippy movement, its emphasis on free choice required the buoyant economy of the 1960s to survive. In the event it did not survive the international oil crisis of 1973 and the massive recession which followed. The last vestiges of the movement were appropriated by wealthy, middle-class consumers, who developed a taste for sushi, lentil loaves, personal growth and staying mellow. In 1976 Cyra McFadden's novel *The Serial* sent up the laid-back lifestyle in Marin County, California. *See also* Alternative Design; Psychedelia.

HISTORICISM

Borrowing from the past, a trend which, in recent years, has become associated with the > Post-Modernist Movement. In the 1990s we have grown used to revivals coming around at shorter and shorter intervals, the most recent looking again at the psychedelic colours and patterns of the 1960s. > Eclecticism, however, has a much longer history. Christopher Wren reworked the medieval past in his Tom Tower at Oxford, while in the 18th century architects and designers borrowed extensively from Egyptian, Greek, Roman and Chinese sources. It was the 19th century, however, that made Historicism its own, and this obsession for the past is reflected in the large numbers of design source books published on the subject. The most famous of these, and now a standard text endlessly reprinted, was Owen Jones's *Grammar of Ornament* (1856). This book provided manufacturers and designers with a diversity of source material, including Elizabethan, Pompeiian, Moorish and Aztec imagery. These styles were all consumed by the demands for decoration and ornament.

The great inspiration behind 19th-century design was the > Gothic Revival, but its architects were at pains to stress that straight copying of imagery was not the aim; they wished to recreate the strength and spirit of the Middle Ages. With the advent of the > Modern Movement any attempt at Historicism was frowned on by the avant-garde. It was not until the development of post-war > Pop Culture that borrowing from the past was made respectable, and it has now come to play a key role in the pluralist approach of design in the 1990s. The British style magazine *The Face* coined the term 'The Age of Plunder' for this direction. Indeed, plunder has played an important role in the inspirational fashion designs of Vivienne Westwood. She has revived the Victorian crinoline, the rococo outdoor fête and imagery from Royal pageantry to create her anarchic clothes. The term plunder was also applied to graphic design of the 1980s. Peter Saville, now a partner with the famous design practice Pentagram, reworked Roman type, > Russian Constructivism and 1960s' Pop for record sleeves and posters, and in doing so reflected a general trend towards what was called 'appropriation of images'.

HOLLYWOOD STYLE

The American film industry was all-powerful in the inter-war years. Its products were the first mass entertainment and cultural export of things American to be shown all over the world. The Hollywood film studios housed a major industry, and a key part of that industry was the army of designers working on sets, props, graphics and fashion. Inevitably, Hollywood was a powerful source of design ideas. Traditionally, however, design commentators have tended to dismiss Hollywood's role, rather as traditional European theatre has dismissed Hollywood standards of acting, and the world of literature has denigrated the Hollywood scriptwriter for 'selling out'. These traditional cultural hierarchies have been undermined since the 1960s. Far from being ephemeral, Hollywood films are now seen for what they really were, and in some cases still are – the most important cultural and visual products of the 20th century.

- Roy Pickard, *The Hollywood Studios*, 1978.

I

ILLUSTRATION

Before World War II illustration was considered to be > commercial art, occupying the middle ground between painting and design. In the post-war period illustration has come into its own as a separate creative activity, and illustrators find work in advertising, packaging, magazines, poster design and books.

The history of illustration goes back to the earliest printed books, such as the works on architecture by Palladio and Serlio in the 17th century. During the 18th century the trend for illustrated books, trade cards and handbills increased, and the status of illustration was enhanced when the poet William Blake illustrated books of his own poems.

As book consumption continued to increase in the 19th century, illustrated books proliferated, helped by the development of colour printing, such as chromolithography, which involved printing from stone blocks (one for each colour), and colour wood-block printing. These techniques made books particularly attractive to children, and the illustration of children's books quickly became an accepted art form. The best-known practitioners included Walter Crane, Kate Green-away and Beatrix Potter. Among illustrators of adult books, Aubrey Beardsley took advantage of photographic techniques to reproduce his erotic, brilliant black and white illustrations for The Yellow Book, a publication devoted to the work of advanced designers. At the same time, well-known artists also worked in the commercial area; Toulouse-Lautrec, for example, produced Art Nouveau posters. If his illustration work can be said to occupy one end of the spectrum, the other end was occupied by thousands of jobbing illustrators paid to produce packaging and chocolate-box lids for industry. Their work was little appreciated and their status as creative illustrators was negligible. More recently that situation has changed. Contemporary illustrators are well known in their own right and can command huge fees for their work. In the 1960s and the 1970s the interest in photography as a medium for illustration looked set to kill off more traditional forms of illustration, but the 1980s saw a tremendous revival of interest in illustration for supermarket packaging, magazines and advertising.

INDEPENDENT GROUP (IG)

A group founded in 1952 by a circle of British architects, writers and artists to explore the world of consumer culture. IG members included Peter and Alison Smithson, James Stirling, Peter Reyner > Banham, Richard Hamilton and Eduardo Paolozzi. Recently a major retrospective exhibition of > Pop design at the Royal Academy has reinforced the group's position as the founders of Pop. They met at London's Institute of Contemporary Art in opposition to the reactionary attitudes of post-war British culture, and organized a now famous series of informal seminars in which they explored all aspects of popular culture. The IG made an original contribution to the analysis of mass-produced design in treating it as seriously as high culture. It looked at such things as cars, advertising and films, and tried to read them as symbols of the new consumer culture. It established the idea that artists and architects could explore the world of consumer culture and the group's writers, particularly Reyner Banham and Toni del Renzio, published a series of influential articles. The group's other important contribution to design theory was a reassessment of the > Modern Movement in which it challenged the movement's authority.

The IG stopped formal meetings in 1955, but continued to meet and collaborate on an informal basis, working together in the following year on the Whitechapel Gallery exhibition, 'This Is Tomorrow'. It is true to say that the ideals and aspirations of the IG remain an ongoing project for the remaining members, including Paolozzi and Hamilton.

● David Robbins (ed)., *The Independent Group, postwar Britain and the aesthetics of plenty*, 1990.

INDUSTRIAL AESTHETICS *See* High Tech.

INTERDISCIPLINARY DESIGN

Almost any designed environment demonstrates the essential importance of the interdisciplinary team. Electrical engineers, for example,
developed the workings of the computer, industrial designers the
casing, while a graphic designer helped prepare the user's manual.
Although the principle of team work is an old one, the potential of the
interdisciplinary team is currently being revised and many of the
industrial giants, such as IBM and Sony, exploit this work method to
expand their international markets. For such companies design teams
permit simultaneous input from different perspectives and disciplines,
combining the talents of, say, artists, philosophers, production
managers and service personnel. Interdisciplinary teams are expected
to take responsibility for the whole project rather than a narrow slice.
The emphasis on design as a team activity also helps to define the
nature of the design profession. As a team activity, the recent cult of
the lone design star has become a dubious concept. The idea of the
designer as celebrity could be on the decline, reinforcing the important
message that design, unlike art activities, is a shared, mutually
dependent activity.

INTERIOR DESIGN

Interior design relates to the decoration and furnishing of spaces within
buildings. Human beings have always created interior spaces for
themselves, but the concept of a professional designer manipulating
and decorating the interior space of a building is relatively new,
emerging only in the 20th century. An 18th-century forerunner was the
ensemblier, who came from an upholstery or furniture background.
During the 1760s, for example, Thomas Chippendale, the British
cabinet-maker, in effect ran an interior design practice from his shop in
St Martin's Lane. Clients ordered their furniture, but could also
purchase carpets and draperies, and hire craftsmen to repaint interior
walls. Fontaine and Percier, Napoleon's interior decorators, brought
together furniture, textiles and painted decorations within his state

living quarters. Similarly, during the 19th and early 20th centuries, furniture retailers such as the London firm of Waring & Gillow would provide reproduction antiques and, if required, create a total environment in keeping with such pieces.

Interior design has always been overshadowed by the architectural profession, and still is today. Leading architects of the 20th century, including Charles Rennie Mackintosh, succeeded in creating stunning interiors for the buildings they designed, including the furniture, floor coverings and light fittings. This approach flourished with the > Modern Movement of the inter-war years, when the architect exercised total control over the open-plan interiors and created such classics of 20th-century design as Le Corbusier's *Grand confort* chair and Mies van der Rohe's Barcelona chair. After World War II, the new profession of interior design acquired stature with the creation of the British Institute of Interior Design and new, high-level courses on the subject at national art schools. In the early 1950s Sir Hugh Casson and Margaret Casson set up the first postgraduate school of interior design at the > Royal College of Art. They faced opposition from the Royal Institute of British Architects (RIBA), who still saw interior designers as decorators, but gradually change came about. Figures such as David Hicks in Britain and Billy Baldwin in the USA became publicly known as interior designers. With the founding of specialist journals like *The World of Interiors*, *Interior Design* and *Designers Journal*, the identity of the profession became more firmly established.

With the retail boom of the 1980s, which was to a certain extent design led, interior design helped to establish a new identity for banks, retail shops and building societies. The 1980s saw the rise of the powerful interior design practice. Rodney Fitch, for example, was the first to employ over 1000 people. Other practices, such as David Davies, Din Associates, Conran Associates and Peter Leonard, ensured that interior design was at last taken seriously as a powerful marketing tool for the retailer. The British took the lead in this transformation of the High Street, curtailed only by the recession of the 1990s. Interior design, however, is now taken seriously and on the same level as graphic, product and fashion design.

● Anne Massey, *Twentieth Century Interior Design*, 1990.

INTERNATIONAL STYLE

Another name for the > Modern Movement. It was 'invented' by Philip Johnson for an exhibition held at the Museum of Modern Art in New York in 1932, but he had borrowed the description from a book by Walter Gropius called *Internationale Architektur* (1925). In the 1930s the label stuck and architects in particular began to describe their work as international. Modernism and the Modern Movement are now more widely used to describe changes in art and design during the 1920s and 1930s.

● H.R. Hitchcock and Philip Johnson, *The International Style*, 1966.

INDUSTRIAL DESIGN

A term covering the products of post-Industrial Revolution society. The concept of the industrial designer is therefore relatively new, and his or her role is to adapt the new products of industry to the mass market. Before the Industrial Revolution this did not exist. The task of creating objects for the home belonged to artisans and craftsmen. During the 19th century the three major industrial powers – Britain, the United States and Germany – gradually saw the emergence of industrial designers. The first step towards this was to develop education for designers. Britain set up a > School of Design with the objective of training designers for industry. The best-known industrial designer from this school was Christopher Dresser, who created designs for mass production for companies as diverse as Minton and Elkingtons.

At the turn of the century in Germany the electrical company AEG appointed Peter Behrens as its industrial designer, and there was a growth in professional organizations such as the Deutsche > Werkbund, founded in 1907. It was the USA, however, that saw the real revolution in manufacturing techniques and the role of design. Henry > Ford developed methods of standardization into 24-hour assembly lines for the production of his Model T car. The USA also produced the first generation of industrial design professionals, including Raymond Loewy, Norman Bel Geddes and Walter Dorwin Teague. Such people were now part of production teams working on the cars, trains, aeroplanes and other hardware of the > Machine Age. The term 'industrial design' was becoming widely used and was seen as a way of increasing sales and profit. The status of the profession continued to increase in the post-war years when designers played a key part in rebuilding devastated Europe. New approaches to educating the industrial designer, begun at the > Bauhaus, were also developed at > Cranbrook Academy, the > Royal College of Art and > Ulm.

Although each industrialized country developed its own national design identity, they all shared a determination to set up professional and government organizations promoting industrial design. Now that the battle to establish industrial design as a legitimate professional activity has been won, the debate in the 1990s has shifted. Manufacturing companies in Japan, for example, regard the industrial designer as an anonymous, although important, member of the whole production team, while in Italy industrial designers like Ettore Sottsass enjoy the creative status of an opera singer or film star.

● John Heskett, *Industrial Design*, 1980; Herbert Read, *Art and Industry*, 1934.

INFLATABLE DESIGN

A term applied to inflatable furniture, which was part of 1960s' > Pop Design. Designers attempted to make furniture as ephemeral fashion items, and experiments also included paper chairs and tables. Part of the Pop aesthetic was that furniture could be expendable, and the final manifestation of that expendability, made possible by the invention of the welded PVC seam, came with the appearance of 'blow-up' items, which could simply be deflated when not needed. Italy led the way with the famous Blow chair, designed by Jonathan de Pas, Donato d'Urbino and Paolo Lomazzi. Britain followed with chairs by Bernard Quention and Roger Dean. Conran Associates marketed a version for Habitat as a 'picnic chair', which came with its own pump and repair kit. The transparent, inflatable chair became *the* accessory for the Pop environment. In the 1980s Ron Arad experimented with the inflation principle in reverse by designing a chair from which air could be removed by the sitter in order to form an imprint of the sitter's body. These days inflatable furniture is made in a variety of colours and sculptural shapes for the swimming pool and beach.

INFORMATION TECHNOLOGY

'*IT*' embraces two main areas, computers and telecommunications, and there is little doubt that they have transformed the process and production of late 20th-century design. Current thinking is that these two sectors are on the point of converging, but in practice this has been hard to achieve because the two industries have very different profiles. By and large telecommunications are dominated by large corporations while the computer industry is a more open-market, with numerous small companies like Apple.

In industrial design terms the microchip revolution has upturned the old idea that form follows function. In theory at least form has been liberated by the microchip, and designers are looking at new ways to develop the person-machine interface. One problem they are exploring is the development of a clear and sensible language between person and machine. Perhaps as Bang and Olufsen have done with their hi-fi systems, placing the most important functions up-front is a good example to follow. Apple Mac have also broken new ground in using icons to convey information about computer screen layout. For example, unwanted material is dumped in a trash can icon, while menus, a concept borrowed from Rank Xerox photocopiers, list options about the presentation of material. However, there is still much work to be done on improving the features and functions of screen-based icons. Meanwhile, the coming thing is > Virtual Reality, the fusion of multimedia, including computers, videos and television.

● P. Zorkoczy, *Information Technology*, 1990.

INSTALLATION

A fine art term used to describe an environment built by an artist. In this context interior designers of the 1980s were attracted to the concept of installations as a way of describing their own design work. Consequently the word installation was used in both an art and a design context.

Marcel Duchamp's installation for the first Surrealist exhibition in New York in 1942 provided the prototype for the artist installation and became the basic form for many late 1960s' movements such as > Pop and > Minimalism. Some artists, including Joseph Beuys and Edward Kienholtz, deliberately used the multimedia aspect to break down traditional hierarchical views of art and its function. The term installation is now commonly used to describe an artist's or designer's exhibited work, whether it is all of one medium taking up a complete space or uniting various art forms. This is evident in the refurbishment of major department stores, where the installation has become a way of using an important designer's work. (The Way In boutique by Eva Jiricna for Harrod's is a good example.) Installations have become the perfect form in which to work across the divides of artist, architect and designer, and as such are in keeping with the fragmented montage effect of the Post-Modern period.

ISOKON

A furniture company founded by Jack Pritchard to manufacture laminated plywood items, of which the lounger chair by Marcel Breuer has become a classic. In design terms Isokon typifies 1930s' Modernism.

ITALIAN DESIGN

Italy is now synonymous with good design, and Milan is regarded as the undisputed capital of style. This reputation has only developed in the post-war period, and by any standards it is a remarkable achievement. As recently as the 1850s Italy was divided into several autonomous principalities and kingdoms; Rome was a Papal state, the Bourbons ruled the south and the Austrian Empire controlled the northern territories. Led by popular heroes like Garibaldi, however, there was a gradual movement towards unification called the Risorgimento, but it was not until after World War I that Italy emerged as an independent sovereign state, although one with enormous problems. The country had been slow to respond to the changes of the Industrial Revolution. Its economy was basically a rural one, and at the end of the 19th century over 60 per cent of the population still worked the land, with varying degrees of success. Southern Italy, for example, was one of the poorest areas of Europe. Another major problem was language. At that time Italy had no universal tongue; each area had its own local dialect. Needless to say, a single national identity proved slow in coming.

None the less, 19th-century Italy responded to wider European design ideas. Iron and steel industries developed in the north and the railway system began to spread throughout the country. Some of these changes could be seen at the 1881 National Exhibition held in Milan. Certainly the products on display showed off traditional Italian strengths − a strong workshop craft tradition in marble, glass and ceramics − but in general the designs looked back to Italy's past achievements. More important was the Turin International Exhibition of 1902. Here Italy, with buildings like Raimondo d'Aranco's Rotundo and the furniture of Carlo Bugatti, showed off an original version of > Art Nouveau called *Stile Liberty* in honour of the London department store. This new confidence and affluence can be seen in the gallerias of Umberto I in Naples and Vittorio Emmanuele in Milan, both built at the turn of the century. This period also saw the foundation of companies that were later to develop international profiles. These included Fiat, established in 1899 in Turin by a group of ex-cavalry officers, Lancia, set up in 1905, Olivetti, founded in 1908 by Camillo Olivetti, and Alfa-Romeo, established in 1910.

In the early years of the 20th century Italy made its own original contribution to the > Modern Movement with > Futurism. This radical movement of artists, architects and poets demanded a complete break with the past, that the museums and libraries should be burnt and embrace a commitment to the glories of the new technology. This intellectual movement inspired a search for a new Italian spirit, a need which was to be exploited by the new Fascist movement led by Benito Mussolini (1883–1945). Fascism, with its twin values of tradition and modernity, proved an irresistible force and it was in the 1930s that the concept of Italian design finally emerged. At first it was dominated by a version of the Modern Movement called > Rationalism, but this was replaced by the more conservative > Novecento Movement, inspired by classical sources. Under Mussolini Italian industry rapidly expanded and saw the first serious attempts to introduce the new principles of mass production. Fiat in particular introduced the principles of Henry > Ford to its manufacture of cars such as the 1939 Fiat 508C. In 1932 Olivetti produced the MP1 typewriter, with a simple body shell adapted for the new production techniques. Indeed, the company was committed to Modernism: former > Bauhaus staff were responsible for publicity, the innovative Marcello Nizzoli was taken on as chief consultant designer and between 1939 and 1941 at Ivrea the company built a Modernist steel and glass factory. Mussolini also reformed transportation, famously making the trains run on time. In design terms trams, trains and ships were among the most aggressively modern objects Italy produced in the inter-war years.

The devastation of post-war Italy prompted the Ricostruzione – a rebuilding programme characterized by remarkable determination. American money from the Marshall Plan helped the effort, but the achievement was Italian. In less than 10 years Italy had become a modern industrial state to compare with France or Germany. Almost immediately distinctive Italian goods appeared on the market, including Corradino d'Ascanio's Vespa scooter for Piaggio in 1946, Gio Ponti's 1947 expresso coffee machine for La Pavoni and Marcello Nizzoli's 1948 Lexicon 80 typewriter for Olivetti. By the end of the 1950s the distinctive Italian approach to design was established. Moreover, Italian cinema, fashion and literature also attracted international admiration. It was the decade of La Dolce Vita, and from here on the status of Italian design only increased. In the 1960s Italy produced some of the best-known icons of > Pop design: the see-through inflatable Blow chair of 1967 by Lomazzi, d'Urbino, Scolari and de Pas, the sag bag or Il Sacco, and the 1965 Brionvega radio by Achille Castiglioni.

In 1972 an exhibition called 'Italy: The New Domestic Landscape' held at the Museum of Modern Art in New York paid tribute to Italy's immense contribution to post-war design and confirmed the dominance of Italian design ideology. When the massive economic recession of 1973 brought to a close many of the more experimental design groups, Italy consolidated her position with a return to classic design, a move best expressed in the work of Mario Bellini and Vico Magistretti for such companies as Olivetti and Cassina. It was in response to this direction that Ettore Sottsass and a group of friends started the now legendary > Memphis group. It was a direct attack on the good-taste, conservative aspects of late 1970s' design. In the 1980s' designer decade Italy held on firmly to her design reputation. Each September saw the Italian Furniture Fair, which attracted buyers, designers and journalists from around the world. The Milan Fiera developed into a celebration of designer culture that was stylish and breathtaking. Indeed, for the last 10 years only what happened in Milan really mattered.

● Andrea Branzi, *The Hot House: New Wave Italian Design,* 1984; Penny Sparke, *Design in Italy: 1870 to the Present,* 1988.

J

JAPANESE DESIGN

When the American naval captain Commodore Perry arrived in Japan in 1854, he ended 250 years of isolation imposed by the Tokugawa shoguns. After a trade agreement was signed between the two countries, the USA presented Japan with a model locomotive, an electric telegraph and a daguerrotype camera. The impact of the West's Industrial Revolution had begun. Some 20 years later the English industrial designer Christopher Dresser visited Japan to record that impact. He travelled over 2800 kilometres, visited 68 potteries and published an account of his travels called *Japan, its Architecture, Art and Art Manufactures* (1882). This book is a unique account of early Meji Japan and reveals a country on the edge of major transition.

At the end of the 19th century Japan's new trading wealth was used to build up the commercial infrastructure of a modern society, with banks, railways, printing presses, telegraphs, education and post offices. The Japanese government actively encouraged the establishment of Western industries. It offered merchants incentives to build Western-style factories and imported skilled labour from abroad, at the same time sending young Japanese to England and the USA to study engineering and science. Many famous Japanese companies were founded at this time. Seiko, for example, was established in 1881, while Toyota has its roots in a company established in 1897. Japanese trade prospered. The late 19th-century European obsession with the Cult of Japan opened up a prosperous export market for luxury products, such as fans, prints, porcelain, and lacquer work. More importantly, European designers began to recognize that Japanese design and culture offered a unique aesthetic approach. Charles Rennie Mackintosh, for example, was inspired by photographs of Shinto temples, and it is interesting to note that the individual style of the > Glasgow School was copied almost immediately in Tokyo.

The Japanese were eager to learn, and books on such diverse topics as Cubist theory and architecture appeared in Japanese translation as soon as they were printed in Paris and London. Gradually this East-West exchange increased as more and more designers travelled. The American architect Frank Lloyd Wright was a key player in this exchange. In 1906 he visited Japan and the experience had a profound effect on the development of his work, and in turn on the development of European Modernism. In the early 1920s he designed the Imperial Hotel, one of Tokyo's major buildings. Ten years later the Modernist architect Charlotte Perriand also visited and worked in Japan. In the inter-war years European dress and customs were introduced into Japanese life, including American films, jazz music, flapper dresses and > Art Deco advertising. Japan also shared another widespread development in the 1930s – a build-up of fierce nationalist tendencies and a massive military investment. But for most Westerners Japan was still perceived as a 'backward' country. Its status as a significant world power became apparent only with the onset of World War II. That period of Japan's history came to a tragic end in 1945 with the atomic bombing of Hiroshima. General Douglas MacArthur supervised the American occupying force there until 1952. Subsequently, the impact of American ideas and US help in the reconstruction of the country were to have enormous effects. By the late 1950s Japan had developed into a major industrial nation. The new Japanese industries of the late 1950s concentrated on capital intensive goods such as cars, motor-cycles, radios, television sets, fridges and washing machines. It was an economic miracle.

Under American guidance the Japanese set up the Ministry of International Trade and Industry (MITI), which granted the newly founded Sony Corporation permission to buy the manufacturing rights to a new invention, the transistor. In 1955 Sony produced its first transistor radio, and in 1959 introduced the world's first solid-state television receiver, which had an 18-inch screen and weighed only 13 pounds. Japanese products began to be associated with the latest technological advances, particularly miniaturization. Japanese industry also had a different profile from that of the West. The country's economic boom was reliant on the intense company loyalty of Japanese employees and their rigorous work ethic. The role of the designer was also different. The post-war period saw a rapid expansion in design education, but the Western model of lone designer superstars and large design practices was not copied in Japan. Instead, designers joined huge companies and their role was largely anonymous. At the same time Japanese design was reliant on Western ideas, which it freely copied. It was not until the 1970s that a distinctive Japanese quality to design began to emerge. Japan has retained its unique approach to colour and form, but has integrated these elements with Western culture and the new technologies the Japanese have pioneered.

● Penny Sparke, *Japanese Design*, 1988.

JUDENSTIL

This is the German equivalent of > Art Nouveau. It comes from the title of a magazine launched in Munich in 1896, and although not exclusively a design magazine, it did act as a showcase for the Art Nouveau style in Germany.

JUNK AESTHETIC

Recycling discarded industrial scrap is not a new design idea, but in the 1980s it became fashionable. It was a strong British design theme, particularly in furniture, with a group of young designer/makers, most notably Ron Arad and Tom Dixon. Arad used old leather car seats for his Rover chair, and off-the-shelf car aerials for domestic lights. Dixon coined the term > Creative salvage to describe this design trend. Young fashion designers, including Judy Blame, made hats decorated with cigarette packets and the foil caps from champagne bottles. Also interesting in this context is the Mutoid Waste Company, a group of young artists who used junk to create > installations in derelict London warehouses, and the Crucial Gallery in Notting Hill Gate, which specialized in selling furniture and artwork by such makers as Jon Mills, using recycled materials. The same spirit can also be seen in British interior design, with > found objects integrated in the work of Nigel Coates and Ben Kelly. Kelly's famous Hacienda nightclub in Manchester incorporated traffic bollards into the scheme, while Coates shipped over to Japan an Edwardian revolving door for the entrance to his Tokyo Metropole restaurant, and a section of an aeroplane hung as a sculpture in his Café Bongo in the same city. During the late 1980s the junk aesthetic went mainstream. Dixon's work appeared in expensive retail design schemes such as Din Associates' design for the Next store on Kensington High Street, and Ron Arad was given a one-man show at the Pompidou Centre in Paris.

K

JOHN MAYNARD KEYNES

Keynes (1883–1946) was best known as an economist, but his theories found an interesting parallel with the design philosophy of the > Modern Movement. Keynes's view was that enlightened intervention of liberally minded intellectuals in the State could improve the economy and turn it round. These ideas were written up in his *General Theory of Employment, Interest and Money* (1936), set against the historical background of Roosevelt's New Deal, which employed artists, designers and architects. Keynes was also a member of the Bloomsbury group, an art speculator and the founder of what is now known as the *New Statesman and Society* magazine. During and after World War II many of Keynes's ideas were put into practice when the Labour government supported the idea that design and designers could help regenerate the post-war economy.

KITSCH

From the German verb *Verkitschen* (to make cheap), Kitsch has had various meanings since the term was first coined. Originally it referred to objects of no real use, such as knick-knacks, souvenirs, non-functional tableware, glass ornaments and novelties. In 1939, however, the American art critic Clement Greenberg used Kitsch to include jazz, advertising and trash novels – broadly speaking, the areas we now define as > Popular culture. In the 1960s Kitsch became an umbrella term for bad taste and vulgarity to be embraced by people of sophisticated sensibilities. In the 1970s this ironic approach led to young, middle-class couples decorating their homes with plaster flying ducks and carefully selected 'witty' and 'amusing' items. Placed in the context of an affluent home, Kitsch could be safely enjoyed and admired. Kitsch was also an area appropriated by admirers of > Camp. The 1980s saw a fashion for the florid religious imagery of southern Europe and South America, typified by 3-D illustrations of the Madonna and the Sacred Heart.

Kitsch is a sensitive area because enjoyment of it relies on a sense of knowing superiority, which can be nauseating. To put it simply, an object that enjoys the status of Kitsch in a smart city drawing-room may at the same time be on display as an object of reverence in another home. Several mainstream critics object to Kitsch because in their opinion it somehow dupes the weak and poor. Greenberg felt that Kitsch betrayed the consumer because it is ultimately undemanding and unsatisfying. Censorship to exclude the cheap, tacky and tasteless is still the driving force behind the design establishment. None the less, playing with the crossovers between conventional good taste and Kitsch has enriched the language of contemporary design.

• Gillo Dorfles, *Kitsch*, 1969.

L

LIBERTY DEPARTMENT STORE

Liberty in London is much more than a shop. Since it was founded in 1875 it has pioneered innovative retail trends, helping to shape contemporary taste. Indeed, by the end of the 19th century the Italians called the new > Art Nouveau movement the 'Stile Liberty'. The shop's founder, Arthur Lasenby Liberty (1843–1917), started his career as an importer and helped to create the vogue for all things Japanese. James McNeill Whistler and Oscar Wilde shopped at Liberty's, and for the Gilbert and Sullivan musical The Mikado the store sent buyers to Japan to get exactly the right costumes. In 1884 a costume department was opened, headed by the architect E.W. Godwin, and it sold children's clothes in the Kate Greenaway style and unstructured gowns for women. Liberty's employed leading > Arts and Crafts designers, of whom Archibald Knox is perhaps the best known. He was responsible for a range of silver and pewter inspired by Celtic forms. The other important area Liberty pioneered was textile design, commissioning George Walton, Charles Voysey, Lindsay Butterfield and Arthur Silver. The quality of these designs has meant that many have remained in continuous production ever since.

● Alison Adburgham, Liberty's, a biography of a shop, 1975.

M

MACHINE AGE DESIGN

A popular description of products from the inter-war period, particularly those from the USA. The Machine Age was marked by a belief in new technology that was not shaken by the Depression years of the 1930s. The American public, influenced by designers such as Raymond Loewy, Buckminster Fuller and Norman Bel Geddes, saw an image of 20th-century America take shape, an image that reflected the visual appearance of the machine. Automobiles became as sleek as spaceships and trains; even ships and buses acquired the new > streamlined look. The same shapes were also used for domestic appliances such as fridges, radios, televisions and washing machines. Artists such as Alexander Calder and Joseph Stella, photographers such as Margaret Bourke White, and film-makers, manufacturers and engineers celebrated the new, machine-dominated world. Their work and the work of the other important innovators, such as the architects of skyscrapers, factories, service stations and bridges, shaped new attitudes and a new culture. Machine Age design was not a single style, but took on board > Art Deco, > Moderne, > International style, streamlining, > Constructivism and > Functionalism. American achievements in industry and technology had helped to create a new modern style, but the romance with machines was not destined to last. However, it did create a powerful and influential new culture.

● *The Machine Age in America, 1918–1941*, exhibition catalogue, Brooklyn Museum, 1986.

MAIL ORDER *See* Retailing.

HERBERT MARCUSE

Marcuse (1898–1979) was a German philosopher whose ideas were referred to by design writers – a development attributable to > Post-Modernism, which opened up design to influences from leading academics in many fields. Marcuse argued that modern 20th-century society generated artificial needs. In particular, he argued that industrial capitalism did not allow the existence of the individual or a full spiritual life for the working class.

MARS

The Modern Architecture Research group was a short-lived British organization to promote the ideas of the > Modern Movement. Formed in April 1933 by British architects as a response to the French > CIAM group, its members included Wells Coates and the historian Sir John Summerson, and its first exhibition was held in the Burlington Galleries early in 1938. The group published plans for the radical redevelopment of London, which were largely ignored, and in 1957 the MARS group disbanded.

● Anthony Jackson, *The Politics of Architecture*, 1970.

MARXISM

A theory of political economy and history developed by Karl Marx in the 19th century in response to the industrialization of production achieved by capitalism. The theory, which went on to be applied to many areas of intellectual life, including design, divided society into the two antagonistic classes – the bourgeoisie and the proletariat. Either you owned the means of production or you were exploited by those who did. Marx placed profit motive at the centre of capitalist production. The proletariat, a class of wage labourers, sold their labour for a fixed sum, while the capitalists pocketed the difference between the price of the labour and the price of the product as profit. This means of production, and the economic base on which it relied, became the foundation for the whole of society, including legal and political structures and forms of social consciousness and ideology. Marx developed a theory of history as the history of class struggle, ancient, feudal and modern bourgeois. He thought that capitalism, in using the proletariat as its labour force, created the seeds of its own destruction. Marx's analysis of capitalism was a theory complemented by his political practice, as shown in *The Communist Manifesto*, which he co-wrote with Friedrich Engels.

Despite general disillusionment with the development of the Communist State after 1945, Marxism has remained both a tool of analysis in many areas of intellectual life, and a theory for social change, most notably put into practice by the Russian Revolution in 1917. Some designers, in common with some artists and architects, subscribe to Marxist beliefs. William Morris, while not strictly a Marxist, certainly held revolutionary socialist beliefs, and many designers sought to create individual, utopian and often rural social experiments. In the 1960s Italian designers became famous for their espousal of Marxist ideas, but the capacity of the designer to change society was and is severely limited. In the 1980s Designer Marxism was the cynical description of a fashionable belief in left-wing causes. In fact, that decade saw the collapse of any attempt by the design profession to express serious political views. The last 10 years have not been the design profession's finest hour.

MATT BLACK

The designer decade of the 1980s was obsessed with black, and many products and accessories were sold only in that colour: televisions, cameras, Filofaxes, cars . . . Since the 1960s Braun products designed by Dieter Rams had used black and it came to be identified with good taste and a purist > minimalism that went hand in hand with the decade's prosperity. Only the rise of a new interest in colour with > Post-Modernism has challenged the supremacy of matt black in these areas.

MEMPHIS

In 1981 the Italian architect Ettore Sottsass launched a radical new design group which he called Memphis. The name combined references

143

to American pop music and to the ancient Egyptian capital. It was the kind of irony and ambiguity Sottsass loved. He launched Memphis with the help of a group of collaborators, employees and friends, among them Michele de Lucchi, George Sowden, Martine Bedin, Hans Hollein, Michael Graves, Arata Isozaki, Nathalie du Pasquier, Marco Zanini and Matheo Thun. The group launched its collection in a showroom in Milan to coincide with the September 1981 Furniture Fair. It was an overnight sensation. The objects and furniture shown resembled children's toys; they were playful and used a bright palette of colours. Decoration was given a new importance, mixing different patterned laminates together appropriated from 1950s' Milanese coffee bars. The furniture challenged basic assumptions. Why, for example, should the legs of a table be identical?

Right from the beginning the media gave Memphis some amazing coverage and in turn the group delivered exciting, newsworthy shows with wonderful photographs that appeared on the pages of the international press from New York to Tokyo. However, Memphis was not without its critics. Some felt it was élitist and had turned its back on the Modernist tradition of design. Leading curators at the > Victoria and Albert Museum and at the Museum of Modern Art in New York felt Memphis was an exclusive avant-garde whose work was a cul-de-sac without any influence on mainstream design. They were to be proved totally wrong. The impact of Memphis, albeit via quirky details on Ikea furniture or graphic patterns for such companies as HMV, proved extraordinarily influential. Barbara Radice, Sottsass's companion and a well-known design writer, became the group's spokesperson and unofficial archivist. In 1988 the Memphis group formally wound up, but not before it won an important position in the history of design. Memphis objects influenced a whole new generation of designers and its products are collected by leading museums all over the world.

• B. Radice, Memphis, 1985.

MILAN TRIENNALES

During the 1950s the Milan Triennales became the main showplace for modern Italian design. The tradition of Italian exhibitions had begun in 1923 in Monza, leading to the first triennale in 1933 held at Milan's

Palazzo d'Arte, which showed the work of Italian Futurists alongside other exponents of the > Modern Movement. In 1957 the theme was Europe, in 1961 compulsory schooling, and in 1964 leisure. These triennales reflected the vigorous Italian debates concerning the nature and direction of design, and they attracted international press attention. More recently the annual furniture fairs have replaced the triennales as the arena for displaying Italy's continuing dominance in design.

MILITARY DESIGN

While it is easy to believe that many civilian products and systems reap the benefits of military design developments, it is less easy to provide specific examples. One of the most obvious spin-offs is the space programme, which for Russia and the USA has always been dominated by military and surveillance considerations. It is certainly true that military design has attracted enormous resources and dominated certain aspects of East–West culture. In 1961, the middle of the Cold War period (1946–89), President Eisenhower described the Bomb, the Pentagon, missiles and bomber aircraft as the military industrial complex. In Russia the space/military programme is undoubtedly the only area in which a designer can work with the same resources and prestige given to Western industrial designers.

The influence of military products on design styling is easy to spot. During the 1950s and 1960s atomic motifs were on everything from cars to coffee tables. The space race sparked off futuristic visions of the kitchen and also led to spacesuit mini-dresses and visors. Military uniforms and accessories were also appropriated by alternative groups like the hippies, who combined combat jackets with long hair and beads. The 1970s also saw a trend towards radio and hi-fi styling that evoked the utility feeling of field equipment in the Vietnam War. In the 1990s these military allusions are simply part of a general repertoire of visual references the designer can plunder. However, the real divide between military and civilian design is carefully maintained to be distinct and separate.

MINIMALISM

In its broadest sense minimalism applies to art and design of the 1960s that seemingly reduced either the 'art work' involved in an object or used a limited range of materials and expression. More specifically the term denotes a primarily American movement that deliberately avoided references to the meaning or content of works in order to emphasize the 'object quality' of art: that it existed like any other object without needing grand metaphysical statements. This was in part a reaction to previous soul-revealing paintings of the 1950s by such artists as Willem De Kooning and Jackson Pollock, but it was also a rejection of the hallowed status of art. Artists like Donald Judd and Carl André (infamous for his 'pile of bricks' at the Tate Gallery) often choose to work with mass-produced, easily accessible materials such as stainless steel, prefabricated sheet metal or copper floor tiles. Often arranged in predetermined mathematical series, unworked on by the artist except for sequence of placement, these artworks denied the convention of the hand-crafted, beautiful art object. Variously named Primary Structures, Serial Art, ABC Art and just 'good design', Minimalism can be seen as a rejection of artifice and therefore part of an earlier, anti-illusionist modern tradition.

Minimalist objects were often shown as > Installations, the concern with surface detail suppressed in favour of a broader awareness of the object and spectator relationship in space and time. Influenced by Gestalt theories, questions of perception and experience were to become important and were applied to writing, dance and theatre, as well as art and design.

● K. Baker, *Minimalism*, 1988.

MODERN MOVEMENT

The term used to describe architects and designers who set about creating a new aesthetic for the 20th century. This spirit of change and innovation took hold around the world and led to the movement often being described as the > International Style. However, the Modern Movement was certainly more than a mere style; for its adherents it was an article of faith. Their attitude to design did not separate form from social purpose. They believed in the city, in a secure future for all made possible by the new inventions and progress of the > Machine Age. This strong relationship with design and social function, the reverence the Modern Movement placed on the mass-produced object for all, has, for example, linked the Modern Movement with socialist values. Certainly the Nazis believed this to be so, and in the late 1930s many leading Continental Modernists fled for their lives. These included Walter Gropius, Marcel Breuer, Lazlo Moholy Nagy and Mies van der Rohe, who emigrated to the USA via Britain in the period after 1936. This particular group had all taught at the > Bauhaus, and certainly the Modern Movement was strongest in Germany. France also made a significant contribution to the movement, led there by the architect Le Corbusier. Other countries adopted less extreme versions. For example, the Finnish architect Alvar Aalto adapted natural materials to the new forms of Modernism. Meanwhile, countries like Britain proved extremely resistant to the ideas of the Modern Movement, generally preferring the traditions handed down from the > Arts and Crafts Movement of the late 19th century. Exceptions included such designers as Wells Coates and Maxwell Fry, and writers Herbert > Read and Nikolaus > Pevsner. The Modern Movement never really had a group manifesto. The nearest it came to that was in architecture with > CIAM, a campaigning body of architects, writers and designers sympathetic to the new ideas. In a series of conferences held in the 1930s the ideas and direction of the Modern Movement in architecture were debated. Sigfried > Giedion, a founding member of CIAM, was a leading writer of the movement. It was not, however, until after World War II that the Modern Movement found massive acceptance in Europe. In the huge rebuilding programmes of the 1950s and 1960s architects and town-planners came out almost unanimously in favour of the high-rise apartment block and the office skyscraper, which were the essential Modernist vision. By the 1970s these buildings had led to massive social failure and widespread condemnation. The Modern Movement, however, had been the dominant architectural and design ideology for nearly 50 years. Alternative ideas and approaches were now widely discussed. The age of > Post-Modernism had begun.

● P. Reyner Banham, *Theory and Design in the First Machine Age*, 1960.

MODERNE

This term was first used in the 1930s by design commentators who wanted to distinguish between the high moral ambitions of the > Modern Movement and what they saw as a corruption of its ideals into mere decorative details. Moderne was dismissed as mere pastiche. Interesting in this context is Nikolaus > Pevsner's condemnation of the now much-loved > Art Deco Hoover factory on the Great Western Road leading out of London.

The word Moderne is no longer widely used; most writers substitute the umbrella term > Art Deco. Moderne-style products were produced on a huge scale in the USA during the 1930s. The style can best be seen in Hollywood films of the period, and in the cities of New York and Los Angeles. Ironically, the products of this 'commercialization', once seen as rather downmarket, are now revered and collected. The 1960s saw a revival in Moderne style. The famous London boutique Biba adopted a house style which used the black and gold favoured by Hollywood. In the 1970s Post-Modernist architect Michael Graves reworked the vocabulary of Art Deco into his language of architectural components. So far Moderne has survived the test of time and popular taste rather more successfully than Modernism.

● Alistair Duncan (ed.), *Encyclopedia of Art Deco*, 1988.

MODERNISM *See* Modern Movement.

MORRIS & CO.

Brainchild of William Morris (1834–96), writer, designer, craftsman and political activist, the 'Firm', as it was to become known affectionately by those associated with it, was originally called Morris, Marshall, Faulkner & Co. Founded in 1861, the original partners included Edward Burne-Jones (1833–98), Dante Gabriel Rossetti (1828–82), and Ford Madox Brown (1821–93) – all painters – and the architect Philip Webb (1831–1915), who had designed the Red House at Bexleyheath for Morris and his wife Jane in 1859. Peter Paul Marshall (1830–1900) was a surveyor, and Charles J. Faulkner (1834–92), who was to become business manager, was a mathematics don at Oxford.

The Firm began as an informal working agreement among close friends 'who were also artists'. They described themselves as 'Fine Art Workmen in Painting, Carving, Furniture and Metals', which, given their inexperience, was somewhat optimistic. The Firm claimed to be proficient in:

I   Mural decoration . . . in dwelling-houses, churches, or public buildings.
II   Carving generally, as applied to architecture.
III Stained glass, especially with reference to its harmony with Mural Decoration.
IV   Metal work.
V   Furniture either depending for its beauty on its own design . . . or its conjunction with Figure and Pattern Painting. Under this head is included embroidery . . . besides every article for domestic use.

Morris, Marshall, Faulkner & Co. first attracted public attention at the South Kensington International Exhibition of 1862. However, the Firm had its greatest early successes with stained glass, which often displayed a distinctly Pre-Raphaelite innocence and youthful energy. Excellent examples of it can be seen at the > Victoria and Albert Museum in what was once called 'The Green Dining Room' (1866). However, the bulk of the Firm's stained glass was predominantly ecclesiastical. As enduring were the wallpapers and textiles produced by the company, which were widely imitated by late 19th-century designers like Lindsay Butterfield. Many are still in production, some in the original colourways.

In 1875 the partnership of Morris, Marshall and Faulkner was dissolved and Morris became the sole proprietor of the Firm, now called Morris & Co. The company's showrooms were at 449 Oxford Street, which was close to the centre of London's luxury trade. In the main it enjoyed commercial success and weathered the recession of the early 1880s, which drove a number of leading competitors into bankruptcy. With the outbreak of World War II in 1939, the company was finally wound up. Fortunately, much archival material relating to its history was preserved, together with many of the wooden blocks used for printing wallpapers.

Morris & Co.'s clients were generally prosperous members of the middle-class intelligentsia – a class which had burgeoned in the 1870s and 1880s. Nevertheless, Morris sometimes complained of having to work for the 'swinish rich'. He and his Firm undoubtedly exercised a great influence on interior design for the last three decades of the 19th century. During the 1890s – through the medium of such journals as *The Studio* – his work became well known in Europe. The Belgian architect Henry van de Velde was an admirer of Morris & Co., as was Josef Hoffmann, the Viennese architect who was to be associated with the > Wiener Werkstatte, a cooperative of artists and craftworkers.

- G. Naylor, *William Morris by himself*, 1988.

N

NATO

Narrative Architecture Today is a British architectural group, founded in 1983 by students and staff of the Architectural Association, London's most prestigious school of architecture. It presented its ideas via a magazine and exhibition of the same name using what it described as a narrative method. Nigel Coates, the group's most famous and out-spoken member, describes narrative architecture as 'the absurdity of the way things are' from 'the city's moments of high culture to the backyards of decay'. In this way NATO is part of an international movement, looking at ways in which to reinterpret architecture for the city and citing their influences from the wold of fashion, film and contemporary culture.

● Nigel Coates, 'Gamma City Manifesto', NATO *Magazine*, No. 3.

NATURALISM

In 1550 Giorgio Vasari described nature as 'the beautiful fabric of the world' and the most important source of inspiration for the creative artist. Naturalism was part of the then prevalent belief in a world of beauty made by God. The impact of nature on design has been a continuous one with a long history, providing an inexhaustible supply of decorative shapes and forms adapted by designers ranging from Gothic to Renaissance. If the study of Naturalism reflected deeply held religious beliefs about the world, there was an alternative view of nature that also had an important impact on design. The scientific analysis of nature was a secular approach, but one which designers were to exploit more and more. The painter William Dyce (1806–64) explored this approach for design education. He saw nature as a laboratory which should be investigated by scientific methods and its principles applied to design. Dyce's viewpoint was widely accepted and expanded in the 19th century, although critics like John > Ruskin viewed this approach as horrible and barbaric. Nature, he argued, was not a machine. Other Victorians took up the application of science to design with more enthusiasm, as shown by Christopher Dresser's important botanical work on plant structure.

The > Great Exhibition of 1851 was a celebration of an extreme form of Naturalism, which some felt had gone too far. The artist Ralph Wornum (1812–77) strongly objected to what he saw as the improper adaptation of natural forms – a gas jet, for example, coming from a flower. The reformist ideas of the > Arts and Crafts Movement recommended nature as a source for design. Certainly William Morris followed that line, and the designers of the > Aesthetic Movement and > Art Nouveau were equally committed to Naturalism. In the 20th century Naturalism has not been at the forefront of design innovations. Art Deco developed a stylized approach to natural forms, while in the post-war period 1950s' design was inspired by atom and crystal structures. Naturalism received a final boost with the 1960s' revival of Victorian patterns, but in the 1990s it has taken its place as simply another style option in the available range.

NEW AGE

A term used to describe the 1990s, which has found the consumer boom values of the 1980s inappropriate. New Age suggests a return to social concern, a rejection of hard-edged materialism, a revival of interest in ecology and a more sympathetic examination of 1960s' issues such as alternative lifestyles.

NEW JOURNALISM

Refers to design writing of the 1960s, which sought to describe the influence of > Popular Culture. During the 1950s the British > Independent Group had encouraged critics and writers to develop a creative approach to writing which would give it a place alongside the new Pop Art activities. Important in this context is Peter Reyner > Banham. The New Journalism, like the new Pop Art, challenged the tradition of serious academic writing which used its own language and addressed a small and exclusive audience. A number of post-war critics now wanted to look at, and treat seriously, areas of > Popular Culture which previously had been ignored or denigrated – subjects such as soap operas, pop stars, customized cars, pulp fiction and Las Vegas. While all of this now seems perfectly ordinary, it was then revelatory to a new generation of readers and writers. The most important American exponent of New Journalism was Tom > Wolfe, who established a writing style that was a Pop form in its own right, a combination of creative writing and reportage. There are very few contemporary writers on design who have not been influenced by New Journalism.

NEW LOOK

Refers to the extravagant post-war clothes designed by Christian Dior. Wartime shortages had led to the government laying down fashion rules in order to conserve precious resources. Clothing tended to be austere, almost military in appearance, and colourful fabrics were in short supply. It is not hard to see why designers and women turned to more romantic, feminine styles when the war and rationing ended. What was surprising was that Christian Dior launched his New Look collection so quickly – on 12 February 1947. In opulent contrast to wartime austerity he produced narrow shoulders, padded hips and extremely full, ankle-length skirts. The New Look caused a sensation. In Britain questions were asked in the House of Commons about the ethics of a style that used up to 50 metres of fabric per dress. Royal approval of the New Look came when Princess Margaret wore a full skirt, and almost immediately mass-produced copies, using less fabric, appeared in chain stores everywhere. Dior's New Look was an international success and re-established Paris as the fashion capital of the world. Dior died in 1957, but the fashion house which bears his name is still one of the world's top couture houses.

NEW TOWNS *See* Satellite Town.

NEW ROMANTICS

A British post-punk youth movement which turned its back on > Punk aggression in favour of glamour, dressing up, developing the art of the pose and cultivating a total dedication to hedonism and night-clubbing. Pop groups such as Kraftwerk and Bauhaus set the tone and the music style at clubs like Blitz, whose patrons included Boy George, later to form Culture Club, a New Romantic band. Boy George wore make-up, Rasta dreadlocks, Hassidic hats and skirts. In the New Romantic movement it was possible to be famous just for dressing up, and Leigh Bowery's ensembles are an example of this trend.

The names of the cult bands – Bauhaus, Culture Club and the Eurythmics – suggest the origins of the movement in London's art schools, including St Martin's and the > Royal College of Art. The excesses of New Romanticism were faithfully recorded in early 1980s' style magazines like *The Face*, *i-D* and *Blitz*. Malcolm McLaren was also a prime mover behind New Romanticism, restyling pop singer Adam Ant in the image of a pirate and highwayman. In the video *Stand and Deliver* he appears as Dick Turpin, period clothes accessorized with a Sony Walkman. Vivienne Westwood produced her Pirate Collection and talked about the concept of plundering, the designer going out into the world and stealing ideas. Westwood's series of Paris catwalk shows were an international success and did a great deal to launch London as the new source of fashion ideas.

Once again British youth culture had inspired new design trends and these were not exclusive to fashion. Interior design changed emphasis, a direction which can be seen in Westwood's shop World's End. The design was David Connor's, combining traditional vernacular elements such as slate and paned glass, with an *Alice in Wonderland* clock whose hands never stopped turning. Connor and his partner Julian Powell-Tuck also developed a more abstract fine art approach to interior design drawings.

New Romantics set the tone for the good-time decade that followed. But by the end of the 1980s people who dressed in New Romantic style, wearing quirky hats indoors with outrageous designer accessories, were now called fashion victims. The style was too extreme to go mainstream and earlier proponents of it, like Boy George, cleaned up their act and went > New Age with a taste of Buddhist chanting.

NEW YORK WORLD FAIR 1939

The largest international exposition ever held. Sixty foreign nations and hundreds of American exhibitors celebrated 'The World of Tomorrow'. The exhibition's futuristic theme, streamlined architecture and displays of the most advanced scientific and technological gadgetry pointed the way forward. The origins of the New York World Fair were in business and financial interests, the aim being to stimulate trade and develop the city as a tourist centre. The timing of the fair, on the eve of World War II, meant that it reflected the design, architecture and cultural themes that dominated the USA in the mid-20th century. The theme of a technological future was perfect for the pioneering industrial designer Walter Dorwin Teague, who was given the job of overseeing the project. Teague commissioned the great designers of the period, including Donald Deskey, Raymond Loewy, Russell Wright, Norman Bel Geddes and Egmond Aren. In this respect the project was the United States' last great statement of the > streamlined style which dominated the country in the 1930s and 1940s, and found expression in the fair's two set pieces – the 610-ft Trylon and the huge, domed Perisphere. The fair's cultural theme was expressed in its commitment to functional architecture, the planning of the site as an overall park design and the relationship between technology and the new forms of artistic expression. Teague was particularly committed to the idea of showing Americans a vision of the future in education, the home and family, transportation and urban planning. Indeed, the fair presented a confident view of every aspect of the American way of life. In 1939, however, the outbreak of war brought with it rather different priorities and concerns.

● *Dawn of a New Day: New York's World Fair 1939–40*, exhibition catalogue, 1980.

NICHE MARKETING

A selling strategy for design. It refers to the practice of recognizing a gap in the market and targeting the consumer with a single specialized product. While not in itself a revolutionary marketing idea, the strength of this new trend during the retail boom of the 1980s was very interesting. Chains of shops such as the Tie Rack and the Sock Shop were shining examples of successful niche marketing, and were later sad examples of its failure. With the recession of the 1990s both these groups were declared bankrupt.

NOVECENTO MOVEMENT

The refined architectural style of the Italian Fascist party of the late 1930s. Mussolini did not share Hitler's personal interest in architecture and design, but he did share a desire to promote Italian nationalism and unity, and Novecento revived references to the glories of Rome reworked in a modern idiom. Mussolini ordered Italian new towns to be built in the style, the most impressive of which was Sabaudia, named after the ancient kings of Italy, in the new province of Latina. Associated with Fascism, Novecento and its exponents are not widely loved. It did, however, encourage Italian industry to employ architects to design new products, and these include Gio Ponti, Carlo Scarpa and Pietro Chiese. One of the classic products from this period of Italian design was the faceted Moka Express coffee-maker designed by Alfonso and Renato Bialetti in 1930.

Novecento was not a popular idiom after 1945, but indirectly it had an important effect on post-war Italian design. For Italians it meant that design had important ideological and political meanings in a way which is difficult to understand in Britain. The implications of design were deeply serious and encouraged a tradition of debate and criticism which has enriched the development of Italian design and helped to give it a distinctive culture unique in Europe.

O

OMEGA WORKSHOPS

A British group of painters, writers and designers associated with the Bloomsbury Group. The art critic Roger Fry organized Omega, which opened in July 1913 at 33 Fitzroy Square in London, with the idea of encouraging artists to design furniture, carpets, pottery and textiles. The designers included Fry, Duncan Grant, Vanessa Bell, Frederick Etchells and Nina Hammett. It was always rather an amateur organization, devoted to bright colours and a painterly technique that owed something to > Cubism and Fauvism. The Omega Workshop was liquidated in 1921, but its work lives on in the Sussex farmhouse called Charleston, where Duncan Grant lived with his wife, Vanessa Bell. Recently restored, the house is full of decorative murals, painted furniture and fireplaces, a style which was very much outside the 1920s' and 1930s' struggle to establish the > Modern Movement. The Courtauld Institute Galleries also have a good collection of Omega-type objects.

Opinion about Omega and Charleston is divided between those who think it self-indulgent and amateurish, and those who admire its energy and use of colour and decoration. A revival of the style is well under way in the 1990s, with reproduction textiles and wallpapers, and a revival of painted decoration for the interior.

OP-ART

An abstract painting style of the mid-1960s, which was recycled almost immediately by textile and graphic designers. 'Op' did not derive from > Pop, but was an abbreviation of optical illusion. The best-known

157

exponent of the style was Bridget Riley, and her paintings of parallel wavy lines set against a white background were simply copied direct as fabric designs for mini-skirts and jumpsuits, and for mural decorations in trendy city apartments. Op-Art techniques were also widely copied on 1960s' record sleeves and on psychedelic posters. Op-Art remains one of the most ephemeral and trendy styles of the decade.

ORIENTALISM

A fashion for all things Eastern, particularly from China and Japan. The interaction between East and West has a long history, starting with the legendary explorer Marco Polo. Europe has always highly valued imported Oriental objects such as silks and porcelain. It was China which dominated the imagination, but travel there was difficult, so first-hand knowledge of the country was extremely rare. When the craze for Chinoiserie reached its height in the 18th century, it was largely inspired by adapting imagery seen on imported and expensive wall-papers and textiles. The designs from Thomas Chippendale's 1754 *Director* indicate the romantic spirit in which things Chinese were adapted for European tastes. His furniture in the Chinese taste can be seen in David Garrick's bedroom, which is reconstructed in the > Victoria and Albert Museum. One of the very few people to visit China and bring back a first-hand account was the architect William Chambers (1723–96). In 1757 he spent some time in Canton, and on his return his drawings were published in *Designs of Chinese Buildings, Furniture, Dresses, Machines and Utensils . . . from the Originals Drawn in China*.

The expanding British Empire was to play a major part in bringing Orientalism to the forefront of public taste. In the 18th century the East India Company encouraged the study of Indian culture and encouraged a vogue for the exotic, seen in the Royal Pavilion at Brighton, built for the Prince Regent. A little later eminent Victorians began to chart the archaeology and culture of Islamic countries. Orientalist Edward William Lane (1801–76) was fascinated by modern Egypt and in 1836 published *An Account of the Manners and Customs of Modern Egyptians*. A similar interest was reflected by contemporary 19th-century artists as diverse as Delacroix, Holman Hunt and Alma Tadema. Books like Lane's study precipitated a flood of material on Oriental art and a huge growth in imported goods. Travel, in the form of Thomas Cook's famous tours, and the expansion of the colonies opened up trade and a cross-fertilization of ideas that has integrated Oriental ideas with those of the West and vice-versa.

A reverence for things Oriental remained a constant theme in the 20th century, reaching a new height in the 1960s with the > Hippy movement, which identified with the spirituality and craft ethic of Eastern countries. Pop icons such as Jimi Hendrix wore Indian clothes and the Beatles paid homage to the trend by visiting the Maharishi, a Hindu spiritual guide. More recently India, China and Thailand have developed as major package tour destinations, allowing increasing numbers of Western tourists to experience the fascination of the Orient for themselves.

ORNAMENT

An immense variety of ornament has been produced throughout the ages, which has created a rich heritage for designers to draw on. From the Industrial Revolution onwards ornament and decoration have generated intense controversy. Is ornament appropriate? How much and when should it be used?

Ornament was central to 19th-century design, and an attempt was made by Victorians such as Owen Jones, whose *Grammar of Ornament* still provides the best taxonomy of the subject, to raise ornament to an authentic art form in its own right. Traditionally, the 20th-century > Modern Movement has been opposed to ornament, but it is difficult to understand this fall from grace. German architect Adolf Loos set the ball rolling with his famous essay 'Ornament Is a Crime', but this was intended to be ironic and not necessarily an ideological opposition to ornament. Loos himself favoured classical ornament on many of his buildings, while his personal taste in furnishings tended towards such items as oriental carpets.

There is really nothing in the Modern Movement which precludes ornament, and while Le Corbusier ridiculed decoration in many of his writings, disapproval stemmed from an attack in the 1920s on outmoded > Art Nouveau details that refused to die. One explanation why ornament occupied such uneasy territory for the Modern Movement was the new design teaching established at the > Bauhaus, and widely copied, which emphasized individual creativity through a basic

159

design course which excluded ornament. Teaching ornament was viewed as retrogressive, harking back to outmoded 19th-century design schools. (Art schools in the 1960s went through something similar in attempting to abolish traditional life-drawing techniques.) None the less, pattern books of traditional decoration such as Seguy's > Art Deco designs, continue to be produced. Ornament and decoration became key issues for 1960s' > Pop Design, and as early as 1966 Robert Venturi's *Complexity and Contradiction in Architecture* argued for a reconsideration of ornament. With the rise of the Post-Modern Movement he was soon to be joined by many other writers and critics, including Charles Jencks, Robert Jensen and Tom > Wolfe. The Post-Modernist campaign in defence of ornament is now over and won. Ornament is firmly back on the design agenda.

● Stuart Durant, *Ornament: a Survey of Decoration from 1830,* 1986.

P

VANCE PACKARD

Packard (b. 1914) was a journalist and key critic of American consumer culture in the 1950s and 1960s. He was born in Pennsylvania and graduated from Columbia School of Journalism. In the early 1950s he began to investigate the work of the Institute for Motivational Research in New York State. His observations on the new world of American supermarkets and television advertisements were published in 1957 in *The Hidden Persuaders*. As a populist exposé of the world of hard selling, the book was a bestseller. Packard upturned the formal conventions of the serious sociology book by using the language of the popular press. Typical of his style was a chapter describing research which measured the rate of eye blinks of housewives in supermarkets and suggested they fell into a light hypnosis called 'Babes in Consumerland'. It was an approach much imitated in the 1960s with the rise of the so-called > New Journalism. Packard was a prolific writer and published a whole series of critiques on consumer culture, including *The Status Seekers* (1959), *The Waste Makers* (1960), *The Pyramid Climbers* (1962) and *The Naked Society* (1964).

VICTOR PAPANEK

Austrian-born designer (b. 1925) who emigrated to New York aged 14. He trained at the Cooper Union and the Massachusetts Institute of Technology, going on to work as a teacher and consultant designer for UNESCO. However, he is best known for his bestselling book *Design for the Real World* (1971), which became the text for the > Alternative Design movement. Written while teaching design at Purdue University, Papanek's book was a plea for design to be seen as a moral activity,

161

not as a marketing device, and in this context the book's subtitle, 'Human Ecology and Social Change', is particularly revealing. Papanek suggested that young designers dedicate themselves not to designing yet another fridge or sofa, but to directing their talents to the problems of the old and the underprivileged. He also advocated recycling techniques, the use of natural forms and a closer relationship between design and the work of sociologists and anthropologists. It was a powerful message for its time.

Papanek's mentor was Buckminster Fuller and he abided by Fuller's adage that 'you have to make sense or to make money if you want to be a designer'. Although Fuller is by far the most important theoretician of the design for need movement, Papanek popularized these alternative ideas. However, he was a controversial figure, always regarded with deep suspicion by the design establishment, but his teaching influenced a generation of students in the 1970s. None the less, his cult status was short-lived and *Design for the Real World* remained a one-off contribution to the design debate.

PENGUIN BOOKS

A British publishing company with a distinguished design history. During the 1930s the rise of the Nazi party caused many leading German designers to flee to Britain. Many went on to the USA, but some stayed and of these perhaps the most important was Jan Tschichold (1902–74). Tschichold was one of the most influential typographers of the 20th century, and when he was employed by Penguin in 1935 to design books, he effectively changed the face of British publishing. His best-known achievement was designing the series style for a whole range of Penguin paperbacks. This approach made the ideas and images of the > Modern Movement accessible for the first time to a wider audience. Well-known writers in the series included J.M. Richards on architecture, and John Gloag and Anthony Bertram on design.

NIKOLAUS PEVSNER

Pevsner (1902–83) arrived in Britain as a refugee in 1936, but went on to become the country's most important writer on architecture and design. In addition to this, Pevsner virtually invented the history of architecture and design as subjects worthy of serious academic study. In fact, his book *The Pioneers of Modern Design*, originally published in 1936, has become standard reading for every design undergraduate. Very few students realize that this manifesto of the > Modern Movement is approaching its sixtieth birthday, and its success, due in a large part to its accessible and rational approach, has given Pevsner a legendary status in the field of design studies. The book, however, is much more than a history. It has helped create a popular perception of design history, which has shaped common tastes and ideas. Pevsner saw the development of design as a road that led to Modernism and Walter Gropius. His book was a single and powerful ideology.

Pevsner was born in Leipzig, the son of academic Jewish parents. In the early 1930s he taught at Göttingen University, and after fleeing to England introduced rigorous German methods to British academic life. His first job, for Birmingham University, was to prepare a research report into the role of design in British industry. It made sobering reading. After the war he was appointed Slade Professor of Fine Art at Cambridge from 1949 to 1955. During the 1960s and 1970s he worked on his mammoth survey of *The Buildings of England*. Inevitably Pevsner's dominance and his defence of Modern Movement principles has come in for criticism. No one, however, can challenge his position as one of the great historians of the 20th century.

PLANNED OBSOLESCENCE

A marketing strategy pioneered in the USA to deliberately limit the lifespan of consumer products. Durability and lifelong service were qualities people once sought when selecting furniture and products for the home. That situation subtly changed in the 1950s when the USA introduced the idea of planned obsolescence into the economy. The idea was simply to encourage people to buy more goods by making products which had a limited life and which would need to be replaced when other and better models came on to the market. There is nothing new about that as a marketing strategy; the fashion business had been doing it for years. What was extraordinary was the extent to which planned obsolescence was introduced into manufacturing in the 1950s. Protest was swiftly voiced by design reformers like Vance > Packard. He wrote *The Waste Makers* in 1960 as a direct attack on obsolescence, which he saw as a social evil, an attempt by manufacturers to exploit the gullible. On the other hand, industrialists and industrial designers saw obsolescence as a wonderful opportunity to provide choice, to stimulate the economy and to create objects of design wonder. In this context the classic American car of the 1950s is an excellent example. Interestingly, the issue of obsolescence was rather diverted by > Pop design in the 1960s, which actively embraced the principle of the throwaway object, but concern has returned in recent years, now linked to a growing interest in > green design.

POMPIDOU CENTRE *See* CCI.

POP DESIGN

Pop design flourished between 1963 and 1971, beginning in London and eventually influencing design throughout Europe and the USA. The essence of Pop design lies in its challenge to the traditions of Modernism, which had dominated international design during the post-war years. At the new Bauhaus in Chicago, and at the Institute of Contemporary Arts and the Council of Industrial Design in London, leading designers and design theorists of the 1930s had a tremendous influence over the burgeoning design professionals. Led by the ideology of the > Modern Movement, design had to function well, be austere, and made to last. This older generation of designers and theorists, including Herbert > Read in Britain and Walter Gropius in the USA, were now to be challenged by a younger generation of design theorists and practitioners.

Beginning with Peter Reyner > Banham and the > Independent Group, who met informally at the ICA from 1952 to 1955, this younger generation evaluated the legacy of the Modern Movement and proposed a new aesthetic criterion for interpreting design, which was based less on functional qualities than on the desires and needs of the consumer. The Independent Group argued that design values need not be universal and everlasting, but could legitimately be ephemeral. This new pluralist approach laid down the critical foundations for Pop design in the 1960s.

164

As a result of higher standards of living, particularly among the 16–24 age group, there was an increased demand for consumer goods which distinguished the younger people from their elders. This had first made an impact during the 1950s and was one of the main catalysts behind Pop design in the 1960s. As the Beatles reached number one in the charts in 1963, so youth consumers sought out design artefacts to express a shared youth culture and identity. Fun furniture, for example, was created in a variety of ephemeral materials. In 1964 Peter Murdoch designed a paper chair constructed out of five-layer laminate and printed with bright polka-dots. It could be stored flat, bought cheaply by the young consumer and easily replaced. There were similar developments in fashion, such as the disposable paper dress which could be washed once or twice and then thrown away.

Typically, surface patterns from the 1960s included flags, bull's-eyes, stripes and other Pop and Op motifs borrowed from painters like Jasper Johns, Bridget Riley and Andy Warhol. Designers favoured surface pattern rather than three-dimensional forms, and themes which emphasized a new optimism in the power of youth culture and innovation. Typical of this new mood were the mini-skirt and the space age outfits of André Courrèges, which incorporated plastic ankle boots and white visored helmets.

Pop design, particularly in graphics, was also characterized by a revival of Victorian and Edwardian forms. A series of exhibitions and books on the decorative arts of those periods provided an important inspiration, as did the desire to challenge the dominance of neat, clean Swiss typography. The swirling lines and decadence of Aubrey Beardsley expressed the hedonistic atmosphere of 1960s' youth culture. Reyner Banham continued to attack outdated Modernism and support Pop design in his writings for New Society throughout the 1960s. By the end of the decade, however, the witty, ephemeral and often superficial aspects of Pop design no longer seemed relevant when environmental issues and the oil crisis of 1973 presented more pressing concerns. Charles Jencks, a student of Reyner Banham's, developed the Independent Group's approach into a more sophisticated > Post-Modernism with his book Modern Movements in Architecture.

The sharp wit of Pop Design became submerged in the 1970s by Post-Modernist theory, which was found largely in architecture, and developed into a new concern for > Classicism. More recently, however, the 1990s has seen a revival of interest in Pop, particularly in

165

fashion design. The artefacts of the 1960s are now eagerly collected, and young designers attracted by the optimism and confidence of a period they can only study second-hand are looking again at the achievements of Pop design.

● Nigel Whiteley, *Pop Design: Modernism to Mod*, 1987.

POPULAR CULTURE

A distinctly modern phenomenon that developed in Western Europe at the end of the 19th century. An urban working class with access to leisure time and money developed new entertainment forms which included illustrated newspapers, films, music hall, detective novels and, later, radio and television. These forms of popular culture, labelled Low Art, were set in opposition to more élitist art forms such as opera and classical music, labelled High Art. In the first half of the 20th century the division between these two areas was enormous, although artists had always been fascinated by the scope and vigour of popular culture. This situation changed in the 1960s with the emergence of Pop Art, and the relationship between art and popular culture moved from strength to strength in the 1970s with the development of Performance and Video Art. In the Post-Modernist period hostility to popular culture has been replaced by direct engagement with it.

POPULUXE

During the 1950s the American advertising industry invented a number of marketing words to which the suffix 'luxe' was added. For example, 'de luxe' implying elegance and superiority, was applied to products ranging from cars to vacuum cleaners. Populuxe, combined from populism and luxury, is a 1980s' publishing invention to describe design from the American consumer boom years of 1954 to 1964.

● Thomas Hine, *Populuxe: The Look and Life of America in the 50s and 60s, from Tailfins and TV Dinners to Barbie Dolls and Fallout Shelters*, 1986.

POST-MODERNISM

Meaning 'after Modernism', this term was first applied to architecture and design in the 1940s, then to the new pluralism of > Pop in the 1960s. However, it is most closely associated with the 1970s, in particular with a book by the architectural historian Charles Jencks called *The Language of Post-Modern Architecture* (1977). For Jencks and other like-minded critics, the use of the term Post-Modernism also implied a critical position against Modernist principles and values. Nowadays the term's meaning has been so debased that Post-Modernism is used to describe almost anything new or novel.

Until the 1960s Modernist values, embodied in the 1930s' furniture of Marcel Breuer and Alvar Aalto and in the 1960s' industrial designs of the Braun company, remained the dominant ideology. Although the Pop aesthetic to some extent overturned those values, the real revolution in design came in the 1970s and 1980s. Taking a broader perspective outside design, many Post-Modernist theorists felt Modernism marked an important transition in the 20th century taking on board key social and technological changes. In this context Modernism can be seen as a response to the early 20th-century industrial machine age, and Post-Modernism to the age of computers and electronic information design. Indeed, Post-Modernism signalled an important shift away from technological optimism to a crisis of confidence in the benefits of technological progress.

Building directly on the ideas of the 1960s, Post-Modernist designers revived a whole series of ideas, materials and imagery which had been rejected by the Modernists. Post-Modernism believed in cultural pluralism, and that principle had important repercussions affecting the way design looked, the way designers thought about themselves and the way design was debated and discussed in the media. The best-known examples of Post-Modernist design came from Italy and the work of Ettore Sottsass and Michele de Lucchi for > Memphis. Their furniture used mixed materials, combining plastic laminates with expensive wood finishes, and played around with such conventions as table legs always being identical and shelves always being horizontal. Another Milan-based design group, Studio Alchymia, also reflected the stylistic > eclecticism, wit and irony of Post-Modernism. Other design disciplines began to reflect the new freedom. Graphic design, for example, heavily influenced by the fixed and purist rules of Swiss

167

typography, began to mix typefaces, play around with printing conventions and freely retrieve imagery from virtually any source. Textile designers experimented with scale and with mixing patterns, often combining diverse imagery on the same design in the manner of a chaotic collage. Another important change Post-Modernism had on design was its insistence that the traditional divide between art and design should be challenged. Graphic designers like Peter Saville now felt confident about showing their work in a traditional art gallery context, while furniture-makers such as Danny Lane referred to the crossover their pieces make into the realm of sculpture. While it has been common practice for artists to move into design, Post-Modernism gave designers the confidence to take on the world of art.

Theorizing about design also saw an important shift of emphasis. Post-Modernism heralded a serious attempt to break down the divisions between anthropology, philosophy, sociology and science. The methodologies and ideas from these disciplines were introduced into design, albeit in a rather superficial way, and likewise the rich visual culture of consumer products provided academics with important case studies. The most important Post-Modernist theorists include Roland > Barthes, Michel > Foucault and Jean > Baudrillard.

Despite the strong emphasis Post-Modernism placed on theory and its claim to embrace important aspects of cultural change, in design terms it has become just another style. The Post-Modernist style can be identified via the revival of historical detail, bright colour and ornament on products ranging from Zanussi fridges and Alessi kettles to Japanese transistor radios.

● H. Foster, *Postmodern Culture*, 1985.

PREPPY

A term used to describe the lifestyle of a group of largely white, American, middle-class young professionals. Often the product of smart prep schools, this group affected a lifestyle based on a certain kind of Englishness. They admired Shetland sweaters, leather brogues and English country house interiors, but they bought the style via American designers like Ralph Lauren. When Lisa Birnbach published her international bestseller *The Preppy Handbook*, which sold over 4 million copies, preppy aspirations went mainstream and international.

PRIMITIVE INFLUENCES

Primitive influences have played an important part in the development of Western art and design, but only in the late 20th century are we beginning to revise long-held prejudices about so-called primitive cultures. No longer do we regard them as somehow stuck in an evolutionary time warp. An interesting example of this is Aboriginal culture, which research now suggests is full of sophisticated skills which we have been too ignorant to understand. The novel *Songlines* by the writer Bruce Chatwin picks up this theme, as does the 1990 American film *Dances with Wolves*, which also attempts to reverse the traditional viewpoint of the Native Americans as savages. In fact in recent times Western opinions have been turned upside-down.

The Victorians tended to dismiss primitive objects as curiosities, which could be admired so long as they were seen as natural, unfettered by artifice and European corruption. They could be championed only as part of Rousseau's view of the noble savage. Hard information and research were also difficult to come by, although there were sources such as Henry Balfour's Pitt Rivers Museum, the anthropology collection at Oxford, and exhibitions such as the 1886 Colonial and Indian Exhibition in London which showed elaborate African objects from the Gold Coast. There were very few attempts to apply primitive decoration and form to 19th-century design. Owen Jones and Christopher Dresser championed Aztec art, and Dresser copied simple ceramic shapes for the Linthorpe Pottery but still within the terms of primitive. A more powerful effect can be seen on painting. For many artists primitive culture came to represent something untainted, powerful and anti-academic against which they could justify their radical experiments. The romantic myth of escape had begun, the best example being provided by Gauguin's retreat to Tahiti.

Primitive art also helped to trigger one of the most important revolutions in 20th-century art – the development of Cubism. Both Picasso and Braque collected and drew African masks in their quest to develop non-representational art. These minority collecting tastes have since become mainstream interests. Television and the media bring images of remote village life into our homes. Smart magazines on interiors are full of Indonesian shadow puppets or Mexican funeral figures. Having been integrated into the vocabulary of international design, the primitive has lost much of its iconic power.

PSYCHEDELIA

A design style based on the images and colours associated with the hallucinogenic drugs which were popular during the late 1960s. The release of the Sgt Pepper Lonely Hearts Club Band album by the Beatles in 1967 is generally credited with launching Psychedelia as a style. Hallucinogenic drugs, especially LSD, were used to explore the subconscious and release the imagination, much as the drug Ecstasy was used to release inhibitions in the > Acid House movement of the late 1980s.

In the late 1960s Psychedelia as a style had its biggest impact on graphic design. In 1967 the poster designer Michael English formed a partnership with Nigel Weymouth called Hapdash and the Coloured Coat, and their work epitomized the style, using fluorescent colours which conjured up the images of an LSD 'trip'. The emphasis was on free-floating, flowing forms, many of which were borrowed from > Art Nouveau images. The intense sexual imagery of Aubrey Beardsley was especially important, combined with the posters of French artists Alphonse Mucha and Toulouse-Lautrec. Another important graphic designer was Martin Sharp, who worked for Jimi Hendrix and Bob Dylan.

For designers Psychedelia was a liberating exercise in creativity, which stressed the importance of the individual through improvisation, free-form composition and technical innovation. The pop poster was the perfect expression of the new drug culture; it was a mass medium, it was cheap and accessible and it communicated the new consciousness. Also important was the graphic style of Oz magazine, launched in 1967 by editor Richard Neville. The magazine layout was a pure psychedelic vision, combining hallucinatory lettering, favourite shades of turquoise and magenta, and illegibility, which was achieved through superimpositions and out-of-focus images.

The influence of psychedelia spread, being used to decorate the outside of buildings such as English and Weymouth's Red Indian façade for Granny Takes a Trip and the Beatles' Apple boutique. Psychedelic fashion was produced by, among others, the Fool, a group of fashion designers who made clothes for the Apple boutique. This group was committed to visual > eclecticism, drawing on medieval ideas and ethnic influences from gypsy culture and India, all in bright, clashing colours. Psychedelic design was too intense a style to last for long, but its influence continued to be felt in the multimedia world of pop concerts and nightclubs.

PUNK

The name used to describe a British youth cult of the late 1970s, which saw a fashion for aggressive make-up, shaved heads, safety pins worn through the cheek and ripped clothes. It was partly a reaction to a massive economic recession which undermined the confidence and optimism of the previous decade. Values of the 1960s, especially those associated with Hippy Culture, were despised by the teen generation of the 1970s. Punk inspired a new raw music, produced such bands as the Buzzcocks, the Clash and, most notorious of all, the Sex Pistols. The Pistols, managed by Malcolm McLaren, enjoyed a high media profile. Jamie Reid designed their record sleeves and Vivienne Westwood their clothes. Although Punk was popularly seen as the product of working-class, urban and essentially deprived youth, the involvement of Reid, McLaren and Westwood is interesting in that they were not young (all three were in their thirties) and they had all trained at art college. McLaren and Reid were typical art college products and this link between Punk and art college is important. Radical performance art, as well as Dada events, influenced Punk and the student political attitudes of the 1960s. Many famous Punk slogans of the period, for example, 'Never trust a hippy' and 'Anarchy is the key, do-it-yourself the melody', were inspired by the slogans from Situationist writings of the 1960s. Punk had a rich intellectual background, which at the time was ignored in favour of the media view of Punk style emerging from the council flats of Brixton, Manchester and Liverpool. None the less, British youth developed a unique style seen in the rich club and music

171

scene which flourished in the late 1970s and early 1980s. It also proved to be a creative influence on British fashion, graphics and furniture in the 1980s.

● Griel Marcus, *Lipstick Traces: A Secret History of the Twentieth Century*, 1989; Jon Savage, *England's Dreaming*, 1991.

Q

QUEEN ANNE REVIVAL

An architectural style which used red brick and details from Dutch vernacular architecture. Philip Webb's Red House, built for William Morris, pioneered the revival of red brick, together with the use of terracotta decorative panels, elements which formed the basis of the style revival called Queen Anne. The best-known exponent of the style was Richard Norman Shaw (1831–1912), who designed Swan House on Chelsea embankment. The façade played with picturesque fenestration details, especially the revival of paned glass windows, and the building had Dutch-inspired gable roofs and dormer attic windows.

R

RADICAL CHIC

A term of ridicule invented by Tom > Wolfe to describe the rather cynical fashion adopted by the rich and famous in the 1970s of flirting with revolutionary groups. John Lennon and Yoko Ono, for example, took up with black activist Malcolm X, while Leonard Bernstein hosted a party for the notorious Black Panthers. The taste Establishment figures had for fêting known terrorists was short-lived, but the term radical chic survived and is now a way of putting down design and designers who appropriate ideas and cultural influences in their work while having no real commitment to their source.

RATIONALISM

Italy's version of the > Modern Movement in architecture and design emerged in 1926 in the form of a manifesto written by a group of young architects called Gruppo Sette (the Group of Seven). Its members were Sebastiano Larco, Guido Frette, Carlo Enrico Rava, Luigi Figini, Gino Pollini, Giuseppe Terragni and Adalberto Libera. Their work was well received in the early 1930s. In Como Terragni built the famous Casa del Fascio for the Fascist party, and Mussolini himself appeared sympathetic and supportive of the group's aims. For a brief period their work reflected the revolutionary and socialist aspects of the early Italian Fascist party. However, the influence of Rationalism was short-lived; it proved to be too international and radical. By the mid-1930s it was clear that the Fascist party no longer subscribed to socialist ideals, but had become the party of middle-class values. Mussolini now preferred the more conservative > Novecento style, which used refined classical and therefore Italian sources. Rationalism, however, did not die completely. Its values were to prove an inspiration and a training ground for the new era of Italian design that emerged after 1945.

HERBERT READ

Read (1893–1968) was Britain's most important avant-garde critic of art, literature and design from the 1930s to the 1960s. He was, in fact, the only British critic of his generation who had worked out an all-embracing view of art and design. Although most of his writings were concerned with a defence of modern art, he also wrote one of the most important books on design, *Art and Industry* (1934). At that time he was living in Hampstead, a stone's throw from Henry Moore, Barbara Hepworth and Ben Nicholson, and during that period met Piet Mondrian, Laszlo Moholy-Nagy and Walter Gropius.

In *Art and Industry* Read helped to popularize design, or machine art, as he so tellingly called it. Although he profoundly disliked industrial culture, he championed the idea that utilitarian objects, such as metal operating tables, could and should be beautiful. For a whole generation of 1930s' British designers Read's book was a significant turning point. It was not surprising, then, that when Milner Gray set up one of the country's first design practices – the Design Research Unit – Herbert Read was invited to become its first director. In the post-war period Read's views did not remain popular. The new generation of > Pop writers and critics took exception to his idea that the artist was the sole possessor of eternal truths and to his implicit rejection of the world of > Popular Culture to which they were so strongly committed.

READY-MADE

Objects or images removed from their normal environment and function and re-presented in an art or design context. The ready-made was introduced in 1913 by the iconoclastic Marcel Duchamp with his bicycle wheel exhibit. The ready-made challenged existing concepts of art, such as the supremacy of the original, hand-crafted object, as well as giving a new idea to the object by its placement in a gallery. For Duchamp the ready-made supposedly possessed no aesthetic qualities and was one of many indistinguishable, mass-produced objects, unlike the > found object which was chosen for its uniqueness. The concept of appropriating an already made object or image was part of the late 1950s' neo-Dada revival and was to be crucial to > Pop imagery. In more recent years, with the development of > semiotics and > feminism, the ready-made has become a way of revealing, confronting and deconstructing the tenets of contemporary capitalist culture across all the arts. Marcel Duchamp became a hero for many young designers educated in the late 1960s and 1970s, particularly those who wanted to inject some intellectual life into the discipline of design. Into this group fall Daniel Weil, professor of industrial design at the > Royal College of Art, and interior designer Ben Kelly.

READY-TO-WEAR

A development that revolutionized the clothing industry. Until the late 19th century, if you wanted new clothes, you either made them yourself or employed a dressmaker to do so. The concept of buying 'off-the-peg' took some time to develop. It was partly stimulated by the Victorian obsession with formal mourning clothes; indeed, there were shops which specialized in mourning attire and could supply everything needed for a sudden bereavement. Ready-to-wear was also stimulated by women's growing taste for tailored clothes, inspired by the cutting skills of the male tailor, not the traditional draping skills of the female dressmaker. The 1860s, however, saw some important technological breakthroughs, including the development by a Leeds menswear company of a bandsaw capable of cutting through many layers of cloth. Triggered by the demand from women for comfortable travel clothes, this technology was applied to women's serge walking suits and ready-to-wear took off. Its development led to a boom in retailing, the growth of department stores and the emergence of > mail order.

RETAIL DESIGN

The history of retail design can be traced back to the great department stores of the 19th century. The 1860s in Paris saw the opening of the Bon Marché and Printemps stores, followed by Marshall Fields in

Chicago, Selfridges in London and Macy's in New York. These enormous emporia provided an affluent, middle-class market with new places to shop. The next retail design innovation, aimed at a working-class market, swiftly followed. It was the chain store. The first of these was opened at the turn of the century by Frank Winfield Woolworth, and by 1919 he had opened 1081 more across the USA. Chain stores were cheap and cheerful, but they did establish an important retail design trend – the idea of a strong shop identity using bold company logos. In Britain during the 1930s an increase in branches of chain stores such as Boots the chemist appeared on many high streets. The post-war period saw the next important retail design change with the development of the shopping centre. The United States pioneered the out-of-town shopping centre, which catered for the family and had generous parking facilities. Meanwhile, Europe pioneered the city-centre shopping precinct. Rebuilding bomb-damaged cities provided an opportunity for new city planning ideas, and the shopping centre, with a traffic-free zone and light, airy shops, made its first appearance in Rotterdam in the early 1950s. In contrast to these early shopping centres, the 1960s saw the rise of the individual retailer-designer, such as Barbara Hulanicki, who founded the Biba boutique, and Sir Terence Conran, who pioneered a new approach to shop design in his Habitat stores.

During the last 20 years the developed world has seen important social and cultural changes affect the patterns of shopping. It has now become a hugely successful leisure activity, and the shopper has come to expect constantly changing, high-quality shopping environments complete with cinemas, cafés, restaurants and leisure facilities. These changes have led to a huge boom in retail design. During the 1980s, for example, the massive expansion of British design was led by the retail sector. Design practices such as Fitch, David Davies and Din Associates enjoyed massive patronage from retailers, completely redesigning national chain stores such as Next and British Home Stores. It is estimated that something like 70 per cent of British multiple retailers had their shops completely redesigned during this period. In addition, the design of expensive, one-off designer shops, representing the couture end of retailing, also attracted massive media attention. Examples include Sir Norman Foster's shop in London for fashion designer Katherine Hamnett and Eva Jiricna's work for the influential British retailer Joseph.

If the 1980s was the shop-till-you-drop decade, the recession-ridden 1990s is surely just the opposite. The economic climate has called for a new look at retailing. The boom years are over and the future of retail design is difficult to foresee. Many designers and pundits predict the rise of shopping alternatives like mail order and teleshopping. However, although it looks likely that the balance of consumer shopping patterns may shift, the role of the retail designer is firmly established. Design is now seen as the key element in enticing shoppers into stores, and the retail designer looks set to remain part of the late 20th-century culture of shopping.

● Rodney Fitch & Lance Knobel, *Fitch on Retail Design*, 1990.

RETAILING

The last 200 years have seen the introduction of new methods of retailing and marketing design, which include the development of chain stores, supermarkets, shopping malls and mail-order services.

The principle of mail order relied on the establishment of postal services to succeed, but ordering from catalogues had a longer history. In the 1760s it was possible to visit Thomas Chippendale's studio on St Martin's Lane and select furniture designs from his printed *Director*. Josiah Wedgwood also equipped his travelling salesmen with a sample case and a catalogue to take orders from customers over a wide area of the country. However, posting orders direct to a company was a 19th-century retailing development devised in the USA to help overcome the huge problems of shopping at a distance. The first to offer the service was Montgomery Ward, founded in 1872, followed in the 1890s by Sears, Roebuck and Company. By 1900 Sears was receiving and dispatching over 100,000 orders a day, and to cope with this demand it pioneered new methods of dispatch and customer service. These were the first distinctive mail order companies.

In Britain mail order tended to be an extension of the service well-known department stores offered to their customers. For example, Fortnum & Mason mailed out food hampers, while the Army & Navy department store catered for the needs of the Empire, shipping clothes and goods to far-flung British colonial families. This specialist, luxury retailing trend remains strong in the 1990s, but mail-order firms supplying goods to ordinary families continued to grow with companies such as Littlewoods and Brian Mills. In the recession years of the 1920s and 1930s catalogue companies essentially became credit brokers for families on limited means. They offered extended credit terms and relied on a local agent to organize the collection of money and to distribute the ordered goods.

The link between mail order and poor sections of the community is one that the companies have tried to shake off in recent years. The best-known attempt has been the Next mail-order catalogue, launched in 1987 by influential retailer George Davies. The catalogue was produced as a designer item, with a hardback cover, smart photography and slick graphics. It also offered an updated service. No longer did orders have to be made through a local agent; it was now possible to phone in direct, and delivery was promised within 48 hours. In spite of such updates, mail-order sales have declined in the 1990s. Companies are now exploring the possibilities of direct sales by television. In France the government paid for 5 million sets to be converted for a trial selling system, which seems to have been a modest success. Mail-order companies believe that families will continue to have less time to shop and will require the facilities of home selection. Technology promises a revolution but the precise changes to direct shopping remain unclear.

Chain stores and supermarkets had their origin in the late 19th century. The first chain store group was Woolworths, founded in the 1880s. It was followed by the A&P Company, which grew from 585 stores in 1913 to 11,500 during the 1920s. The earliest English chain stores, such as Sainsburys, operated like traditional grocery shops, with a shopkeeper and assistants serving behind a counter. The change came with the introduction of supermarkets. Early in the 20th century the USA introduced the concept of cash-and-carry stores. In the recession of the 1920s and 1930s the low overheads of these outlets, reflected in lower mark-ups on the stock, made them very popular. In 1916 Clarence Saunders introduced a turnstile and the idea of self-service at a store in Memphis called Piggly Wiggly. It was the beginning of an international revolution in retailing. The development of huge supermarkets closed the small store and market and brought to an end the era of personal service. *See also* Boutiques; Retail Design.

ROBOTICS

The development of machines which resemble human beings and are designed to perform routine tasks. Information about robotics usually falls into one of two categories: science fiction or technology. Currently, Japan leads the world in the science of robotics. In fact, the popular film *The Terminator* ends with two Japanese-made industrial robots fighting it out.

The word robot was first used by the Czech playwright Karel Čapek in the 1920s, but clockwork mechanisms for mechanical dolls had first been developed in the 16th century. By the 18th century the mechanisms had become very sophisticated; some dolls could play the harpsichord, write and draw pictures. This tradition of mechanical toys and gadgets remained popular into the 19th and 20th centuries. From the 1950s, however, the progress in computer technology led to advanced automated machines and eventually to the building of industrial robots. The first experimental models were introduced in the 1960s in Japan. These early robots performed single tasks such as spot welding or paint spraying. In Japan today it is possible to see robots making sushi and performing sophisticated factory assembly tasks. However, it is not yet possible to create a totally human-like machine using current technology. Robots need wheels or crawlers to 'walk', but the movement is currently far from smooth. Most of the robots in use reproduce a sequence of pre-recorded movements, and have sensors which can detect changes in temperature, pressure and texture. The most critical research, in the area of artificial intelligence, is still to be completed, but it will eventually make robots capable of making decisions. This means that future robots will not be limited to working in factories. They will be able to deal with dangerous work in nuclear power stations, engage in rescue operations and space travel, and care for the special needs of handicapped and old people. Eventually robots will be commonplace both at work and in the home.

• Frederik L. Schodt, *Inside the Robot Kingdom*, 1988.

ROCOCO REVIVAL

Rococo is an 18th-century European decorative style characterized by curving, asymmetrical ornament based on nature, with three-dimensional scrolls, shells, cartouches and waterfalls. In the 1820s the style enjoyed a revival, and 10 years later it was picked up as an international design trend across all classes.

ROYAL COLLEGE OF ART

One of the world's best-known design schools. Jocelyn Stevens (rector until 1992) is a businessman with no background in education, and he has kept the college in the public eye with his controversial management style. Opinions vary as to whether he has provided a much-needed shot in the arm to design education, or whether he has effectively killed off a distinguished British institution. Controversies of this kind, however, are part of the Royal College's long history of fierce debate and public resignations.

In 1835 the government, worried that standards of British design needed to be improved, ordered the appointment of a Select Committee on Arts and Manufactures. One of its primary recommendations was the establishment of a central school of design to train teachers. An advisory board of industrialists was appointed, including the pottery manufacturer William Copeland. When the school opened at Somerset House in 1837, there were deep divisions about how and what design students should be taught. The first director, the architect and designer J.B. Papworth (1775–1847), lasted only a year, to be replaced by the painter William Dyce (1806–64). Dyce had been sent to France and Germany to study their methods of design education and he came to the conclusion that design students needed direct contact with industry. In 1842 he published a teaching manual called *Drawing Book*, which put forward the guiding principle of the School of Design – that ornament should have a geometrical basis. At the same time Dyce also believed that students should be taught life drawing. Controversy about the syllabus continued to rage, and led, in 1849, to a re-organization of the school. During the 1850s and 1860s, the school, run by Henry Cole (1808–82) and Richard Redgrave (1804–88), enjoyed tremendous success. By 1860 the number of design schools throughout the country had risen from 20 to 80 and student numbers had grown from 3200 to 85,000. Famous teachers of that period included Owen Jones and Gottfried Semper, and Christopher Dresser was a famous former pupil. Towards the end of the century, however, the School of Design moved away from radical design education towards the education of fine artists, a direction confirmed in 1896 when Queen Victoria granted the title Royal College of Art. By the 1930s it was recognized that a shake-up was long overdue. This finally came after the war with the appointment in 1948 of Robin Darwin as principal, and with him returned the college's international profile in design.

● C. Frayling, *The Royal College of Art, 150 years of art and design*, 1987.

JOHN RUSKIN

Ruskin (1819–1900) was the most important design writer and critic of the 19th century. His only serious rival to that claim was William Morris. Ruskin, an intense, complex, almost neurotic man, helped to shape the taste and attitudes of his century more than anyone else. He was a precocious child, the son of a prosperous wine merchant, and in 1837 went to study at Oxford. At the age of 24 he published his first volume in the series *Modern Painters*, a defence of his hero J.H.W. Turner. Six years later, in 1849, he published his monumental defence of the Gothic style, *Seven Lamps of Architecture*. This was followed by *Stones of Venice* (1851–3). Ruskin despised the industrial world England had pioneered. He was a vocal critic of the > Great Exhibition of 1851 and reserved particular dislike for machine-made ornament. In his famous notes reviewing Holman Hunt's painting *The Awakening Conscience*, Ruskin attacked the 'fatal newness of the furniture'.

Like Morris, Ruskin held views that showed a strong social conscience; in fact, his Guild of St George was a failed attempt to put his ideas of social reform into practice. None the less, his writings became sacred texts for the > Arts and Crafts Movement. Ruskin and Morris met in 1857 and became allies 20 years later when they worked together for the Society for the Protection of Ancient Buildings.

Ruskin was a gifted amateur artist, and although his own attempts at design were largely unsuccessful, his belief that ornament should be based on conventional natural forms proved influential. Indeed, his writings were widely translated abroad, and Walter Gropius was inspired by his books. John Ruskin's attitudes to art, architecture and design, and their relationship to society and morality continue to have a lasting effect on the 20th century.

● Tim Hilton, *John Ruskin*, 1985.

RUSSIAN CONTRUCTIVISM

Constructivism was the famous Russian contribution to the ideas of the > Modern Movement. After the 1917 Revolution in Russia the Bolsheviks deprived landowners and landlords of their property and replaced the previous capitalist system of production and distribution of goods. They sought the means to feed, clothe and adequately maintain the huge population of the Soviet Union as befitted the new workers' state. Thus, after 1917, socially organized production was coupled with democratic planning through the soviets (workers' committees). These organizations had developed during the Revolution as the most democratic means of decision-making. Delegates from local soviets would represent their views at regional and national levels, but were subject to recall and replacement by the locality. Using this system, the production of goods could be related to the needs of the population both at a local and a national level. The Revolution led to a huge burst of energy in all the arts with a range of styles given free rein. Art and design were seen as linked, along with architecture, film, theatre and photography. Painters and sculptors who had previously worked within the confines of their own discipline now worked alongside designers and architects in helping to rebuild the new society. Few large projects were realized in the early days as the Revolution suffered invasion, civil war and terrible economic problems. The provision of food and shelter, together with defence of the Revolution, had to be put before cultural activity. Finally, this situation led to the rise of bureaucracy and its political representative, Josef Stalin. Stalinist measures sounded the death knell of the social and artistic aspirations of the Russian Revolution. Sixty years later, however, Russian Constructivism remains a powerful force on modern design. In the late 1970s a series of books and exhibitions brought this work to the attention of Western designers. Contemporary graphic designers continue to be inspired by the work of Aleksandr Rodchenko (1891–1956), El Lissitzsky (1890–1941) and Kasimir Malevich (1878–1935).

RUSSIAN DESIGN

For most of the 20th century Russian design has been dominated by the communist regime. Since the collapse of communism in 1991 the old Soviet Union has broken up and Russia is once again a single, independent country, but the legacy of communism will linger for many years yet. Not only did it shape the country's culture, it particularly affected the production and sale of consumer goods. The rise of Stalin after 1925 led to authoritarian and bureaucratic rule, and centralized planning. This command economy excluded the producers from the decision-making process, and although the system enabled the Soviet Union to industrialize at a rapid rate, the costs were enormous, not least to the millions who died from famine as farming was forcibly collectivized. The producers, having no role in the planning of production, lost interest in the process itself, while the planners, lacking this democratic input, made decisions based on arbitrary quotes rather than real needs. As centralization became more inefficient and corrupt, it led to economic stagnation and loss of quality and innovation in the goods produced. At the same time Stalin imposed Soviet Socialist Realism across the whole of cultural production, including design. This was regarded as the only style appropriate to the working class, but in reality corresponded to the needs of the State. Any elements of the avant-garde and innovative styles of > Russian Constructivism were replaced with a narrative realism based on the art and literature of the 19th century. It was in this atmosphere that post-war designers had to train. After graduation they were assigned to a factory or to work in State design practices called Vniite. Opportunities for personal creative development were limited. Some relief came in the 1960s under Khrushchev, but long-term hopes for change in the 1970s were dashed. Change was finally to come with the introduction of *perestroika* (restructuring) and the era of *glasnost* (openness) under Mikhail Gorbachev. Western companies and Western designers looked forward to the opportunities an open Russian market would offer, but despite the promises, change has been slow in coming. The recession in the West has meant that companies are reluctant to invest in Russian projects that show little sign of return. As well as this, the political implications of the 1991 break-up of the old Soviet empire are still not clear.

The present situation for designers and for the country looks grim. However, designers have been allowed to organize themselves into the Union of Soviet Designers, with offices in Moscow and St Petersburg. A few were also allowed to set up in private practice. Nevertheless, the prospects of work are extremely limited in the present climate. In 1990

Kingston Polytechnic organized 'Soviet Design in the West' at the > Victoria and Albert Museum. This conference, the first of its kind, provided a fascinating but depressing insight into this period of Russian change. The economic and geographical problems facing the former Soviet Union are immense, and designers are expected to function with virtually no equipment. Western technology in the form of computers and fax machines are scarce. The rouble remains a non-convertible currency and free trade with the West has yet to be realized. None the less, Western manufacturers and designers are beginning to explore the possibilities of working in Russia, while at the same time a generation of talented Russian designers are hoping to play a key role in the regeneration of the economy. *See also* Marxism; Russian Constructivism.

● C. Gray, *The Great Experiment: Russian Art 1863–1922*, 1982.

S

SATELLITE TOWN

This post-war term was coined to give the outer suburbs of large cities an identity of their own. Croydon outside London is an example. Satellite town is sometimes interchangeable with New town, a name given to such places as Harlow and Peterlee, which were part of the expansion programme of post-war Britain.

SCANDINAVIAN DESIGN

The products of Denmark, Finland, Sweden and Norway share common design features, such as a love of natural materials, particularly wood, and a commitment to rational form, which have created a look both stylish and adaptable. In the post-war period there was a deliberate attempt to market the designs of these countries as a single design movement. They appeared at the Milan Triennales, for example, and at exhibitions in the USA and Europe, including 'Formes Scandinaves' at the Louvre in 1958. During the 1950s and 1960s Scandinavian designers came into their own, and the range and virtuosity of their work in glass, ceramics, textiles and furniture made Scandinavian design the domestic style of the period.

This design tradition has its roots in the late 19th century, when all the Scandinavian countries reflected their own version of the > Arts and Crafts Movement, being essentially craft-based. There were, however, attempts to come to terms with industrial change. In 1915 Sweden set up the Svenska Sjlodforeningen, modelled on the German > Werkbund. The result was the first sign of a new 20th-century Swedish style, illustrated in the work of Wilhelm Kage (1889–1960) for the famous ceramic factory Gustavsberg, and Edward Hald (1883–1981) for Orrefors glass. The 1930 Stockholm Exhibition showed off the new Swedish design, and its combination of the traditional with a new rational aesthetic was seen in the furniture of Bruno Mathsson (1907–88) and Josef Frank (1885–1967), as well as the architecture of Gunnar Asplund (1885–1940). The exhibition made an enormous impression on the rest of the world, and the work was admired for being rational and moderate, qualities that Sweden continued to exemplify in the post-war period.

During this time Denmark was also gaining an industrial reputation for the design of furniture. The first important Danish name is Kaare Klint (1888–1954), who ran the Copenhagen Cabinet Makers' Guild in the 1930s. In the post-war period Finn Juhl (b. 1912), inspired by modern sculpture, pushed wood to its limits in a series of chairs, using loosely woven textiles with natural polished surfaces, while Arne Jacobsen (b. 1902) is best known for his plywood stacking chairs, Egg and Swan, from the early 1950s. More recently Verner Panton (b. 1926) has continued this tradition of innovative Danish furniture. Also important is the Danish family company that Georg Jensen inherited in 1936 from his father, a famous > Art Nouveau silversmith. The Jensen company produced modern tableware and jewellery that was minimal, practical and tremendously influential.

Finland moved into the international design spotlight rather later. Before the war the country's most important designer, the architect Alvar Aalto (1898–1976) became famous for his plywood furniture designs, which remain in production as classics. In the post-war period, however, Finnish designers were considered the most radical in Scandinavia with the work of Tapio Wirkkala (1915–85) and Timo Sarpaneva (b. 1926) for the glass company Iittala, and Kaj Franck (b. 1911), who designed ceramics for Arabia. Textiles were another strong area, with the Marimekko company founded in 1951 and Vuokko Oy in 1964 achieving an international reputation for their bold, striped fabrics and simple dress designs.

Of the Scandinavian countries, only Norway failed to produce a contribution to interior design in the 1950s. This was partly because Norway has a small population and has not enjoyed the economic expansion of the other Scandinavian countries.

Scandinavian design dominated world taste in the late 1950s and early 1960s, when no contemporary interior was complete without a

Danish chair and a Swedish rug. Shops with names like Dansk and Svensk appeared in cities all over the world. More recently, however, Scandinavian design has failed to produce inspirational work to compare with the decades after the war.

● D.R. McFadden, *Scandinavian Modern Design: 1880–1980*, 1982.

SCHOOL OF DESIGN *See* Royal College of Art.

SCIENTIFIC MATERIALISM

A theory developed in the 19th century which claimed that everything could be explained in scientific and technical terms without the agency of divine intervention. Charles Darwin's *Origin of the Species* (1859) and his theory of evolution is the supreme example of the genre. The impact of such theories encouraged designers to see design as an evolutionary process, and the concept that certain rational designs deserved to survive was particularly important in the 19th century when designs were often mindlessly > historicist.

In the 20th century the heritage of scientific materialism is reflected in the work of Raymond Loewy, whose design charts show the evolution of the train and automobile. Another indirect influence from the 19th-century school of thought is the concept of the design classic – the survival of an object which embodies enduring qualities of form, function and appearance. The survival of the design fittest? Finally, it must be said that important design critics such as John > Ruskin vehemently opposed scientific materialism and stressed the spiritual nature of creativity. Ruskin's position on this is also up for revival in the late 20th century.

SEMIOTICS

The science of signs. During the 1960s designers began to be interested in semiotics as a way of understanding the visual world. Language itself is the most universal system of signs, and in the early 20th century key studies were carried out by the Austrian philosopher Ludwig Wittgenstein and the Swiss linguist Ferdinand de Saussure. This pioneering research did not analyse the concepts on which ideas were based but the language in which they were expressed, in search of underlying bias – a bias that might be expressed in terms of race, class or gender. Semiotics therefore provided an analytical tool with which to explore the visual world. Umberto Eco used it to analyse architecture and Roland > Barthes applied it to photography. Designers began to feel that semiology was a possible tool to help reveal the needs and wants of the consumer. Unfortunately, most writers on semiology have concentrated on the theoretical issues of the subject, and designers have little real understanding of how to apply these theories to the practice of design.

SHAKER DESIGN

The Shakers were originally an English nonconformist community established by Ann Lee in Manchester in the 18th century. In 1774 she and a small group of followers emigrated to the USA and founded a series of communities on the East Coast, some of which survived until the 1960s. A severe sect, they translated their beliefs into a series of refined, austere buildings and furniture, which have now become part of the vocabulary of modern design. Shaker carpenters and craftsmen took the metaphor of moral perfection – straight, upright and foursquare – and translated it into a series of a simple ladder-back chairs, tables, boxes and cupboards that owed something of their inspiration to the tradition of English 18th-century furniture. One distinctive feature of their rooms was a high wooden rail from which pegs protruded at regular intervals. On these were hung chairs and clothes. Shaker design abhorred any decoration and used plain, natural wood. Although quirky and extremely idiosyncratic it is not hard to see why this anonymous, elegant and rational furniture has attracted many devotees. In the 1970s Shaker reproduction designs became very popular in smart shops in London and New York.

• June Spriggs, *By Shaker Hands*, 1975.

SIMULATION *See* Baudrillard.

SITUATIONISTS *See* Chaos.

SIXTIES DESIGN *See* Pop Design.

ADAM SMITH

Smith (1723–90) was a Scots economist, whose major work on economics, *An Inquiry into the Nature and Causes of the Wealth of Nations*, was the first analysis of the implications of the Industrial Revolution. Smith was the first to recognize that manufacturing industry had overtaken agriculture as the most important area of production, and he pointed out the changes that the Industrial Revolution was to bring about in the areas of labour, production and marketing. One of his most important theories concerned the division of labour. Using the simple example of manufacturing a pin, he suggested that a worker responsible for all stages of a pin's production would have a small output. If, however, he concentrated on a single aspect of the operation, his output would increase 100-fold. This principle was applied by manufacturers like Josiah Wedgwood, whose ceramics factory in Staffordshire overturned the previous craft practice of a single worker controlling the production of a pot. It also led to the production lines of the > Ford car factory in the early 20th century.

Smith also discussed the idea of supply and demand, pointing out that increased production on its own was not enough; selling and marketing the product were vital to the new manufacturing industries of the Industrial Revolution. Smith's theories were to be extremely influential on economic theory in the 19th century and subsequently on design and industry.

SOVIET DESIGN *See* Russian Design.

SPANISH DESIGN

Over the last ten years Spanish design has emerged as an area rich in innovative new ideas. During the post-war period, Spain remained a relatively underdeveloped country, dominated until the 1970s by the right-wing regime of General Franco. However, it has a rich architectural and design heritage, which in the 20th century includes the work of the architect Antonia Gaudi (1852–1926) and Modernist painters such as Salvador Dali (1904–89).

In the latter part of the 20th century, a new generation of designers has helped to raise Spain's design status. The work of the internationally acclaimed designer Javier Mariscal has led to a revival of innovative graphic design based around the Catalan city of Barcelona. Spanish fashion has also attracted much attention, with the work of such designers as Sybilla and Roberto Verinno and Alberto Dominguez. Dominguez, who lives and works in Galicia, enjoys hundreds of outlets throughout the world (including 300 in Spain), selling the unstructured, softly-tailored clothes that have become his hallmark.

This new confidence is reflected in all areas of Spanish design. In Madrid, the developments in music, fine art, fashion and film have been labelled *La Movida*. Barcelona has also moved to the forefront of Spanish design, blossoming during the 1980s with new architecture, shops, designer bars and nightclubs. In 1992 Barcelona hosted the Olympic Games, the staging of which resulted in the renovation of many historic buildings and an enormous project to build new transport and communication systems.

During 1992 Madrid was nominated Culture Capital of Europe and the World's Fair was held in Seville. Spain has now secured its role in the modern world, and its design achievements fully reflect this new confidence and prosperity.

● Emma Dent Coad, *Spanish Design and Architecture*, 1990.

STILE LIBERTY *See* Art Nouveau; Italian Design.

STREAMLINING

A design process developed in the USA during the 1920s and 1930s by designers such as Raymond Loewy and Walter Dorwin Teague. Streamlining promoted smooth, aerodynamic shapes for industrial products ranging from cars, ships and aeroplanes to simple pencil sharpeners. The designers claimed a scientific rationale for these streamlined shapes, citing natural forms such as ice floes and wind-tunnel experiments in the car industry. However, while there was some substance to these claims, the reality was that streamlining merely evoked the period's romance with technology and the machine. The European > Modern Movement tended to dismiss streamlining as a mere style and claimed it was not a serious contribution to the development of 20th-century design. Nowadays the products of the American designers involved in streamlining have come to evoke a heroic age of confidence in design.

• *The Machine Age in America, 1918–41*, exhibition catalogue, Brooklyn Museum, 1986.

STRUCTURALISM

A sociological perspective that aims to provide an understanding of human conceptual activity. The best known exponent of structuralism is the anthropologist Claude Lévi-Strauss (b. 1908), a member of a largely French intellectual movement that looked at anthropology, sociology, linguistics and design. The theorists of structuralism examine social structure, but from a position that has often been criticized as ignoring the random, irrational quality of human creativity and has led to a counter movement called De-Structuralism. *See also* Semiotics; Foucault, Michel; Barthes, Roland.

SUBCULTURE

A group within a larger established culture. In a design context the style, attitudes and aspirations of subcultures have received a great deal of research and attention. Groups as diverse as the Freemasons and > Punk rockers could be classed as subcultures. The word signals defiance towards accepted cultural norms, and often includes minority and oppressed groups such as Rastafarians and gay communities. What is important in design terms is that the code, dress and style of subcultures can often have important influences. For example, the dreadlocks worn by male Rastafarians later became a fashion style for white women. The word 'subculture', however, has come to have a particular meaning applied to Britain's post-war, white, working-class youth movements, ranging from Teddy Boys to Mods, Skinheads and Punks.

• Dick Hebdige, *Subculture: The Meaning of Style*, 1979.

SUPERMARKETS *See* Retailing.

SURREALISM

Founded by the poet André Breton in 1924, Surrealism was one of the most influential art movements of the 20th century. An admirer of the revolutionary ideas of Karl > Marx and Sigmund Freud, Breton defined Surrealism as 'Pure psychic automatism . . . Thought's dictation, in the absence of all control exercised by the reason and outside all aesthetic or moral preoccupations.' Emerging from the Paris Dada group of the early 1920s, Breton, along with the poets Eluard and Aragon, continued to experiment with various techniques, including automatic writing, trances and the cultivation of dream imagery in order to explore the unconscious systematically so that a new reality or 'surreality' could exist. This was not intended to be a dream world, but one of surprises, where the most ordinary object could be transformed by the artist's perception.

Surrealism was the most vital movement in 1920s' Paris and included such artists as Jean Arp, Joan Miró, Max Ernst, René Magritte, Bellmer, Salvador Dali, Man Ray and Alberto Giacometti. There was no single Surrealist style, but a tendency to use automatic methods, dream imagery or a startling juxtaposition of objects in painting, poetry or > assemblages. Freudian concerns, such as fetish, desire, repressed emotions and sexuality, were the focus of much Surrealist work.

The anti-Establishment quality of Surrealism was shown at the 1938 International Exhibition in Paris, which consisted of a total environment designed by Marcel Duchamp, a 'Surrealist street' lined with female mannequins dressed by male members of the group and leading to the main exhibition hall. Dali, who had joined the movement in 1929, was certainly the most well known of the group through his films with Luis

Buñuel and his often bizarre public exhibitionism. World War II led to most of the group moving to the USA, where the Surrealist Exhibition of 1942 in New York placed them firmly in the annals of modern art. Dali, by now expelled by Breton for his anti-communist tendencies, was sought after as a designer of fashion accessories and creator of such items as the famous Mae West Lips Sofa.

Surrealism's freedom of technique and content had a major influence on young, New York-based artists like Ashille Gorky, De Kooning and Jackson Pollock. It also had an international following, and the ideas and methods of Surrealism are now integrated in advertising, fashion and design. One famous example of its integration is the British advertising campaign for Benson & Hedges cigarettes.

T

TASTE

Taste involves the critical judgement of human objects and culture and it suggests a well-trained appreciation of what is aesthetically pleasing. The philosophical arguments about exactly what taste constitutes have a long history. Early theories are linked to the science of aesthetics and the concept of what the Greeks defined as 'the beautiful'. The orator Cicero (104–43 BC) declared: 'There is a certain apt disposition of bodily parts which, when combined with a certain agreeable colour, is called beauty.' For the philosopher Plato (427–347 BC) beauty was associated with what is to be admired and desired.

From antiquity, then, principles of taste were developed to help establish what was good. The 18th century, for example, saw the publication of many essays on aspects of taste, including treatises on the picturesque, the sublime and the beautiful. Theories of taste put forward ideals to imitate, such as the Roman villa, the landscapes of Claude Lorrain, Greek sculpture and Arab pattern-making. In the 19th century, and particularly for the > Modern Movement in the 20th century, these theories of taste were often linked with function. For the Modern Movement choices and taste in materials and form reflected theories revered as a moral truth. With the arrival of > Post-Modernism, taste, in its more traditional sense, is once more openly discussed. In spite of this, taste remains somewhat controversial, and the traditional subject of aesthetics is seldom taught at educational establishments. This is partly due to another underlying problem, namely the implication that good and bad taste are determined by social environment. Taste therefore has strong social and political implications. Many people feel that good taste is largely the preserve of the rich and well educated. Unquestionably this is not the case. Good taste is culturally determined, but during the 1960s this idea was fundamentally challenged. > Pop design implied that artists and designers were prepared to jettison traditional canons of taste in favour of a more populist aesthetic. In the post-war period high and low art were kept in distinct categories, but by the 1990s those distinctions had broken down. Opera, for example, traditionally a high art, crossed the divide when an operatic aria was used as the theme song for the 1991 Football World Cup. More recently taste, so long avoided as a subject for discussion, is back in fashion and a number of books about it have been published.

• Stephen Bayley, *Taste*, 1991; Peter Lloyd Jones, *Taste Today*, 1991.

TAYLORISM

A theory of management developed by Frederick Winslow Taylor (1856–1915). Taylor, an American industrial engineer who pioneered time and motion studies, wrote an influential book called *The Principles of Scientific Management* (1911), which was widely read by leading industrialists and manufacturers. One of its main ideas was that industrial production could be made more efficient by breaking down the labour process into its smallest component parts, not just on the assembly lines, but also in the office. Taylorism was intended to be a streamlining of capitalist production which would improve production and profits, but it was also adopted by many European progressives as a means of making production benefit working people. Taylor's book was read by designers and artists, including Lèger, who used the author's models of production as metaphors in his own painting. Taylor's ideas also influenced the development of American industrial designers.

TECHNOCRATS

A group of middle-class professionals working in and around Los Angeles during the 1930s, who developed some individual ideas about industrial production. In the main they were industrial technicians who had studied the American capitalist system and concluded that much of the productive capacity that was around in the Depression years was unused, and that improved efficiency in production techniques would eventually make manual labour unnecessary. The Technocrats, who sped around in grey suits, grey hats and grey cars, envisaged the abandonment of the distribution system with its use of money once the maximum capacity of industry could be unleashed. They were part of the era of > streamlining, which shaped the New York design practices of such men as Walter Dorwin Teague. They were also part of the debate about the disparity of consumption, which dominated the 1930s. As a movement, however, the Technocrats of the 1930s need to be distinguished from the Technocrats around today, who believe that the technological management of details rather than broad ideologies is the way to improve the world and design.

TIFFANY'S

A world-famous store fixed in popular imagination by the story 'Breakfast at Tiffany's' written by Truman Capote. It was originally founded by Louis Comfort Tiffany (1848–1933), the son of a well-known New York silversmith. During the 1860s Tiffany travelled to Europe and studied painting, but became increasingly interested in the decorative arts. On his return to the USA, he set up a professional interior design firm, Louis C. Tiffany & Associated Artists, in 1879, and experimented with elaborate, iridescent glass design in naturalistic forms of flowers and birds. Tiffany glass became one of the best-known products of the > Art Nouveau movement and won prizes at the Paris 1900 Exhibition and at Turin in 1902. For the company, and in the same style, Tiffany also designed ceramics, textiles, electric light fittings and mosaics. After his death in 1933 the Tiffany store specialized in expensive, luxury items.

U

ULM

The Hochschule für Gestaltung (high school for design) in the town of Ulm became Germany's most celebrated post-war design school. Its ambition was to take over where the > Bauhaus left off, and it became famous for a rigorous, disciplined and purist approach to industrial design. The school was founded in 1953 by Inge and Grete Scholl, two sisters who had suffered at the hands of the Nazis. In 1955 Ulm was formally opened, with new buildings designed by Max Bill, and was divided into four areas of specialization: product design, architecture, visual communication and information. Max Bill was a product of the Bauhaus and believed strongly in the creative and individual nature of the designer, ideas that brought him into conflict with Thomas Maldonado, who replaced Bill as director of the school in 1956. Maldonado believed that design should be explored using teamwork and intellectual enquiry. To this end he extended the school's curriculum to include anthropology, > semiotics and psychology.

Ulm's great achievement was in establishing strong links with post-war German industry and the school's greatest success story was their collaboration with the Braun company. Braun employed a young student of Maldonado's, Dieter Rams, and it was Rams who gave Braun household products their distinctive form. In fact, his stylized and formal radios and razors have come to express industrial design in the post-war period. In 1968 Ulm, like the Bauhaus before it, was forced to close because of political pressure. However, this did not prevent the spread of its influence, particularly in Japan.

UNDER-CONSUMPTION

A doctrine which states that what is produced is never matched by what people are able to pay for. The term actually comes from the notorious, late 18th-century English economist Dr Thomas Malthus, but its real importance came about in the USA of the 1930s, when factories were idle and workers impoverished. The industrial design profession at the time made a great point of emphasizing that design could effectively solve the problem of under-consumption. The theory was revived in the late 1950s by writers such as Vance > Packard when the USA entered a recession and there appeared to be too many goods and not enough money to buy them. In his book *The Hidden Persuaders* Packard criticized the methods industry used to stimulate more sales, including the introduction of > planned obsolescence for such goods as cars, fridges and other domestic appliances. The theory of under-consumption is important for design because it reinforces the idea that design can solve economic problems by encouraging higher levels of spending and consumption. Linked in this way to the doctrine of supply and demand, under-consumption describes part of the overall picture, but in the final analysis explains very little.

UTILITY

The name given to the furniture and household products designed in Britain during World War II. When Hitler's bombing campaign began in earnest in 1940, Churchill was anxious that civilian morale should not be further undermined by the prospect of no consumer goods in the shops to replace those destroyed by the bombs. In 1941 he introduced the Utility scheme, a unique experiment for Britain, in that everyone was given the same choice, at the same price and with a strictly allocated number of coupons depending on your family circumstances, not your income. For Britain it was a dangerously socialist experiment, and only the direst of war circumstances could have explained its introduction.

The design of Utility goods was largely placed in the hands of a small band of progressive designers who had worked, generally in a small way, as Modernist designers in the 1930s. In 1941 they got their chance at mass production. Sir Gordon Russell (1892–1980) had grown up in the Cotswolds, where he had gone to school with children whose parents were members of Charles Ashbee's Guild of Handicrafts. Although committed to the principles of industrial production, Russell's furniture for the scheme (two ranges called 'Cotswold' and 'Chiltern' suggest the tone) applied sensible > Arts and Crafts ideas to the range. Fashion and textiles were also interesting – fashion because top couturiers like Norman Hartnell, Hardy Amies and Victor Stiebel designed clothes for the mass market, and textiles because designers like Enid Marx worked on fabrics for Utility sofas and curtains.

Utility was a fascinating design experiment. It also ingrained into a whole generation of people the ethic of 'Make do and mend', a slogan taken from a propaganda poster series. Anyone who lived through the 1950s will recognize the impact Utility attitudes had on their lifestyles. Later, for the social revolution of the 1960s, it proved a powerful force against which to rebel.

• Geffrye Museum, *Utility Furniture and Fashion*, exhibition catalogue, 1974.

V

VANK *See* Dutch Design.

THORSTEIN VEBLEN

(1857–1929) was an American economist who coined the term 'conspicuous consumption' to describe the behaviour of the fabulously wealthy American dynasties at the turn of the century. He was born in Wisconsin of Norwegian parents and went on to study at Johns Hopkins and Yale universities. It was in his influential book, *The Theory of the Leisure Class* (1899), that he first referred to 'conspicuous consumption' to describe spending which satisfies no real need but is a mark of prestige. Veblen's work on cultural analysis provides a key description of the mode of behaviour by which a leisure class maintains its separate cultural identity – in this case, by indulging in the excesses of that gilded age.

Veblen was a populist radical, who attacked the outward excesses of the rich and their design accoutrements. Most importantly, he became a prominent source of dissenting American economic theory in the 20th century, and his ideas went on to influence post-war design commentators such as Vance > Packard and Victor > Papanek. It is rather ironic, however, that in the 1980s Veblen's thoughts on conspicuous consumption were appropriated to rather different ends by the prevalent > Yuppie culture of the shop-till-you-drop decade.

VICTORIA AND ALBERT MUSEUM (V&A)

The world's largest collection of decorative art and design. With the support of Prince Albert, it was founded on 6 September 1852 as the Museum of Manufactures in Marlborough House, and Sir Henry Cole was appointed as its first director. The museum's declared purpose was to help educate young designers and the public, and Cole received a grant of £5000 to buy objects from the > Great Exhibition of 1851. In 1857 the museum moved to its present site in South Kensington, housed at first in a building of iron and glass, and later in a more permanent building designed by Captain Francis Fowke. Owen Jones designed the Oriental Galleries, the Morris Company designed the Dining Rooms and Sir Edward Poynter designed the Grill Room. The museum was imitated all over Europe. In 1863 the Paris Union Centrale des Arts Décoratifs opened, and was followed the next year by the Vienna Museum of Applied Arts. In 1899 Queen Victoria laid the foundation stone for the present buildings and directed that the museum should be renamed Victoria and Albert.

In the 20th century the museum's design role shifted emphasis. After World War I the museum's collecting policy concentrated on historical objects. By the 1960s the museum had become out of touch; it relied on Edwardian curatorial methods and was becoming more and more remote. In the 1970s Sir Roy Strong brought a different approach to the museum and encouraged a limited policy of support for modern design exhibitions and acquisitions. In the 1980s, however, the museum faced a crisis. Government policy required museums to become more financially self-sufficient, and this was linked to a general feeling they should be more accessible to the public. In 1988 the museum appointed its first woman director, Mrs Elizabeth Esteve-Coll, to introduce radical changes to the museum structure. In terms of design this has meant a return to the museum's original commitment to promoting contemporary work.

- J. Physick, *The Victoria and Albert Museum*, 1982.

VICTORIAN DRESS REFORM

A fashion movement that contributed to the liberation of women. In the 1860s clothes for women were restrictive. The fashion for the crinoline was at its most extreme, with skirt hoops reaching a width of 6 feet, and boned corsets, tightly laced, were obligatory wear to produce the then fashionable nipped-in waist. The reaction against this was a Dress Reform movement advocating loose clothing made of natural materials coloured with vegetable dyes. William > Morris encouraged his wife Jane to take up the cause, and she was photographed in the style by Rossetti in 1862 – lots of gathered fabric, medieval details in the styling and definitely no corsets or waisting. The development of cycling and sporting activities for women also encouraged change. Women began to adapt items of dress from traditional men's tailoring, which allowed more freedom.

Health was another argument raised in dress reform. In 1884 Dr Gustav Jaegar, whose name lives on with the chain of fashion shops, aired his views at an International Health Exhibition held in the Albert Hall. He advocated wool next to the skin to stimulate circulation, absorb perspiration and entice noxious substances from the blood. This theory was perfectly practical, but some of his other ideas were more extreme, for example five-toed socks, or the idea that you should not wash wool but simply leave it to breathe. He was also firmly opposed to wearing dyed fabric, except in winter when body perspiration was low. Men, too, were part of the Dress Reform Movement. The > Arts and Crafts writer Edmund Carpenter is credited with the invention of open-toed leather sandals for men, an idea he may have picked up from India. Collars were also looser and ties knotted more like scarves. Contemporary photographs of Charles Rennie Mackintosh show off the style.

Dress reform of the Dr Jaeger variety was associated with cranks rather than fashion, and this prejudice continued into the 20th century. Then, new technologies rather than ideologies brought about the biggest dress revolution for ordinary people, with the appearance of artificial fabrics like rayon and nylon, which were easy to wash and drip dry. Quirkiness, however, remains apparent even in contemporary fashion. Dr Scholl sandals are sold in chemists to emphasize their 'medicinal' attributes, and the 1960s' revival of folk dress included items like Red Indian moccasins and Lancashire mill clogs. Science was also allowed a role, with the campaign for gravity-correct Earth shoes. More recently, in the New Age mood, claims have been made that wearing specific crystals can control moods and ward off illness.

VIRTUAL REALITY (VR)

The name for new developments in media integration. It was initially developed by the military for flight simulation in the training of astronauts and fighter pilots. As a leisure product VR creates real-life experiences in which the viewer is no longer a passive spectator, but an active participant. VR is a tactile, noisy and animated 3-D world. This new breakthrough in interactive computers allows the user access to sophisticated technology, including surround-vision helmets with stereophonic sound, and gloves studded with motion sensors. Soon students will be able to study Norman England using VR, the disabled person will be able to experience the world with no physical obstacles, advertising companies will devise interactive advertisements for the consumer. One commercial system is Dimension International's VR Toolkit, which makes it possible to create 3-D objects and place them in a 'virtual' world. The system has already been used to create a British television programme called *Cyberzone*, a game show where contestants' actions are mimicked in the virtual world by Cyborgs, which run or walk when the contestant does. The first British 'virtuality machine' was produced by W Industries. So far VR equipment is basic and cumbersome, but that situation will change in the very near future, when the VR world truly mimics the real one.

VOGUEING

Madonna popularized this cult, which involves a mannered, posturing style of dancing, and sometimes dressing up as a fantasy figure. She had actually stolen the craze from New York gay culture. Manhattan's fashionable gay crowd combined catwalk shows with break-dancing, and pop entrepreneur Malcolm McLaren also used the craze for his *Waltz Darling* album. Vogueing is now used to describe anyone putting on the style at a smart opening or party.

W

WERKBUND *See* Deutsche Werkbund.

WHITE GOODS

The industry term for consumer products such as washing-machines, dish-washers and refrigerators traditionally made out of white sheet steel. Although there have been attempts to introduce colour into the design of these domestic products, most notably in the 1950s, white remains the preferred finish. *See also* Brown goods.

WIENER WERKSTATTE

The German equivalent of C.R. Ashbee's Guild of Handicrafts. Founded in Vienna in 1903, the Werkstatte encouraged craftspeople/designers to develop their own style, unlike Ashbee's guild where the medieval ideal of the anonymous worker was the norm. In general, the work of the Werkstatte was far more avant-garde than contemporary British > Arts and Crafts work. Another key difference lay in the fact that the Werkstatte was concerned primarily with matters of taste rather than the transformation of society through the Morris ideal of joyous labour.

The Wiener Werkstatte enjoyed a considerable international profile and the British magazine *The Studio* publicized its work in a special 1906 edition called *The Art Revival in Austria*, which introduced an international audience to the achievements of the Werkstatte and to Austrian architects and designers in general. The banker Fritz Warndofer financed the group, which was formally set up in June 1903 as the Wiener Werkstatte Productiv – Gemeinschaft von Kunsthand-Werken in

Wien (Viennese Workshops – Production Cooperative of Art Workmen of Vienna) with Koloman Moser and Josef Hoffmann as artistic directors. By 1905 it employed over 100 workers and had become the Viennese centre of progressive design. They produced small, domestic objects in ceramics, glass, wood and leather, as well as jewellery, none of which was intended for machine production. More importantly, under Hoffmann's artistic direction the Werkstatte was associated with a distinctive aesthetic, using simple geometric forms based on repeated grid motifs and rectilinear shapes. Hoffmann's geometric simplicity combined with rich decoration produced a rich design heritage of cutlery, glass vases, teapots and furniture which continues to influence contemporary design.

In the 1920s the Viennese design movement was taken to the USA by émigrés, who included Hoffmann's son Wolfgang. Here it was integrated into the > Moderne style that dominated American decorative arts of that period. The severe rectilinear style dominated Werkstatte products until 1915. After this date objects began to show a more eclectic and curvilinear style. Hoffmann himself moved in this direction, as did fellow designer Dagobert Peche. In 1928 the Werkstatte celebrated its twenty-fifth anniversary, but it closed four years later because of financial difficulties.

● J. Werner, *Wiener Werkstatte*, 1984.

TOM WOLFE

Wolfe (b. 1931) is part of the post-war generation of writers on design. He is also the inventor of a new style of design writing called > New Journalism, which emerged in the USA during the 1960s as the writing equivalent of > Pop design. The idea was to use an accessible writing style that picked up on slang, advertising jargon and the vernacular. The approach is suggested by the titles and subjects of some of his most famous books – *The Kandy-Colored Tangerine-Flake Streamline Baby* and *The Electric Kool-Aid Acid Test*, both published in 1968. Wolfe's books became essential reading during the Swinging Sixties, and his influence as a writer and critic has proved an enduring one. Wolfe invented the 'me-decade' to describe the 1970s, but his satire on social aspirations shifted to architecture in the 1980s with the popular critique *From*

Bauhaus to Our House (1981). More recently Wolfe has developed into a serious writer of fiction. The publication of his novel exploring the social mores of New York life, *Bonfire of the Vanities* (1988), caused a sensation. This savage satire was Wolfe's attempt at writing a novel with the style and scope of Victorian writers such as Dickens and Thackeray, and the ripples it caused continue into the 1990s with the release of a film based on the book.

WOMEN'S MOVEMENT *See* Feminism.

WORLD FAIRS

International design exhibitions. The best-known 20th-century examples include the 1925 Paris Exposition des Arts Décoratifs, the 1929 exhibition in Barcelona, the 1930 International Modern Style exhibition in Stockholm, the 1939 > New York World Fair, the 1958 exhibition in Brussels and the 1960 exhibition in Osaka. The Montreal Expo of 1967 was notable for Otto Frei's German pavilion with its steel mesh roofs, and for Buckminster Fuller's geodesic domes for the USA pavilion. The 1992 World Fair was hosted by Seville.

Y

PETER YORK

Real name Peter Wallis, a well-known writer and broadcaster on British style and society. Alongside his successful career as a journalist he runs a successful marketing company in London called SRU. In the early 1980s he wrote a series of articles for the society magazine *Harpers & Queen*, and in one of the these pieces invented the word 'Sloane Ranger' to describe a certain type of debby woman, and her upmarket accoutrements: Barbour jackets, Hermes headscarves and green wellington boots. York went on to identify the Princess of Wales as the perfect example of the species. He later developed the article into a best-selling book called *The Sloane Ranger Handbook*, described by Tom > Wolfe as a 'seminal sociological study'.

York developed a writing style in the manner of Wolfe, but because he worked largely for magazines is often dismissed as an ephemeral commentator. In fact, York's writings remain acute observations on British society and in 1988 he was invited to give the South Bank Lecture on television on the subject 'Punk or Pageant', which highlighted two diverse but simultaneous aspects of British style. More recently the Peter York persona has been dropped to develop his career as Peter Wallis, business consultant. For those in the know he remains an extremely important commentator.

YOUTH CULTURE

The study of youth culture is a post-war development encouraged by the emergence of a new category of consumer – the teenager. Changed economic circumstances meant that young people, previously forced to

208

adopt parental norms and taste, suddenly had the financial means to develop a lifestyle of their own. This phenomenon, first seen in the USA, quickly spread to Europe during the 1950s, and Britain has played an important role in the emergence of a recognizable youth culture. The 1950s saw a trend for draped jackets, greased-back hairstyles, crêpe-soled shoes and brightly coloured shirts associated with the Teddy Boy 'uniform'. This was followed by a series of youth cults, including Beatniks, Mods, Skinheads, > Hippies, > Punks, > New Romantics and more recently > Acid House. Sociologists and contemporary culture commentators have studied these youth movements and their conclusions fall into two camps. The first believed that youth culture was an original, spontaneous development, which had its roots in working-class life, while the second believed youth culture to be the result of commercial manipulation by advertising and the media. Whatever the truth, youth culture has affected mainstream design and cultural attitudes. According to Malcolm McLaren, it remains Britain's most original contribution to post-war design, and it is certainly true that images of Punks in their full regalia have become instantly recognizable as British icons.

● D. Hebdige, *Subculture: the Meaning of Style*, 1979.

YOUNG FOGIES

A 1980s' description applied to young men who wore traditional suits and enjoyed a taste for nursery food. In the early 1980s the film *Chariots of Fire* and the television series of Evelyn Waugh's *Brideshead Revisited* revived a fashion for > English Style of the 1920s and 1930s. Well-to-do young men, nicknamed Young Fogies, aspired to Georgian houses, the architecture of Quinlan Terry, well-worn tweed jackets and brogue shoes. Although tailor-made for satire, the Young Fogey movement revealed some interesting footnotes to 1980s' taste. It inspired a preference for second-hand clothes, restaurants specializing in nursery food of the jam roly-poly variety and a vogue for elaborate drape curtains. More seriously, its adherents espoused right-of-centre Conservative values and tended to denigrate anything new, particularly in architecture.

The founding father of this school of thought was David Watkin. He and his disciples, including the historian Gavin Stamp, campaigned through such organizations as the Georgian Society and Thirties Society to preserve the nation's architectural heritage, and at the same time maintained a successful attack on most contemporary architecture. With the latter they were helped by Prince Charles and his now famous intervention in the National Gallery competition when he described one entry as a 'carbuncle'. At the heart of Fogeyism was a group of privileged and influential individuals with a powerful voice.

YUPPIES

Young, Upwardly mobile Professional People, who cared only for personal promotion and gain. Anyone in the consumer-oriented 1980s who drove a BMW, had a mobile phone and used a Filofax personal organizer was called a Yuppie. *i*-D magazine called it the '80s cult that dare not speak its name'. The media used the name as an all-purpose description for middle-class values, and in the USA it caught on in a big way. *The Yuppie Handbook* was published in 1984 and a series of Hollywood films, such as *Desperately Seeking Susan* and *Wall Street* explored the phenomenon. Somewhat later a television soap called *thirtysomething* cashed in on Yuppie lifestyles. The movement eventually came crashing down with the recession of the late 1980s.

BIBLIOGRAPHY

1. BIBLIOGRAPHIES, DICTIONARIES, MANUALS AND DIRECTORIES

Ambasz, E., (ed.), *The International Design Yearbook 1968/7*, New York, 1985, London, 1986

Bayley, S., (ed.), *The Conran Dictionary of Design*, London, 1985

Conway, H., (ed.), *Design History: a Student's Handbook*, London, 1987

Coulson, Anthony J., *A Bibliography of Design in Britain 1851–1970*, London, 1979

Duncan, Alastair, (ed.), *Encyclopedia of Art Deco*, London, 1988

Fleming, J. and Honour, H., *The Penguin Dictionary of Decorative Arts*, London, 1977, Harmondsworth, 1979

Garner, Phillipe, (ed.), *Phaidon Encyclopedia of Decorative Arts 1890–1940*, Oxford, 1978

Jervis, S., *The Penguin Dictionary of Design and Designers*, Harmondsworth and New York, 1984

Margolin, Victor, *Design History Bibliography*, London, 1987

Morgan, Ann Lee, (ed.), *Contemporary Designers*, London and Chicago, 1984

Sharp, Dennis, *Sources of Modern Architecture: A Critical Bibliography*, 2nd ed. London and New York, 1981

2. NINETEENTH-CENTURY DESIGN

Adburgham, Alison, *Liberty's: A Biography of a Shop*, London, 1975

Aslin, Elizabeth, *The Aesthetic Movement: Prelude to Art Nouveau*, London and New York, 1969

Battersby, Martin, *The World of Art Nouveau*, London, 1968

Callen, Anthea, *Angel in the Studio: The Women of the Arts and Crafts Movement, 1870–1914*, London, 1978 (published in New York as *Women Artists of the Arts and Crafts Movement, 1870–1914*, 1979)

Crawford, Alan, *C.R. Ashbee: Architect, Designer and Romantic Socialist*, New Haven, 1985

Durant, Stuart, *Ornament*, 1987

Greenhalgh, Paul, *Ephemeral Vistas: Expositions Universelles, Great Exhibitions and World's Fairs, 1851–1939*, Manchester, 1988

Hounshell, David A., *From the American System to Mass Production, 1800–1932: The Development of Manufacturing in the United States*, Baltimore, 1984

Kaplan, Wendy, (ed.), *The Art That is Life: The Arts and Crafts Movement in America, 1875–1920*, Boston, 1987

MacCarthy, F., *All Things Bright and Beautiful: Design in Britain 1830 to Today*, London, 1972, rev. ed. London, 1979 (as *A History of British Design 1830–1970*)

MacCarthy, Fiona, *The Simple Life: C.R.Ashbee in the Cotswolds*, London, 1981

McKendrick, Neil; Brewer, John; and Plumb, J.H., *The Birth of a Consumer Society: The Commercialization of Eighteenth Century England*, Bloomington, IA, 1985

Naylor, Gillian, *The Arts and Crafts Movement: A study of its sources, ideals and influence on design theory*, London, 1971

Physick, John, *The Victoria and Albert Museum: the History of its Building*, London, 1982

Schaefer, H., *The Roots of Modern Design: The Functional Tradition in the Nineteenth Century*, London, 1970 (published in New York as *Nineteenth Century Modern: The Functional Tradition in Victorian Design*, 1970)

Schmutzler, Robert, *Art Nouveau*, New York, 1962, 1964

Twyman, Michael, *Printing 1770–1970: An Illustrated History of its Development and Uses in England*, London, 1970

Watkinson, Raymond, *Pre-Raphaelite Art and Design*, London, 1985

3. TWENTIETH-CENTURY DESIGN

Adam, Peter, *Eileen Gray: Architect, Designer: A Biography*, London, 1987

Ades, Dawn, *Posters: The Twentieth Century Poster: Design of the Avant Garde*, New York, 1984

Ambasz, Emilio, (ed.), *Italy: The New Domestic Landscape*, New York, 1972

Anscombe, Isabelle, *Omega and After: Bloomsbury and the Decorative Arts*, London, 1981

Arts Council of Great Britain, *Thirties: British Art and Design before the War*, London, 1979

Banham, Peter Reyner, *Theory and Design in the First Machine Age*, Cambridge, MA, 1980

Battersby, Martin, *The Decorative Twenties*, New York, 1969, London, 1971

Battersby, Martin, *The Decorative Thirties*, London, 1969, New York, 1971

Bayley, S., *Harley Earl and the American Dream Machine*, London, 1984

Bayley, Stephen, (ed.), *Sony: Design*, London, 1982

Benton, C.; Benton, T.; and Scarf, A., *The History of Architecture and Design*, Milton Keynes, 1975

Billcliffe, Roger, *Charles Rennie Mackintosh: The Complete Furniture, Furniture Drawings and Interior Designs*, London and New York, 1979

Branzi, Andrea, *The Hot House: Italian New Wave Design*, Cambridge, MA, 1984, London, 1985 (originally published in Milan as *La Casa Calda*, 1983)

Bush, Donald, *The Streamlined Decade*, New York, 1975

Calloway, Stephen, *Twentieth Century Interior Decoration*, London, 1988

Campbell, J., *The German Werkbund – The Politics of Reform in the Applied Arts*, Princeton, 1978

Clark, Robert Judson et al, *Design in America – The Cranbrook Vision 1925–1950*, New York, 1983

De Noblet, Jocelyn, *Design: introduction à l'histoire de l'evolution des formes industrielles de 1820 à aujourd'hui*, Paris, 1974

Dorfles, Gillo, *Introduction à l'Industrial Design*, Paris, 1974

Forty, Adrian, *Objects of Desire: Design and Society 1750–1980*, London, 1986

Gardner, Carl and Sheppard, Julie, *Consuming Passion: The Rise of Retail Culture*, London, 1989

Gray, C., *The Great Experiment: Russian Art 1863–1922*, London, 1982

Greif, Martin, *Depression Modern: The Thirties Style in America*, New York, 1977

Gresleri, Giuliano, *Josef Hoffmann*, Bologna, 1981

Harrison, Helen A., (ed.), *Dawn of a New Day: The New York World's Fair, 1939–1940*, New York, 1980

Heskett, John, *Industrial Design*, London, 1980, 1982

Hiesinger, Kathryn B., and Marcus, George H., (eds), *Design Since 1945*, New York, 1983

Hillier, Bevis, *The Decorative Arts of the Forties and Fifties: Austerity Binge*, New York, 1975

Hine, Thomas, *Populuxe*, London and New York, 1987

Horn, Richard, *Fifties Style: Then and Now*, New York, 1985

Horn, R., *Memphis*, Philadelphia, 1985

Katz, S., *Classic Plastics: from Bakelite to High-Tech*, London, 1984

Katz, S., *Plastics: Designs and Materials*, London, 1978

Kron, S., and Slesin, S., *High Tech: The Industrial Style and Source Book for the Home*, New York and London, 1978

Lodder, Christina, *Russian Constructivism*, Yale, 1983, London, 1985

Lorenz, Christopher, *The Design Dimension: Product Strategy and the Challenge of Global Marketing*, New York, 1986

Lucie-Smith, E., *A History of Industrial Design*, Oxford, 1983

McDermott, Catherine, *Street Style, British Design in the 80s*, London, Design Council, 1987

McFadden, David Revere, (ed.), *Scandinavian Modern Design 1880–1980*, New York, 1982

Meggs, Philip B., *A History of Graphic Design*, New York, 1983

Meikle, Jeffrey L., *Twentieth Century Limited: Industrial Design in America 1925–1939*, Philadelphia, 1979

Melot, Michel, *The Art of Illustration*, New York, 1984

Myers, Kathy, *Understains: The Sense and Seduction of Advertising*, London, 1986

Naylor, Gillian, *The Bauhaus Reassessed: Sources and Design Theory*, London and New York, 1985

Open University, *History of Architecture and Design, 1890–1939*, Milton Keynes, 1975

Papenek, V., *Design for the Real World: Human Ecology and Social Change*, New York, 1971, London, 1972, rev. ed. London and Chicago, 1985

Paris-Moscou 1900–1930, Paris, Centre Georges Pompidou, 1979

213

Phillips, Barty, *Conran and the Habitat Story*, London, 1984

Radice, B., *Memphis: Research, Experiences, Results, Failures and Successes of the New Design*, London and New York, 1985

Russell, Gordon, *A Designer's Trade*, London, 1968

Sparke, Penny, *An Introduction to Design and Culture in the Twentieth Century*, London, 1986

Sparke, Penny, *Consultant Design: the History and Practice of the Designer in Industry*, London, 1983

Sparke, Penny, *Design in Context*, London, 1987

Sparke, Penny, (ed.), *Did Britain Make it? British Design in Context: 1946–86*, London, 1986

Sparke, Penny, *Ettore Sottsass Jnr.*, London, 1982

Sparke, Penny, *An Introduction to Design and Culture in the Twentieth Century*, London, 1986

Sparke, Penny, *Italian Design*, London, 1988

Spencer, Herbert, *The Pioneers of Modern Typography*, London, 1969

Sudjic, D., *Cult Objects*, St Albans, 1985

Teague, W.D., *Design this Day*, New York, 1940, London, 1947

Thackara, J., (ed.), *New British Design*, London, 1986

Twyman, Michael, *Printing 1770–1970: An Illustrated History of its Development and Uses in England*, London, 1970

Whiteley, Nigel, *Pop Design: Modernism to Mod*, London, 1987

Whitford, Frank, *The Bauhaus*, London and New York, 1984

Whitney Museum, *High Styles: Twentieth-Century American Design*, New York, 1985

Woodham, J., *The Industrial Designer and the Public*, London, 1983

4. THE MODERN MOVEMENT

Banham, Peter Reyner, *Theory and Design in the First Machine Age*, London, 1960

Giedion, S., *Mechanization Takes Command: a Contribution to Anonymous History*, New York, 1948

Giedion, Sigfried, *Space, Time and Architecture*, Oxford, 1941

Hitchcock, Henry-Russell, *Architecture: Nineteenth and Twentieth Centuries*, London, 4th edition, 1977

Hitchcock, Henry-Russell and Philip Johnson, *The International Style*, London, New York, 1966

Itten, Johannes, *Design and Form: the Basic Course at the Bauhaus*, London, rev. ed. 1975

Le Corbusier, *Towards a New Architecture*, London, first published 1923, 1927, Architectural Press Reprint, 1970

Mumford, Lewis, *Technics and Civilization*, London, 1934

Overy, Paul, *De Stijl*, London, New York, 1969, 1991

Pevsner, Nikolaus, *Pioneers of Modern Design: From William Morris to Walter Gropius*, Harmondsworth, 1968 (originally published London, 1936 as *Pioneers of the Modern Movement*)

Read, Herbert, *Art and Industry*, London, 1934

Wilk, Christopher, *Marcel Breuer, Furniture and Interiors*, New York, 1981

Willett, John, *The New Sobriety 1917–1933: Art and Politics in the Weimar Period*, London, 1978

Wingler, Hans M., *The Bauhaus*, Cambridge, MA, 1969

5. POST-MODERNISM

Banham, R., *Design by Choice*, London, 1981

Barthes, R., *Elements of Semiology*, London, 1987

Barthes, R., *The Fashion System*, London, 1985

Barthes, R., *Mythologies*, London, 1972

Berman, Marshall, *All that is Solid Melts into Air: The Experience of Modernity*, London, 1983, 1985

Dorfles, G., (ed.), *Kitsch: the World of Bad Taste*, London, 1969

Eco, Umberto, *A Theory of Semiotics*, Bloomington IA, 1976

Foster, H., (ed.), *Postmodern Culture*, London, 1985

Foucault, M., *Discipline and Punish*, London, 1977

Giedion, Sigfried, *Mechanization Takes Command: A Contribution to Anonymous History*, New York, 1969

Hebdige, Dick, *Subculture, The Meaning of Style*, London, 1979

Jencks, Charles, *The Language of Post-Modern Architecture*, London, 1977, 1984

Lévi-Strauss, C., *Structural Anthropology*, New York, 1963

Thackara, John, (ed.), *Design After Modernism*, London, 1988

Venturi, R., *Complexity and Contradiction in Architecture*, New York, 1966

Venturi, Robert, *Learning from Las Vegas*, Massachusetts, 1979

Williamson, J., *Decoding Advertisements*, London, 1978

Wolfe, T., *From Bauhaus to Our House*, London, 1982

York, P., *Style Wars*, London, 1980

6. WOMEN AND DESIGN

Adam, Peter, *Eileen Gray: Architect, Designer: A Biography*, London, 1987

Anscombe, Isabelle, *A Woman's Touch: Women in Design from 1860 to the Present Day*, London, 1984

Attfield, J. and Kirkham, P., (eds), *A View from the Interior: Feminism, Women and Design*, London, 1989

Callen, Anthea, *Angel in the Studio: The Women of the Arts and Crafts Movement, 1870–1914*, London, 1978 (published in New York as *Women Artists of the Arts and Crafts Movement, 1870–1914*, 1979)

Hayden, Dolores, *The Grand Domestic Revolution: A History of Feminist Designs for Homes, Neighborhoods and Cities*, Cambridge, MA, 1983